# Economics, Natural-Resource Scarcity and Development

## Conventional and Alternative Views

*Edward B. Barbier*

Earthscan Publications Limited
London

*To my father, who understood the ways of the world better than most.*

First published 1989 by
Earthscan Publications Limited
3 Endsleigh Street, London WC1H 0DD

British Library Cataloguing in Publication Data

Barbier, Edward B.
  Economics, natural-resource scarcity and
  development: conventional and alternative
  views
  1. Natural resources. Management. Economic
  aspects
  I. Title
  333.7

  ISBN 1-85383-024-0

Typeset in 11/12 pt Plantin
by DP Photosetting, Aylesbury, Bucks
Printed and bound in Great Britain by Mackays of Chatham

Earthscan Publications Ltd is an editorially independent and wholly owned subsidiary of the
International Institute for Environment and Development.

# Contents

**Acknowledgements**      vii

**Introduction**      ix
     Economics and natural-resource scarcity      ix
     Towards an economics of sustainable development      xv

**1. Historical Approaches to Natural-Resource Scarcity**      1

     Malthusian and Ricardian scarcity      1
     Smith, Malthus and Ricardo      4
     Mill, Jevons and Marshall      11
     The special case of Marx      19
     *Conclusion:* The modern conventional view      22
     *Appendix:* The Malthus-Ricardo theory of diminishing
         returns      26

**2. Non-Economic Influences**      34

     Conservationism      34
     Ecology      38
     Thermodynamics      51
     *Summary and conclusion:* Towards an alternative view      55

**3. Conventional Theory: Optimal Rates of Depletion**      62

     Conventional theories of natural-resource scarcity      62
     Exhaustible resources      63
     Renewable resources      66
     *Summary and conclusion*      70

**4. Conventional Theory: Pollution and Natural Environments**      75

     Pollution as an externality      75
     Optimal pollution control: charges versus standards      78

The preservation of natural environments over time        81
*Summary and conclusion*                                   84

5.  **An Alternative View Of Natural-Resource Scarcity**    92

An alternative view of natural-resource scarcity           93
A theoretical model                                        100
Wider implications: Technology, tastes and time            105
*Summary and conclusion*                                   109
*Appendix:* A model of economic-environmental interaction  110

6.  **Two Examples: Deforestation in Amazonia and the
    Global Greenhouse Effect**                             120

Deforestation in Amazonia                                  120
*Summary and conclusion*                                   132
The global greenhouse effect                               133
*Summary and conclusion*                                   152

7.  **Upper Watershed Degradation in Java**               160

On- and off-site effects                                   161
Incentives for soil conservation                           163
Economic policies and investment strategies                167
*Summary and conclusion*                                   178

8.  *Conclusion*: **An Economics of Sustainable Development** 184
Some definitions and conditions                            184
Sustainable development and advanced economies             189
Sustainable development and developing economies           192
*Summary and conclusion*                                   204
*Appendix:* A model of optimal sustainable economic growth 205

**Index**                                                  217

# Acknowledgements

This book is largely based on my doctoral thesis, *"Alternative" Economic Approaches to Natural Resource Scarcity*, which I wrote between 1982 and 1985 while studying for a PhD in economics at Birkbeck College, University of London. I am therefore grateful to Ron Smith and Dennis Snower, my PhD supervisors, and Partha Dasgupta, my examiner. No words can sufficiently convey my thanks to Ron Smith, in particular, who was so instrumental in helping me develop my ideas and arguments, and whose interest in all new economic ideas is admirable. I would also like to thank Julia Phelan who allowed me to use her word processor and flat.

The converting of my thesis into the present book, plus the additional research required, was conducted over 1987 and 1988 as part of my duties as a full-time economist at the International Institute for Environment and Development (IIED) in London. I am indebted to all my colleagues at IIED for contributing to the stimulating atmosphere that has no doubt greatly influenced this book. I would also like to thank the Swedish International Development Authority (SIDA) and the US Agency for International Development (USAID) for funding my work as an economist at IIED over the last two years; and the International Fund for Agricultural Development (IFAD), the UK Overseas Development Agency (ODA), the United Nations Development Programme (UNDP), USAID and the World Bank for hiring me for various consultancies.

During the writing of this book I have been privileged to work with two excellent environmental and resource economists, David Pearce and Anil Markandya, to whom I owe an intellectual debt. As the three of us have joined together to form the joint IIED/University College London Environmental Economic Centre (LEEC), I look forward to our future explorations of many of the ideas expressed in this book.

I am indebted to Richard Sandbrook, Vice-President of IIED, who has supported my work as an economist – and this book in particular – from the beginning; to Gordon Conway, who insisted that USAID partially fund me through his Sustainable Agricultural Programme at IIED, and from whom I have learned a great deal about sustainable development; and to Czech Conroy, with whom I worked on organizing IIED's Sustainable Development Conference of 28–30 April, 1987.

The task of writing this book was made much easier by Neil Middleton, Director of Earthscan Publications, who combines amazing editorial skills with an eclectic grasp of the subject. I would like to thank all the members of Earthscan Publications who have contributed to ensuring that this book sees the light of day.

I would also like to thank several individuals who facilitated the process of converting chapters of my thesis into this book. I am grateful to Laura Coolidge for assisting me in finding additional research material on Amazonian deforestation and the global greenhouse effect; to Simon Rietbergen for reviewing a draft on Amazonian deforestation; and to Gerry Leach and Jules Pretty for reviewing drafts on the greenhouse effect. I would also like to thank the World Bank for reviewing and clearing Chapter 7 for publication; in particular, I appreciate the effort by Ernst Lutz to ensure a speedy clearance. I am again grateful to Anil Markandya and David Pearce, as well as to Shanti Chakravarty, for commenting on earlier versions of the model in the appendix to Chapter 8, and to Karl-Göran Mäler for his views on the entire chapter.

This book would not have been possible without the inspiration on my life and ideas of my wife, Francine, who has seen the whole transition from intellectual musings to thesis to publication. And of course Lara, who has been a constant reminder of what the book is really about.

*Edward B. Barbier*
*Associate Director*
*IIED/UCL LEEC*

# Introduction

## ECONOMICS AND NATURAL-RESOURCE SCARCITY

Although the analysis of environmental and resource problems is considered a comparatively new field in economics, formal economic analysis of natural-resource scarcity can be traced back to classical political economy and the foundation of economic ideas. Contemporary approaches to problems such as pollution, optimal depletion rates and common-property exploitation are, however, substantially different from the classical concern with the scarcity of arable land and diminishing returns in agriculture. Not only has environmental economics benefited from general developments in modern economics, but it has also been subject to important non-economic influences, namely environmentalism, ecology and thermodynamics. On the one hand, incorporating these influences presents a fundamental challenge to conventional economic analysis; on the other, they can be assimilated into more integrated alternative economic approaches for analysing the trade-off between resource use and environmental problems.

The essential theme underlying these alternative approaches is that environmental degradation arising from economic activity imposes costs on the economic system. These costs may or may not be captured by the markets of that system. Nevertheless, if these costs are increasing over time then they are an indication of a new type of natural-resource scarcity phenomenon. The rising costs associated with environmental degradation also suggest that the current pattern of economic development may not, in the long run, be environmentally sustainable. Thus, the emerging alternative approaches to natural-resource scarcity are essentially responses to a new class of environmental problems confronting the world today such as deforestation, climatic change from global warming, acid rain, desertification and watershed degradation. These problems both result from and lead to more complex economic-environmental interactions than more conventional models of pollution discharge or resource depletion would suggest. This book is essentially about those contemporary developments in environmental and resource economics which are concerned primarily with the long-run sustainability of economic activity.

It is important to remember that these new approaches are just the latest phase in the long evolution of the economic analysis of resource problems. A good way to understand these contemporary developments and appreciate their full potential as a contribution to economic analysis is to contrast them with more conventional approaches and to examine the historical evolution of the economic analysis of natural-resource scarcity. This is the approach taken by this book. Therefore, one is able to identify many common themes arising throughout the evolution of the economic analysis of environmental problems. For example, one important theme that will arise consistently in this book is the distinction between an absolute, or physical, natural-resource scarcity phenomenon and a relative scarcity phenomenon. The former has often been referred to as Malthusian scarcity and the latter Ricardian scarcity.

As the terms absolute and relative scarcity will be used throughout this book, it is important to discuss their distinctions a bit further:

*Absolute* natural-resource scarcity is fairly straightforward. It may occur if an economic activity or a whole system of economic activities depends upon an essential natural resource that has a finite limit on its physical availability. As that resource is depleted through use in the economic process, it may become absolutely scarce in a physical sense: there will be no more of that resource to be used. Absolute natural-resource scarcity is often referred to as Malthusian scarcity because it usually applies to resources of uniform quality and with an ultimate physical limit; however, absolute scarcity may also occur for physically limited resources if there are no substitutes in economic activity for these resources as they become increasingly scarce. Hence, the crucial factor in absolute natural-resource scarcity is the possibility of physical environmental limits on the economic processes of production and the consumption of goods and services.

*Relative* natural-resource scarcity is a slightly more complex concept, yet it goes right to the heart of modern neo-classical economic analysis. According to neo-classical theory, economics is "a science which studies human behaviour as a relation between ends and scarce means which have alternative use".[1] Thus a situation of relative scarcity always exists because resources are "limited" with respect to human wants, and human wants are "unlimited" in relation to resources. However, some resources are more relatively scarce than others. For example, a resource that is relatively abundant, such as air, may be used simultaneously for many activities (e.g., breathing, internal combustion and photosynthesis) such that employing the resource to fulfil one use (e.g., breathing) does not mean sacrificing alternative uses of the resource (e.g., internal combustion and photosynthesis). In contrast, if a resource is relatively scarce, such as coal, allocating the resource to fulfil one use (e.g., generating electricity) will mean less of the resource will be available to fulfil alternative use (e.g., domestic heating).

In a market economy, relatively scarce resources are allocated primarily by means of the price mechanism. The increasing relative scarcity of a resource implies a greater demand for it and therefore a higher price relative to other resources. More formally, if the price of a relatively scarce resource were dropped to zero, then the quantity demanded of that resource must exceed the quantity supplied. Alternatively, if at zero price the quantity demanded does not exceed quantity supplied, then clearly the resource is not relatively scarce. This implies that all potential uses of the resource can be fulfilled even if no price is charged.[2] Thus, under efficient market conditions, the increasing relative scarcity of a resource should translate into higher relative prices being charged for it.

Relative natural-resource scarcity would occur, therefore, if a resource essential to economic activities was used increasingly so that it became scarce relative to demand. If the resource is traded in an efficient market system, its economic value, or price, will rise. The crucial feature of relative natural-resource scarcity is that this phenomenon does not require any absolute physical resource limits. Instead, the total quantity of a resource may be unlimited but the quality of supplies may continuously diminish. That is, as the resource is extensively exploited, the economic process will have to appropriate it at lower and lower quality grades. Since the lower quality grades are generally less productive, more of the resource is required to match previous productivity levels.[3] This requires greater effort in resource exploitation and so leads to a rise in average costs; if this effort does not increase, the result is a decline in effective resource supplies (i.e., they become less and less productive). In both instances, the increasing relative scarcity is reflected in higher prices. For example, as good arable land is used up, marsh land and other less productive marginal lands may be converted to agriculture. By applying greater agricultural inputs (e.g., labour, mechanization, fertilizers, pesticides, etc.) the productivity of the newly converted land can be raised to the level of good arable land – but only at a higher unit cost. In contrast, if both lands receive the same package of inputs, productivity on the marginal lands would be lower and thus unit costs would still be higher.

Relative natural-resource scarcity is sometimes referred to as Ricardian scarcity as it is often thought to arise from the diminishing quality or accessibility of resources without requiring limits on the physical availability of resource stocks. If efficient markets exist for a natural resource, any increase in its relative scarcity will lead to higher relative prices for its productive services. As a consequence, there can only be a long-run economic constraint arising from relative natural-resource scarcity if the lack of these productive natural resources imposes such high costs within the economic system that growth in output cannot occur. In turn, this depends on whether higher relative prices automatically induce the technological substitution of other economic resources for the scarce natural resources and stimulate changes in consumption patterns to reduce demand.

Since the evolution of classical economic theory, economists have frequently expressed concern over whether natural-resource scarcity phenomena display relative or absolute scarcity characteristics. For example, the classical economists considered the scarcity of fertile land relative to the demands of an expanding population to be a key determinant in their theories of economic growth and distribution (see Chapter 1). The association of absolute scarcity with Malthusian scarcity arose because the Rev Thomas Malthus is thought to have argued that the fixed availability of agricultural land eventually leads to physical limits on the growth of subsistence production. Similarly, David Ricardo is thought to have initiated the concept of relative scarcity through assuming that agricultural land has no physical limits but was subject to diminishing quality and hence higher unit-costs of exploitation.

However, the neo-classical economists of the late nineteenth and early twentieth centuries often ignored the possibility of any natural-resource scarcity constraint on growth and chose instead to focus on the efficiency of market systems when allocating all scarce resources used in economic activity. They concluded that specific natural resources used in the process of production and consumption, such as raw material and energy stocks, display the relative scarcity characteristics common to all economic resources used as factors of production.[4] Moreover, under optimal market conditions in a dynamic (i.e., growing) economy, it was generally believed that relative scarcity of natural resources would not operate as a long-term constraint on economic growth. In the neo-classical view of the market system, as a particular resource becomes relatively scarce and its market price rises, this will provide incentives for the technological innovation necessary to exploit marginal stocks more efficiently, to develop cost-effective substitutes, and to conserve the use of existing supplies by curbing demand. Such dynamic economic responses to relative scarcity are often cited as the main reasons why the pessimistic predictions of the classical economists never materialized. Thus, as long as the relative scarcity of a natural resource is reflected in market prices and costs, dynamic conditions should automatically alleviate any such scarcity constraints. This is the conventional view of natural-resource scarcity that predominates in much of contemporary economic thinking (see Chapter 1).

It has long been recognized that the relative scarcity of certain non-renewable natural resources, such as fossil fuels and minerals, may be related to their potential exhaustibility.[5] For these exhaustible resources, eventual depletion of stocks poses the threat of an absolute constraint on available supply. Economists soon noted a similar problem for renewable resources, such as forests and fisheries, where the rate of stock depletion can exceed the natural rate of regeneration. These features underline the potential relative scarcity of economically valuable natural resources; as a result, the problem of natural-resource scarcity was perceived to be fundamentally one of determining the optimal rate of depletion/ management of such exhaustible/renewable stocks so as to maximize utility-yielding consumption over time. This became the conventional economic theoretical approach to the problem of natural-resource scarcity (see Chapter 3).

Modern economists have also recognized that the waste by-products of production and consumption may have a negative impact on human welfare, particularly when such pollution interferes with the health, amenity and recreational benefits provided by the natural environment. It has been acknowledged, however, that these costs are often afflicted externally to the market mechanism.[6] In other words, since the negative impacts, or costs, of pollution are not automatically reflected in the market prices of waste-generating commodities, pollution is considered a classic example of market failure. In modern neo-classical economics, this characteristic of pollution usually affords it separate treatment from the phenomenon of natural-resource scarcity, where the relative scarcity of depletable natural resources is assumed to be reflected in market prices (see Chapter 4). Thus, according to the conventional view, depletion of resource stocks is the real problem of natural-resource scarcity, whereas pollution is primarily a case of market failure.

In the 1960s and 1970s, increased public awareness of global environ-mental and resource problems sparked renewed interest in the economics of natural-resource scarcity. From this emerged what could be termed an alternative to the conventional economic view of the problem. This alternative view was also inspired by developments in ecology and the possible implications of the laws of thermodynamics for the economic process (see Chapter 2).

As noted above, the recent emergence of these alternative approaches is largely in response to a new class of global environmental problems. Essentially, the common perspective underlying these approaches con-tains two distinguishing features. First, resource depletion and waste generation by the economic system tend to be seen as an integral process – the throughput of material and energy resources in the economic system.[7] Secondly, because of this fundamental economic-environmental interaction and the inability of the natural environment to sustain indefinitely the conversion of its resources into waste, an absolute ecological constraint on economic activity leading to the growth of physical output is said to exist. Initial studies portrayed this constraint in terms of the global limits on the physical availability of many economi-cally valuable natural resources such as fossil fuels and timber.[8] More recently, economic analysis has focused on the ecological damage of economic activity, the misallocation of resources and even growth to the biosphere and its natural ecosystems (see Chapter 5). What this means is that, in the long run, an absolute ecological constraint may arise because the increasing environmental degradation inflicted by the economic process irrevocably disrupts natural ecosystems, permanently impairing essential environmental functions on which economic activity and human welfare depend.

This approach is also concerned with a fundamental relative-scarcity problem. As the environment is increasingly being exploited for one set of uses, say, to provide new sources of raw material and energy inputs and to assimilate additional waste, the quality of the environment may deteriorate. The consequence is an increasing relative scarcity of essential environmental services and ecological functions. These range from recreational, health, cultural, educational, scientific and aesthetic services to the maintenance of essential climatic and ecological cycles and functions. Thus the crucial focus of an alternative analysis is on the trade-off between, on the one hand, environmental quality and sustainability and, on the other, resource depletion and waste generation by the economic process (see Chapter 5). The main objective is to demonstrate the physical dependency of economic activity on the sustainability of crucial natural-resource systems and ecological functions, and to indicate the economic costs, or trade-offs, resulting from the failure to preserve sustainability and environmental quality. The result is an emerging theoretical justification, increasingly supported by applied analysis, for incorporating environmental considerations into economic policymaking, planning and project analysis, as part of an overall effort to achieve sustainable economic development (see Chapter 8).

This alternative approach may be particularly applicable to cases where cumulative resource depletion and degradation through economic over-exploitation lead to severe ecological disruption and the collapse of human livelihoods. For example, with continuous tropical deforestation there may be adverse local and inter-regional ecological disturbances that radically alter rainfall patterns, climate and species diversity. The result may be a catastrophic decline in the ability of the forest area and neighbouring regions to support dependent economic systems and human populations (see Chapter 6). Similarly, climatic changes resulting from the excess emission of greenhouse gases from industrial activity may significantly affect agricultural productivity and thus the ability of some regions of the world to feed their populations (see Chapter 6). Intensive agricultural production on marginal lands can lead to accelerating problems of soil erosion and trends towards long-term desertification, which require new policy approaches and investment strategies in order to sustain agricultural development (see Chapter 7).

The alternative approach may be perhaps most relevant to cases in the

Third World where the combination of poverty, unequal distribution of land and other resources, and population growth, are pushing millions of people to over-exploit existing resources in order to survive. Their herds overgraze; their shortening fallows on steep slopes and fragile soils induce erosion; their need for off-season and off-farm incomes drives them to cut and sell fuelwood and to make and sell charcoal; they are forced to cultivate and degrade marginal and unstable land.[9] The result is irrevocable environmental damage with long-term economic losses. Assuming no change in the current distribution of land and other resource assets, the number of subsistence farmers, pastoralists and landless households – groups representing three-quarters of the agricultural households in developing economies – will increase by 50 million, to nearly 220 million, by the year 2000.[10] Without adequate livelihood opportunities, these resource-poor households will continue to degrade the environment in order simply to meet minimum subsistence and income needs.

## TOWARDS AN ECONOMICS OF SUSTAINABLE DEVELOPMENT

This alternative economic view of natural-resource scarcity poses a serious challenge to the conventional view that has prevailed for so long. It also offers a potentially unique theoretical insight into the problem of natural-resource scarcity, one that is distinct from conventional approaches. This book attempts to explore this potential insight by discussing its possible contributions to environmental and resource economics, and also its limitations. In particular, this book will attempt to integrate and develop this alternative perspective into a coherent model suitable for the economic analysis of environmental problems. Thus, much of the final part of the book will be devoted to discussing examples of the new class of environmental problems that are more appropriately analysed through this type of model and approach. The policy implications of such an analysis will also be discussed.

The general theme is that economic analysis of environmental and resource problems may be turning full circle. There may be conditions under which present patterns of resource exploitation have transgressed ecological thresholds. A new class of problems arising from environmental degradation has not been adequately dealt with by conventional economic approaches. These problems are occurring at the global level, such as the warming caused by greenhouse gases; at the regional level, such as Amazonian deforestation; and at the more local level, such as upper watershed degradation on Java. The challenge is to extend environmental and resource economics to analyse these new kinds of natural-resource scarcity and the environmental conditions for sustainable development.

It may still be theoretically possible in the neo-classical system to conceive of scarce resources as being infinitely substitutable so that economic growth, in principle, can proceed forever. However, there is increasing concern that actual economic systems do not always contain the automatic self-regulating mechanisms for ensuring the perpetual environmental sustainability of current economic development paths. Consequently, if a more sustainable development path is our objective, there must be a consistent economic analysis of the problems arising from environmental degradation and the trade-offs implicit in any ecological constraints.

For example, the recent report of the World Commission on Environment and Development makes it very clear that our current global path of economic development is unsustainable.[11] To quote just a few examples: more land has been cleared for settled cultivation in the past 100 years than in all the previous centuries of human existence; over the last 35 years, the consumption of chemical fertilizers increased ninefold, the use of pesticides increased thirty-two fold and irrigated areas doubled; and around 325 to 375 million tonnes of hazardous wastes were generated worldwide, with around 5 million tonnes produced by newly industrialized and developing countries. Dealing with the environmental problems that are inevitably arising from such trends requires a new way of looking at the inter-relationship between the economic process and the environment: it requires an economics of sustainable development. We are not there yet. Nevertheless, this book offers one vision of the way that economic analysis is evolving, and must evolve still further, in this direction.

The book consists of nine chapters, which can be grouped into four parts. The first part (the Introduction, and Chapters 1 and 2) provides an overview of the historical background to environmental and resource economics and analyses the impact of environmentalism, ecology and thermodynamics on contemporary approaches. The second part (Chapters 3 and 4) highlights the more recent developments and extensions of conventional approaches in environmental and resource economics, in particular their concentration on optimal rates of pollution and resource use. Criticism of these approaches leads in the third part (Chapters 5–8) to the development of an "alternative" approach to the economic analysis of environmental degradation. This approach is illustrated by the examples of the global greenhouse effect, Amazonian deforestation, and upper watershed degradation on Java. This last case is developed in order to illustrate the policy implications that can be derived from an analysis concerned with sustainable development. The final part (Chapter 8) discusses the implications of taking a new direction in the analysis of environmental and resource problems – the development of an emerging economics of sustainable development.

## NOTES

1. Lionel Robbins, *The Nature and Significance of Economic Science* (2nd edn), (Macmillan: London, 1952) p. 16.
2. This latter case also fits the neo-classical definition of a free good: "There are things in the external world which are present in such comparative abundance that the use of particular units for one thing does not involve going without other units for others. The air we breathe, for instance, is such a 'free' commodity." Robbins, op. cit., pp. 14–15.
3. Alternatively, the resource may not strictly decline in quality but may instead become more difficult to exploit. For instance, deeper wells or mine shafts need to be dug, more drainage is required for marginal agricultural land, greater exploration is required to find reserves and so on. Nevertheless, the result is effectively the same: greater effort and so greater costs are required to obtain qualitatively the same amount of resource.
4. See, for example, Alfred Marshall, *Principles of Economics; An Introductory Volume* (8th edn), (Macmillan: London, 1949) and Robbins, op. cit.
5. See, for example, Harold Hotelling, "The economics of exhaustible resources", *Journal of Political Economy*, Vol. 39 (1931), pp. 137–75; William Stanley Jevons, *The Coal Question: An Inquiry Concerning the Progress of the Nation and the Probable Exhaustion of Our Coal Mines* (Macmillan: London, 1909); Marshall, op. cit.; and John Stuart Mill, *Principles of Political Economy With Some of Their Application to Social Philosophy*, 1909 edn (Augustus M. Kelley: Clifton, New Jersey, 1973).
6. See, for example, Marshall, op. cit., and A.C. Pigou, *The Economics of Welfare* (4th edn), (Macmillan: London, 1962).
7. The "throughput" concept is usually attributed to Kenneth E. Boulding, "The economics of the coming spaceship Earth", in H. Jarrett (ed.), *Environmental Quality in a Growing Economy* (Johns Hopkins University Press: Baltimore, 1966). The other pioneer of this thermodynamics analogy is Nicholas Georgescu-Roegen, particularly his essays in *Analytical Economics* (Harvard University Press: Cambridge, Massachusetts, 1966) and *The Entropy Law and the Economic Process* (Harvard University Press: Cambridge, Massachusetts, 1971).
8. See, for example, J.W. Forrester, *World Dynamics* (Wright Allen: Cambridge, Massachusetts, 1971) and Dennis L. Meadows, Donella H. Meadows, Jorgen Randers and William Behrens, *The Limits to Growth: A Report for the Club of Rome's Project on the Predicament of Man* (Universe Books: New York, 1972).
9. See Robert Chambers, "Sustainable livelihoods, environment and development: putting poor rural people first", Discussion Paper 240 (Institute of Development Studies: Brighton, Sussex, December 1987).
10. World Commission on Environment and Development, *Our Common Future* (Oxford University Press: Oxford, 1987), p. 142.
11. Ibid.

This book is published in collaboration with the London Environmental Economics Centre and the International Institute for Environment and Development (IIED).

*The London Environmental Economics Centre* is a joint initiative of IIED and the Economics Department of University College London. The main objectives of the Centre are: research into environmental problems of less-developed countries from an economic standpoint; dissemination of research and state-of-the-art environmental economics through publication, public and professional address and specialist conferences; and advice and consultancy on specific issues of environmental policy.

*The International Institute for Environment and Development* is a charitable organization concerned with the environment and how it is affected by development. IIED's sustainable development programmes include policy research, technical assistance and training, institution-building, and information. Its agenda encompass health and living conditions in Third World human settlements, forestry and land-use, marine resources, dryland management, sustainable agriculture and environmental economics.

# 1
# Historical Approaches to Natural-Resource Scarcity

The focus of this chapter is the historical development of economic theories of natural-resource scarcity, from Adam Smith and the classical economics through to the landmark 1963 study by Barnett and Morse, and the contemporary conventional view. These theories have tradition-allly been classified as either "pessimistic Malthusian" models that suggest a long-term absolute natural-resource scarcity constraint or "optimistic Ricardian" models that do not assume any absolute limits but only admit that resources decline in quality and are therefore relatively scarce. The major themes of this chapter are, first, to examine how well these Ricardian and Malthusian labels fit the classical and neo-classical theories of natural-resource scarcity, and secondly, to demonstrate how adoption of the Ricardian perspective on resource availability allowed more modern theories to become increasingly sanguine about the ability of market forces and technological change to overcome any "relative" scarcity.

## MALTHUSIAN AND RICARDIAN SCARCITY

Barnett and Morse are often credited with being the first to draw a distinction between Malthusian and Ricardian economic approaches to natural-resource scarcity.[1] In making this distinction, the authors laid the groundwork for the differentiation between "absolute" and "relative" scarcity, with the former being associated with Malthusian and the latter with Ricardian scarcity:

> Modern views concerning the influence of natural resources on economic growth are variations on the scarcity doctrine developed by Thomas Malthus and David Ricardo in the first quarter of the nineteenth century and elaborated later by John Stuart Mill. There were two basic versions of this doctrine. One, the Malthusian, rested on the assumption that the stock of agricultural land was absolutely limited; once this limit had been reached, continuing population growth would require increasing intensity of cultivation and,

consequently, would bring about diminishing returns per capita. The other, or Ricardian, version viewed diminishing returns as a current phenomenon, reflecting decline in the quality of land as successive parcels were brought within the margin of profitable cultivation.[2]

Thus, Malthusian scarcity is assumed to treat natural resources (e.g., agricultural land) as being homogeneous in quality, whereas Ricardian scarcity portrays them as varying in quality. In the absence of technological change, both scarcity effects eventually constrain economic activity; however, they differ in both method and timing. Modern approaches to natural resource scarcity are assumed to be extensions of the Malthusian and Ricardian doctrines.

In terms of method and the timing of diminishing returns, an important distinction is that, for Malthusian scarcity, diminishing returns do not set in until the absolute limits of the available stock of natural resources is reached. In contrast, "Ricardian diminishing returns take effect from the outset, thus requiring no specification concerning the time horizon and no assumption of an absolute limit to the availability of resources". That is, Malthus "found resource scarcity inherent in the finiteness of the globe", whereas Ricardo "focused upon the differential fertility of the individual parcel of lands; and assuming that the better lands would be used first, he found declining quality to be the cause of increasing resource scarcity".[3]

So in the Ricardian case, increasing production costs set in as soon as resources are used up in order of declining quality; the less fertile the land, the more effort needs to be applied which leads to a rise in the costs per unit of output. In contrast, with Malthusian scarcity , there is assumed to be no difference in the quality of the resource stock; therefore, costs do not rise until the absolute limits of the stock are reached. These contrasting scarcity effects are depicted in Figure 1.1.

As shown in Figure 1.1a, Malthusian scarcity reflects a situation of absolute scarcity. The finiteness of resources – the physically limited stock of land – acts as a constraint on the expansion of output. Moreover, it is only when this absolute limit is reached that this scarcity effect is conveyed by rising costs (prices). Once this has occurred, however, the entire stock of natural resources is fully employed, and the increase in costs is ineffective in encouraging substitution among resources. Economic activity is abruptly halted without any chance of adjustment.

However, Ricardian scarcity exhibits all the characteristics of relative scarcity (see Figure 1.1b). As resources are used in successive grades of declining quality, the costs of resource-use rise. Consequently, as soon as the initial stock of the highest quality resource is fully employed (O A'), physical scarcity is translated into relative scarcity measured by price movements. The economic system should therefore automatically

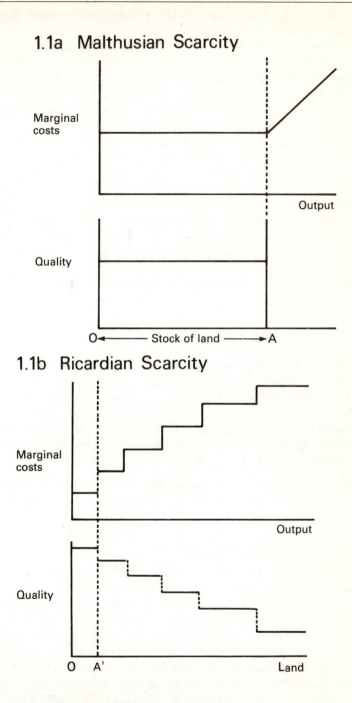

Figure 1.1: **Malthusian and Ricardian Scarcity**

respond to such price signals by substituting for the more expensive, relatively scarce natural resource.

A situation of Ricardian scarcity does not necessarily imply the existence of an absolute limit to resource availability: "There is always another extensive margin, another plateau of lower quality, which will be reached before the increasing intensity of utilization becomes intolerable".[4] As long as there are sufficient factors working to offset the progression of Ricardian diminishing returns, either by making poorer quality resources more economical to exploit or by allowing the substitution of previously unexploited resources and synthetic alternatives, then there should be no long-term constraint on economic activity. The rising relative costs accompanying any Ricardian scarcity effect should stimulate technical progress and thus foster "discovery or development of alternative sources, not only equal in economic quality but often superior to those replaced".[5] This existence of Ricardian scarcity implies that economic growth may lead to a temporary, increasing relative scarcity of a particular stock of resources, but this does not necessarily lead to an absolute constraint on growth.

## SMITH, MALTHUS AND RICARDO

The use of the Malthusian and Ricardian distinction by Barnett and Morse and others suggests that the contemporary debate has its fundamental roots in, and perhaps was even anticipated by, classical economic approaches to scarcity. A brief review of the classical treatment of the problem by Adam Smith, Thomas Malthus and David Ricardo should reveal the extent to which classical approaches anticipated the conflicting contemporary approaches with respect to:

  i) the role of price as a measure of "relative" (exchange) scarcity;
 ii) the role of natural-resource inadequacy as an "absolute" constraint on growth; *and*
iii) the role of technological progress in alleviating any scarcity-induced constraints on growth.

Classical economics differs substantially from modern neo-classical economics. For one thing, the primary concern of the classical economists was not to demonstrate the allocative efficiency of the market system but to explore the social, economic and natural conditions determining economic growth: "... considerations concerning 'allocative efficiency' were eclipsed by broader considerations concerning the means of raising the physical productivity of labor and expanding the total volume of economic activity".[6] Moreover, classical economic views on scarcity were often more consistent with those developed by the "natural law" philosophers (such as Francis Hutcheson, Gershom Charmichael and Samuel von Puffendorf) and the Physiocrats (such as Quesnet), whose writings formed the ideological basis for the classical doctrines. Although in the natural law theories there was some appreciation that the relative scarcity of goods has a determining influence on the structure of relative prices, these theories did not endorse the neo-classical notion of relative scarcity as the fundamental economic problem and the rationale for the existence of prices as indices of scarcity.[7] These fundamental differences with modern economics limit the extent to which classical scarcity doctrines can be compared with the contemporary economic debate over natural resource scarcity.

## Adam Smith

In the *Wealth of Nations*, Adam Smith was searching for an unvarying standard of value that could account for and measure increases in the "real wealth" of nations and, for this purpose, "market values which depended on monetary whims and fashions, on temporary relations between supply and demand, did not appear satisfactory".[8] For this reason, he emphasized the distinction between the true value, or "natural price", of a commodity and its market price, where the former is determined by "the amount of labor commanded in the market" and the latter by the "relative scarcity" of goods in short supply.[9] Thus price may serve in the marketplace as an indicator of the relative scarcity of goods in short supply *versus* those in abundance but relative scarcity was neither the fundamental resource problem nor an explanation of "how prices came to be what they are".

Smith did not consider that the finite limits of the earth, or any other natural-resource scarcity problem, would pose a threat of an absolute constraint on economic growth. Instead, "Smith's account rested on the presupposition that nature was generous ... like the Physiocrats before him, he viewed agriculture as capable of yielding outputs far in excess of inputs".[10] Smith placed great emphasis on the accumulation of capital to raise labour productivity in agriculture.[11] None the less, although he believed that economic stagnation would not arise from diminishing returns in agriculture imposed by absolute resource limits (i.e., on arable land), Smith's writings do suggest that, despite increased productivity, overwhelming economic dependency on agriculture would eventually increase demand for agricultural output in excess of supply. Prolonged excess agricultural demand would lead to profound distributional impacts, in terms of exchange relationships, private property institutions and the pattern of income distribution. It is these distributional and social responses to the relative scarcity of agricultural output – and not the economic dependency on natural resources – that eventually produce a stationary state.[12]

Smith's doctrine does contain some semblance of the modern concern with relative scarcity and constraints on growth. However, the unique role of social relations and distributional consequences in his analysis plus the failure to consider the ameliorating role of technological innovation suggest that Smith's view is far removed from contemporary natural-resource scarcity debates.

## Thomas Malthus

It is not Adam Smith's theories but the ideas of Thomas Malthus, especially those expressed in *An Essay on Population*, that are associated with the concept of an absolute constraint on growth.[13] As Barnett and Morse comment, however, Malthus's *Essay* "is far more an analysis of population than of natural resources, and natural-resource scarcity in effect are more asserted than demonstrated. Moreover, Malthus did not consider the problem of resource depletion, and therefore had nothing to say about the possibility of increasing scarcity and scarcity effect from resource destruction."[14]

At the crux of Malthus's argument that "population has this constant tendency to increase beyond the means of subsistence, and that it is kept to its necessary level by these causes" was his belief that subsistence, and thus humankind, is "necessarily confined in room" by nature.[15] Hence Malthus's concept of a limit to the rate of increase in subsistence as compared to the unlimited expansion of population led to his famous "iron law":

> Assuming, then, my postulate as granted, I say, that the power of population is indefinitely greater than the power in the earth to produce subsistence for man. Population, when unchecked, increases in a geometrical ratio. Subsistence only increases in an arithmetical ratio. A slight acquaintance with numbers will shew the immensity of the first power in comparison with the second.[16]

It was not until his later work, *Principles of Political Economy*, that Malthus applied his concept of "limited territory" and consequent law of population increase to an explicit analysis of the long-term conditions for growth.[17] In doing so, Malthus made several important departures from the "bounty of nature" view shared by the Physiocrats and Adam Smith.

First, Malthus suggested that the limited supply and unevenness in quality of land was an important determinant of landlords' rents in agriculture.[18] In the Malthusian system, as population growth exceeds the growth of subsistence, "cultivation will be extended to less fertile acreages and/or will be intensified on lands already under the plough".[19] However, cultivation of lower-quality land would be unacceptable to the landlord "unless he could, at the least, obtain the same rent as before".[20] As the extension of agricultural land to less fertile acreages would require more effort in terms of capital and labour to produce the same output as before, yet the landlord's rent would not fall, this implies a proportionately smaller return for capital and labour to divide. Given that there is a minimum level of subsistence needed to sustain each labourer, and more labour is increasingly required, then the division of the return to capital and labour eventually favours the latter, causing profits to decline.[21] In turn, as "the cost of producing corn and labour continually increases" relative to "the cost of producing manufactures and articles of commerce", profits and capital accumulation in the non-agricultural sector "must continue to fall".[22]

Consequently, for Malthus, the inevitable constraint on economic growth emerges from two interlinking causes: the advent of diminishing returns in agriculture resulting from the continual expansion of population on limited fertile land, and the decline in the exchange value of manufactures and commerce with respect to labour and subsistence (i.e., "corn").[23] In effect, although the natural-resource (agricultural) scarcity problem is inherently physical (diminishing returns due to the constant application of a variable input, labour, to one fixed in supply, land), it manifests itself as a "relative" scarcity phenomenon (higher prices for subsistence and labour).[24]

This view that physical scarcity must translate into relative scarcity conveyed by exchange relationships is not surprising given Malthus's belief that all value, either real or nominal, is reflected in exchange value.[25] Malthus adhered strongly to the view that market forces determined both product and factor prices and, consequently, incorporated into the measurement of real value "the money price of common agricultural labour". As a result, his theory of value, even more so than Adam Smith's, can be considered "a precursor of neo-classical economics rather than in opposition to it".[26]

Although Malthus believed that agriculture was physically dependent on arable land, he did not envisage the entire economic system, both agricultural and non-agricultural sectors, as physically dependent on other natural resources – and certainly not on raw materials or energy supplies. Instead, if the Malthusian system is physically dependent on anything, it is human labour, which acts as the ultimate constraint on growth. It is only because labour is a necessary input into the system that the high costs of subsistence, and thus of labour, are inescapable. This suggests that the existence of "limited territory" is by itself not sufficient to constrain growth; the key catalyst is the rapid expansion of population on this "limited territory". Without the additional assumption that the rate of population growth must always exceed the rate of subsistence growth, and that the physical dependency of the economic process on labour prevented it from escaping the inevitable consequences of this law, it is doubtful whether Malthus would have considered "limited territory" by itself to be a factor influencing diminishing returns in agriculture. This latter assumption is often overlooked, but it is the crucial mechanism through which the constraint becomes binding. Indeed, Malthus appears to hint at this in his *Essay*:

> In this supposition no limits whatever are placed to the produce of the earth. It may increase for ever, and be greater than any assignable quantity; yet still the power of population being in every period so much superior, the increase of the human species can only be kept down to the level of the means of subsistence by the constant operation of the strong law of necessity, acting as a check upon the greater power.[27]

In fact, without making any additional assumptions concerning resource-saving technological innovations, it can be demonstrated that this constraint on growth in the Malthusian system would be broken through introducing the substitution of capital for labour in agriculture (see the appendix to this chapter). With a declining agricultural labour force, and assuming a fixed subsistence wage, it would no longer be obvious that "a greater proportion of the whole would necessarily go to labour". Consequently, there would be no reason to expect the rate of profit and the accumulation of capital to cease in agriculture. Moreover, if labour-substitution took place in the non-agricultural sector, then manufacturing and commerce could also insulate themselves from any potential rising labour costs. This would, of course, protect the share of profits and ensure capital accummulation. Thus capital-labour substitution in both agricultural and non-agricultural sectors would reduce economic dependency on labour, allowing continued capital accumulation and growth.

Malthus's perception of the process leading to eventual stagnation is fundamentally different from the modern notion of Malthusian scarcity as interpreted by Barnett and Morse, and others. The Malthusian system also differs from contemporary alternative theories of natural-resource constraints on growth, as outlined in The Introduction. A key ingredient in the latter is the assumption that the constraint on growth arises from the *entire* economic process, and not just agriculture, being *directly* dependent on the limited resources of the natural environment. This condition is an external, ecological or biophysical, limit resulting from the increased environmental degradation and ecological disruptions generated by this dependency. The source of the constraint on growth is not population growth *per se* nor the physical dependency of the economic system on labour. It arises from the physical dependency of the economic process on the environment and its impact through environmental degradation on the sustainability of economic activity. In contrast, Malthus's constraint is an internal, economic constraint resulting from the high labour costs accompanying the relative scarcity of subsistence and the dependency on labour. Thus in the Malthusian system, capital–labour substitution is sufficient to allow the economic system to escape stagnation. But capital–labour substitution cannot mitigate the type of scarcity effect envisioned by the contemporary alternative view.

## David Ricardo

David Ricardo's approach to natural-resource scarcity is based on his famous statement that, as the price of corn rises "with the difficulty of producing the last portion of it", total rent of all agricultural land must increase:

> Rent, it must be remembered, is not in proportion to the absolute fertility of the land in cultivation, but in proportion to its relative fertility. Whatever cause may drive capital to inferior land must elevate rent on the superior land; the cause of rent being, as stated by Mr Malthus in his third proposition, "the comparative scarcity of the most fertile land". The price of corn will naturally rise with the difficulty of producing the last portions of it, and the value of the whole quantity produced on a particular farm will be increased, although its quantity will be diminished; but as the cost of production will not increase on the more fertile land, as wages and profits taken together will continue always of the same value, it is evident that the excess of price above the cost of production, or in other words, rent, must rise with the diminished fertility of the land, unless it is counteracted by a great reduction of capital, population and demand.[28]

Thus, in supposed contrast to Malthus, Ricardo is often credited with identifying the scarcity of natural resources (arable land) as a relative scarcity effect conveyed by rising market prices.

The theories of Malthus and Ricardo actually share much in common. For example, Ricardo also concluded that the result of rising agricultural rents and increased employment of labour and capital on less fertile lands must be a decline in the share of profits.[29] In addition, Ricardo was clearly a Malthusianist in that he accepted Malthus's iron law of population expansion as the central ingredient of his system.[30] In both the Ricardian and Malthusian systems, population growth is the primary causative factor leading to the cultivation of less fertile lands and the consequent diminishing returns in agriculture; over the long run, the continual expansion of labour causes profits to decline as a greater proportion of output is distributed as wages and rent. Finally, both Malthus and Ricardo suggest that qualitative differences in the fertility of land are important determinants of rising rent and agricultural prices, although Malthus considered this to be only one of several important factors. In fact, it has been noted that Ricardo gave "full credit to Malthus and Edward West for the authorship of the rent doctrine", as is implied in the above passage.[31]

In contrast to Malthus, Ricardo did not include any explicit concept of an absolute limit to natural resources (land) in his analysis. Whereas Malthus stated that such a limit exists, dictated by "limited territory", Ricardo simply maintained that nature has "limited the productive powers of the land".[32] Although modern writers often infer from this distinction that Ricardo "implicitly doubted the significance of Malthus's ultimate limit",[33] it may have been that Ricardo considered a more interesting aspect of the physical limitation imposed by nature to be quite literally the limited *productive powers* of the land. In particular, Ricardo may have been struck by the unique feature that in agriculture, as opposed to industry, nature is "niggardly in her gifts" of "labour":

> The labor of nature is paid, not because she does much, but because she does little. In proportion as she becomes niggardly in her gifts she extracts a greater price for her work. Where she is munificently beneficent she always works gratis.... Does nature nothing for man in manufactures?... There is not a manufacture which can be mentioned in which nature does not give her assistance to man, and give it, too, generously and gratuitously.[34]

Since the main theme of his *Principles* was to demonstrate that "every increase of the quantity of labour must augment the value of that commodity on which it is exercised",[35] it is not surprising that Ricardo was more interested in describing the resource limitations imposed by nature in terms of the "limited productive power" of nature. As nature "becomes more niggardly in her gifts" of "labor", further cultivation requires a more disproportionate use of human labour, which according to the labour theory of value is the only way this scarcity effect will lead to higher real prices from agricultural output. Hence, in the Ricardian system, it is necessary to describe the natural resource (land) scarcity situation in terms of the limited productive powers of nature in order for it to be consistent with a labour theory of value.

The major dissimilarity between Malthus and Ricardo's views over the concept of the physical limitations imposed by nature may have more to do with their different methods of inquiry, which derived in turn from their different approaches to the problem of value. Ricardo insisted that labour was the fundamental measure of all economic values, whether it is "real" or "market". Consequently, it was important that he construct the methodology of his inquiry in terms consistent with this labour theory of value. Malthus, on the other hand, clearly rejected such an approach. In fact, Ricardo's preoccupation with a labour theory of value indicates that he was actually further from both the neo-classical concept of market price being a true measure of relative scarcity; as "Ricardo's foundation of value is not related to 'scarcity' in any sense of the word", it clearly cannot be compared to "the neoclassical theorisation of the market" that is "based on a concept of inexorable scarcity which provides the neo classical system with its 'foundation' of value".[36] Ricardo's approach is therefore equally incomparable with the relative scarcity approach of the contemporary conventional view of natural-resource scarcity.

If the decline in profits and economic stagnation in the Ricardian system ultimately results from the assumption of labour dependency and rapid population growth, then this prediction must be susceptible to the same weakness as the Malthusian system: if there were substantial capital – labour subsitution and/or a limit to population expansion, then there would no longer be a natural-resource scarcity constraint on growth (see the appendix to this chapter). Significantly, although both Malthus and Ricardo did acknowledge the effects of technological improvements on agricultural production, it was Malthus who appeared more optimistic about the potential ameliorating role of technological change.

For example, Paglin notes that Ricardo considered technological improvements in the short run to be cost-reducing rather than output-increasing; that is, they would allow the same output to be produced with less capital and labour.[37] In the short run, any decline in profits might be "happily checked at repeated intervals by the improvements in machinery connected with the production of necessaries, as well as by the discoveries in the science of agriculture". But over the long run, "the natural tendency of profits then is to fall" as these technological improvements are overridden by eventual diminishing returns in agriculture due to population expansion and economic dependency on labour as a productive input.[38] In contrast, Malthus maintained that technological improvements could, over the long run, increase output.[39] As a result, the inevitable consequences of Malthusian population growth and labour dependency could be postponed to such an extent that "diminishing returns in agriculture were not a problem which need concern anyone for hundreds of years".[40]

## MILL, JEVONS AND MARSHALL

The interpretations of the classical economic theories of natural-resource (land) scarcity by John Stuart Mill, William Stanley Jevons and Alfred Marshall mark an important transition in economic thought between these theories and the contemporary debate. The works of these three writers also reflect the historical transition in modern thought from classical to neo-classical economics. While Mill is considered to be a classical economist, his interpretations of the phenomenon of relative natural-resource scarcity are closer to the modern conventional economic view than either Ricardo's or Malthus's approaches. Similarly, while Jevons's theories on marginal utility and consumer demand were central to the marginalist revolution, he attempted to prove that the finite nature of Britain's coal stocks would ultimately lead to an absolute constraint on growth. Only in the work of Marshall does there appear to be a complete transition both from classical to neo-classical (marginalist) economic thought, and from the classical views on scarcity to the modern conception of the natural-resource scarcity problem.

## John Stuart Mill

As his *Principles of Political Economy* reveals, John Stuart Mill clearly shared the classical economic view that, in the long run, economic expansion would eventually encounter the problem of diminishing returns in agriculture, which in turn would lead to falling profits, rising rents and increasing subsistence costs.[41] Moreover, for Mill, this "impossibility of ultimately avoiding the stationary state" is also grounded in the tendency for population to increase "as it has never yet failed to do so when the increase of industry and of the means of subsistence made room for it",[42] and in the economic "fact" that the "limited quantity of land, and limited productiveness of it, are the real limits to the increase of production".[43]

Unlike his predecessors, Mill acknowledged more explicitly the important counteracting influences of technological "improvements" in postponing the inevitable emergence of the stationary state.[44] In fact, Mill conceded that without the supposed Malthusian tendency of population to increase with increases in subsistence and material wealth, agricultural improvements could be sufficient to support economic growth:

> If population were stationary, and the produce of the earth never needed to be augmented in quantity, there would be no cause for greater cost of production. Mankind would, on the contrary, have the full benefit of all improvements in agriculture, or in the arts subsidiary to it, and there would be no difference in this respect, between the produce of agriculture and those of manufactures.[45]

In addition, Mill extended the classical concept of natural-resource scarcity to non-renewable mineral resources. Although he argued that mining is "more susceptible of mechanical improvements than agricultural production" and that exhausted mines could be replaced by "the discovery of new ones, equal or superior in richness", he nevertheless considered mining to yield diminishing returns and increased costs in the long run.[46] Furthermore, he considered the problem of exhaustible-resource scarcity to be a constraint independent of the Malthusian population problem:

> The only products of industry, which, if population did not increase, would be liable to a real increase of cost of production, are those which, depending on a material which is not renewed, are either wholly or partially exhaustible; such as coal, and most if not all

metals; for even iron, the most abundant as well as most useful of metallic products, which forms an ingredient of most minerals and of almost all rocks, is susceptible of exhaustion so far as regards its riches and most tractable ores.[47]

There are two additional contributions that Mill makes to the contemporary debate over natural-resource scarcity. First, he considered the diminishing returns impact of natural-resource scarcity to be a *current* phenomenon that comes into operation "long before the final limit is reached."[48] Hence, Mill argued strongly in favour of the relative–scarcity approach to natural-resource scarcity as developed by Ricardo (and by Malthus in his *Principles*) based on the assumption that land in agriculture is used in order of declining fertility and that its gradually increasing scarcity must be reflected in "an augmentation of cost and therefore of price".[49]

Mill is also credited with being the first classical economist to consider the impact of natural-resource scarcity on the various amenity services provided by nature to humankind. These services represent alternative uses of natural resources (e.g., land), of which Mill distinguishes two types. On the one hand, there is the specific, more narrowly defined use of land as living space for residential use. Given that this use is subject to private property rights, Mill suggests that its relative scarcity would also be reflected in market conditions: "Land is used for other purposes than agriculture, especially for residence; and when so used, yields a rent, determined by principles similar to those already laid down.... Sites of remarkable beauty are generally limited in supply, and therefore, if in great demand, are at a scarcity value."[50]

In an oft-quoted passage, Mill considers a more general alternative use of natural resources:

> It is not good for man to be kept perforce at all times in the presence of his species. A world from which solitude is extirpated is a very poor ideal. Solitude, in the sense of being often alone, is essential to any depth of meditation or of character; and solitude in the presence of natural beauty and grandeur, is the cradle of thoughts of aspirations which are not only good for the individual, but which society could ill do without. Nor is there much satisfaction in contemplating the world with nothing left to the spontaneous activity of nature; with every rood of land brought into cultivation, which is capable of growing food for human beings; every flowery waste or natural pasture plowed up, all quadrupeds or birds which not domesticated for man's use exterminated as his rivals for food, every hedgerow or superfluous tree rooted out, and scacely a place where a wild shrub or flower could grow without being eradicated as a weed in the name of improved agriculture. If the earth must lose that great portion of its pleasantness which it owes to things that the

unlimited increase of wealth and population would extirpate from it, for the mere purpose of enabling it to support a larger, but not a better or happier population, I sincerely hope, for the sake of posterity, that they will be content to be stationary, long before necessity compels them to it.[51]

In this passage, Mill appears to be suggesting that certain services provided by nature, such as solitude, meditation, natural beauty, spontaneous activity and pleasantness, are threatened by the use of the environment for furthering economic growth. Moreover, the scarcity of such essential services may have a detrimental impact on human welfare long before diminishing returns impose an absolute constraint on economic activity. It should also be noted that Mill does not suggest that the imminent scarcity of these environmental services will be reflected in market prices; instead, he concludes that preservation of these vital services may motivate society to consider the stationary state as a desirable outcome "long before necessity compels them to it".[52]

Mill's analysis of natural-resource scarcity provides an important bridge between classical and more contemporary views.[53] For example, Mill acknowledged the importance of technological improvements in postponing any scarcity constraint on growth, which he portrayed as a gradual relative scarcity phenomenon that would be reflected in market prices. He also recognized that the physical dependence of the entire economic process on (particularly non-renewable) natural resources could lead to a potential scarcity effect independent of that generated by population growth. Finally, Mill's views on the effect of economic growth on environmental quality seem to anticipate the contemporary environmental movement.

## William Stanley Jevons

Jevons's work *The Coal Question* is significant to contemporary views of natural-resource scarcity in several respects.[54] First, in contrast to the classical economists (with the exception of Mill), Jevons considered that the potential exhaustibility of non-renewable resources, particularly coal, was the most important threat to sustained economic growth in industrialized countries such as Britain. In addition, his views on and analysis of the economic implications of the scarcity of exhaustible resources (coal) closely resembles the limits to growth studies of the early 1970s that also predict an absolute scarcity constraint on economic activity.[55]

*The Coal Question* was not just an extension of the special case that Mill made for exhaustible resources in classical analysis, but a fundamental re-orientation of this analysis towards a concern with the role of non-renewable resources in limiting growth. This clearly paralleled the development of Britain from an agricultural to an industrial-based economy, which meant that coal had effectively replaced corn as the means of "subsistence":

> Our subsistence no longer depends upon our produce of corn. The momentous repeal of the Corn Laws throws us from corn upon coal. It marks, at any rate, the epoch when coal was finally recognized as the staple produce of the country; — it marks the ascendancy of the manufacturing interest, which is only another name for the development of the use of coal.[56]

Believing that economic growth in Britain depended on continued coal consumption, which was physically limited by the availability of commercially exploited reserves, Jevons concluded that "should the consumption multiply for rather more than a century at the same rate, the average depth of our coal-mines would be 4,000 feet, and the average price of coal much higher than the highest price now paid for the finest kinds of coal ... we cannot long continue our rate of progress".[57] Jevons consequently believed that the "inevitable exhaustion" of these reserves "will be marked *pari passu* by a rising cost or value of coal; and when the price has risen to a certain amount comparatively to the price in other countries, our main branches of trade will be doomed".[58] The result would be economic stagnation for Britain.

For Jevons, the physical dependency of the economic process on coal was assured, because he considered it "useless to think of substituting any other kind of fuel for coal".[59] As for petroleum, he noted that "it is undoubtedly superior to coal for various purposes, and is capable of replacing it", yet he dismissed the possibility of petroleum as a feasible substitute, for "its natural supply is far more limited and uncertain than that of coal, and an artificial supply can only be had by the distillation of some kind of coal at considerable cost".[60] Jevons was equally pessimistic about the impact of technological change on reducing mining costs and increasing effective reserves. Mine depths could only be 4,000 to 5,000 feet, he reasoned, because of the high capital costs of increasing shafts, the great risks and the prohibitive interest payments on loans.[61] Jevons also maintained that any "economical use" of coal would not reduce but actually increase demand, for the resulting fall in price would only induce a higher rate of consumption.[62] Nor did he believe that Britain could import the coal that it would need in the future, as the high transport and commercial costs would mean a price "three or four times as dear as it now is in England and America".[63]

In retrospect, Jevons obviously failed to anticipate the development of petroleum as an important substitute for coal and the impact of technological innovations in reducing both the costs of extraction and the transport costs involved in the global trade of fossil fuels. He did not appreciate that the relative scarcity of coal and its consequent higher price would induce the necessary technological innovations to increase effective supplies, develop cost-effective substitutes and thus alleviate any potential constraint on growth. Thus the failure of Jevons's predictions reinforces the conventional view that the economic process is not physically dependent on any one exhaustible resource, and hence threatened by its depletion. The relative scarcity of that resource should automatically stimulate the appropriate market conditions necessary to offset any threats to overall economic activity.

## Alfred Marshall

As Barber notes, "From his vantage point in time Alfred Marshall could observe that the gloomier classical prognoses on the fate of the economy had not, in fact, been borne out."[64] Marshall was, however, careful to preserve those aspects of the classical theory that he felt were accurate. For example, in his analysis of land scarcity, Marshall essentially agreed with the classical economists that agriculture displayed diminishing returns. He observed that "an increase in the capital and labor applied in the cultivation of land causes *in general* a less than proportionate increase in the amount of produce raised unless it happens to coincide with an improvement in the arts of agriculture".[65] Nevertheless he qualified this statement by explaining that diminishing returns "may indeed be held in check for some time by improvements in the arts of production and by the fitful course of the development of the full powers of the soil; but which must ultimately become irresistible if the demand for produce should increase without limit".[66] Similarly, Marshall maintained that the real contribution that Ricardo in particular makes to the understanding of diminishing returns in agriculture is that "it shifts the centre of interest from the mere amount of the farmer's produce to its exchange *value* in terms of things which the industrial population in his neighborhood will offer for it".[67]

Although Marshall conceded that the classical economists (or at least Ricardo) understood that any scarcity of fertile land must lead to higher agricultural prices, he rejected the notion that such a scarcity effect would constrain economic growth. Because "they did not allow enough for the increase of strength that comes from organization," Marshall argued, "Ricardo and the economists of his time generally were too hasty in deducing this inference from the law of diminishing return".[68] Higher agricultural prices should lead to improvements in the organization of rural economic life, including the areas of transport, communications, markets, medical care and other services. Since improved organization ultimately augments the "knowledge" of the farmer:

> his efficiency in many ways is increased.... All his produce is worth more; some things which he used to throw away fetch a good price.

He finds new openings in dairy farming and market gardening, and with a larger range of produce he makes use of rotations that keep his land always active without denuding it of any one of the elements that are necessary for its fertility.

Thus "the growth of organization and knowledge" and other innovations flowing from them would prevent land scarcity and diminishing returns in agriculture from constraining economic growth.[69]

As for the extension of the "law of diminishing return" to mining and exhaustible resources, Marshall takes a completely different view to that of Mill and Jevons:

The produce of mines again, among which may be reckoned quarries and brickfields, is said to conform to the law of diminishing return; but this statement is misleading. It is true that we find continually increasing difficulty in obtaining a further supply of minerals, except in so far as we obtain increased power over nature's stores through improvements in the arts of mining, and through better knowledge of the contents of the earth; and there is no doubt that, other things being equal, the continued application of capital and labor to mines will result in a diminishing rate of yield. But this yield is not a *net* yield, like the return of which we speak in the law of diminishing return. That return is part of a constantly recurring income, while the produce of mines is merely a giving up of their stored-up treasures. The produce of the field is something other than the soil; for the field, properly cultivated, retains its fertility. But the produce of the mine is part of the mine itself.[70]

In other words, the concept of diminishing return may be applicable to "the supply of agricultural produce and of fish", which is "a perennial stream", but not to mines, which are exhaustible "reservoirs". As the "produce of mines" exists as finite reserves, the increased effort (and thus cost) involved in mining may not be related just to the "continually increasing difficulty in obtaining a further supply of minerals" as the reserves approach exhaustion, but also to the *rate* of mineral depletion. The same mine could be exhausted at a faster rate over a shorter period of time if more labour and capital were applied initially. That is, if "the requisite specialized capital and skill got ready for the work, ten years' supply of coal might have been raised in one year without any increased difficulty".[71] Hence, a faster rate of depletion would imply more capital and labour being applied initially but less of a rise in costs as the mine approaches exhaustion.

If there are no diminishing returns in mining, then the relationship between scarcity and price in mining is different from that in agriculture. For example "royalties" in mining, unlike rent in farming, "are levied in proportion to the stores that are taken out of nature's storehouse". Thus the royalty on a ton of coal "represents that diminution in the value of the mine, regarded as a source of wealth in the future, which is caused by taking the ton out of nature's storehouse ... therefore the marginal supply price of minerals includes a royalty in addition to the marginal expenses of the mine".[72] As the deposit approaches exhaustion, the higher will be the discounted present value of the mine, the royalty and thus the market price. So even though the relative scarcity of exhaustible resources may not "conform to the law of diminishing return", it is reflected in higher market prices.[73]

Like Mill, Marshall also acknowledged that land and nature might have important functions other than simply providing inputs for production. He wrote, "the natural beauties of a place of fashionable resort have a direct money value which cannot be overlooked; but it requires some effort to realize the true value to men, women and children of being able to stroll amid beautiful and varied scenery". Similarly, Marshall observed that the "services which land renders to man, in giving him space and light and air in which to live and work, do conform strictly to the law of diminishing return". For any "expenditure" to improve or supplement such services (such as the use of artificial means to supplement natural light and ventilation), "there is a return of extra convenience, but it is a diminishing return".[74] Moreover, although "improvement of the environment, which adds to the value of land and of other free gifts of nature, is in a good many cases partly due to the deliberate investment of capital by the owners of the land", Marshall also noted that "in many cases this is not so"; and any increase in the net income derived from the "free gifts of nature", and not from "deliberate" capital investment, "is to be regarded as rent for all purposes".[75]

These brief hints in his writing indicate that Marshall considered environmental services to have a crucial economic role. On the one hand, he appeared to acknowledge that the "direct money value" of some essential environmental services underestimated their "true value". In addition, the externality problem in which there are unaccountable increases in "the net income derived from the free gifts of nature" suggests that natural services often make important contributions to production that bypass market transactions. Finally, the diminishing returns of any artificial improvements in these services highlights their relative scarcity, e.g., "the growing difficulty of getting fresh air and light, and in some cases fresh water, in densely populated places".[76]

Marshall's discussion of the problem of natural-resource scarcity clearly reflects the emerging conventional view that still predominates today. This is particulary true of the assumption that natural resource scarcity, whether in land or mining deposits, must be reflected in market prices, which in turn induce the necessary ameliorating innovations. On the other hand, Marshall's understanding of the economic role of environmental resources is currently emphasized by more alternative contemporary views. However, one should note that compared to the classical economists, Marshall devoted very little space in his *Principles* to the problem of natural resource scarcity, which is perhaps an indication that this was no longer considered by the new school of neo-classical economics to be such a major concern.

## THE SPECIAL CASE OF MARX

This review of the historical development of economic theories of natural-resource scarcity has focused largely on their emergence within the classical and neo-classical schools of thought. This is because most of the contrasting contemporary and alternative views of natural-resource scarcity by and large follow in the tradition of these schools. Immediately, this begs the question as to what was the contribution of Karl Marx to contemporary theories of natural-resource scarcity.

The standard reading of Marx is to assume that the one thing he had in common with the neo-classical school emerging in the late nineteenth and early twentieth centuries was little regard for the role of natural resources in the economic process. In other words, "Marx's dogma that everything nature offers us is gratis" stems from his "well-known tenet that nothing can have value if it is not due to human labor", from which it follows that "things supplied by nature 'gratis' and the services of capital proper have no value."[77] This is indeed the impression one obtains from *Capital*:

> The land (and this, economically speaking, includes water) in its original state in which it supplies man with necessaries or means of subsistence ready to hand is available without any effort on his part as the universal material for human labor. All those things which labor merely separates from immediate connection with their environment are objects of labor spontaneously provided by nature, such as fish caught and separated from their natural element, namely water, timber felled in virgin forests, and ores extracted from their veins. If, on the other hand, the object of labor has, so to speak, been filtered through previous labor, we call it raw material. For example, ore already extracted and ready for washing. All raw material is an object of labor [*Arbeitsgegenstand*], but not every object of labor is raw material; the object of labor counts as raw material only when it has already undergone some alteration by means of labor.... With the exception of the extractive industries, such as mining, hunting, fishing (and agriculture, but only in so far as it starts by breaking up virgin soil), where the material for labor is provided directly by nature, all branches of industry deal with raw material, i.e. an object of labor which has already been filtered through labor, which is itself a product of labor.[78]

For Marx, only "raw material", which is both a product of natural resources and of labour, has value, whereas other natural-resource products are "spontaneously provided by nature" and thus cannot have value as they are not products of labour. This view is not surprising, given Marx's attempts to establish a labour theory of value as a key to explaining the exploitative nature of capitalist society. This produced a completely different theory of value from that of the classical and neo-classical schools.

For example, as pointed out by Desai, in neo-classical economics, the role of value theory is to provide a theory of relative prices, whereas in the classical theory of value, prices of all goods (that is, their exchange values) are thought to be derived from the current labour input and the labour input embodied in materials of production.[79] In contrast, for Marx, value is a social relationship, based on the relationships of production that arise historically and are specific to certain societies or modes of production. In particular, value relationships are not valid for feudal or communist societies but are found only in capitalist societies. In capitalist modes of production, the exploitative social relationship between the labour and capitalist classes is hidden by the seemingly free and equal commodity relationship of the exchange of labour power for money. This transformation of social into commodity relationships is referred to by Marx as commodity fetishism. The role of his value theory, therefore, is to reveal the exploitative social relationship concealed by commodity fetishism. This is why Marx sought to explain exchange value in terms of the process whereby labour power is purchased and transformed into a final product which is exchanged against other final products embodying labour power, and how the surplus generated by this process is appropriated by the capitalist class.

Although it is clear that Marx believed that labour power is the source of all exchange value, he did not necessarily assume that it was the source of all use values, or wealth. For example, in the *Critique of the Gotha Programme*, he argues that "labor is not the source of all wealth. Nature is just as much the source of use values (and surely these are what make up material wealth!) as labor. Labor is itself only the manifestation of a force of nature, human labor power."[80] As emphasized by Gowdy, such a framework allows for the possibility of going beyond merely considering the impact of social relations of production on resource scarcity to examine the limits imposed by nature on exchange relationships.[81] Unfortunately, Marx never really developed this line of thinking, although in *Capital* he did fault capitalist agriculture for leading to premature exhaustion of arable land:

> According to Marx the premature exhaustion of the soil occurs because there are economic disincentives to maintaining long-lived capital investments. With increasing resource exhaustion, the rising

cost of raw material depresses the rate of profit. Furthermore, the fact that the "marginal cost" of a non-renewable resource is in reality only the marginal cost of extraction and not production creates a surplus for the producer. This surplus arises from the fact that the marginal social cost of producing a unit of an exhaustible resource is much greater than the private cost.... Marx faults the price system for misallocating natural resources over time. The time horizon for non-renewable and semi-renewable resources is not compatible with the time horizon for the prices the market system imposes on these resources.[82]

As argued by Redclift, modern followers of Marx approach the problem of natural-resource scarcity primarily through the process which use values (that is, wealth in the form of nature) are converted to exchange values (that is, in the form of labour power).[83] The commitment to commodity production under capitalism makes environmental externalities inevitable and misallocates natural resources inefficiently over time. As a result, natural-resource scarcity will disappear only when the necessity to make commodities in order to generate surplus value (profit) disappears.

On the other hand, "the 'externality' effects that have attracted the attention of economists in western societies are far more central to the 'survival algorithm' of many households in the South than many Marxists have acknowledged ... the point at which the costs in destroying the environment and non-market social relationships exceed the benefits of further commodity production has already arrived."[84] In developing countries, "environmental degradation is seen as a *result* of underdevelopment (of poverty, inequality and exploitation), a *symptom* of underdevelopment, and a *cause* of underdevelopment (contributing to a failure to produce, invest and improve productivity)" and may therefore lead to ecological collapse before the full development of capitalist modes of production.[85]

Herein lies the dilemma for modern orthodox Marxists. As noted above, although Marx did write about processes of environmental degradation – notably soil erosion – he did not consider the possibility of an absolute natural-resource scarcity constraint on an economic system resulting from ecological collapse. Rather, his concern – and the concern of modern Marxism – is with the collapse of capitalism arising from the inherent contradictions found in the social relationships that, in Marx's own view, stem from fully developed *capitalist* modes of production. This view may be compatible with the notion that the ecological crisis in fully developed industrialized countries also invariably stems from the capitalist process of commodity production (and, indeed, is often interpreted as an indication of the impending collapse of this process), but the orthodox Marxist approach is difficult to apply to the resource scarcity problems faced by societies in the Third World that do not have a fully developed capitalist mode of production.

As some writers have pointed out, the serious analytical problem that Marxism faces in dealing with the partly or wholly subsistence agricultural modes of production in developing countries is that it is difficult to apply the labour theory of value so long as producers have some degree of independent control over the means of production of their livelihoods.[86] The idea that these societies and their institutions closely resemble aspects of feudalism, as identified by Marx as one of the stages of pre-capitalist economies that immediately preceded and led into the capitalist commodity market system, has also been challenged.[87] As Kitching observes for Kenya, "this need not inhibit the development of a theory of exploitation suitable for Kenyan conditions. But clarity about the meaning and limits of value theory is the prerequisite of such development."[88]

Whereas theories of natural-resource scarcity based on neo-classical economics tend to abstract from social and political relationships, the Marxist contribution is to make these relationships explicit. In particular, Marx's labour theory of value offers a method of focusing on the exploitative process of transforming use values (that is, in the form of natural-resource wealth) into exchange values (that is, in the form of labour power). It is important to realize, however, that "in a real world where commodities exchange through money, and where relations of production assume the apparent form of monetary relations, rates of exploitation are necessarily unmeasurable".[89] Thus modern Marxist theories of exploitation and class analysis must necessarily be less explicit in their analysis of the social relationships surrounding natural-resource scarcity than Marx's original use of the labour theory of value allowed. Nor are pure Marxist theories the only possible interpretations of these relationships. Instead, these theories have to vie with more neo-Marxist interpretations that focus on the international system and the historical processes contributing to environmental problems, and other interpretations that, for example, may examine the power, class and general social relationships contributing to problems of soil erosion in developing countries – but primarily from a non-Marxist perspective.[90]

## CONCLUSION: THE MODERN CONVENTIONAL VIEW

By exploring classical and early neo-classical theories of natural-resource scarcity, this chapter has questioned the legitimacy of using the Malthusian and Ricardian labels to distinguish between contemporary views on resource and environmental problems. For one thing, in following the classical tradition established by Adam Smith, it is clear that the approaches adopted by Malthus and Ricardo have more in common with each other than with more modern views of natural-resource scarcity. The unique feature common to all the classical theories, including Ricardo's, is the central role of the Malthusian theory of population expansion and the assumption that economic growth, particularly in agriculture, is dependent upon increasing labour inputs. These two factors were seen to interact with the relative scarcity of land to produce unavoidable distributional consequences – notably the decline in profits with respect to wages and rent – that would lead to economic stagnation. Compared with these similarities, the much-emphasized differences between these two classical views (i.e. that Ricardo seems to shy away from Malthus's original absolute scarcity formulation of the problem and instead stresses the relative scarcity of land) appears less significant.

In contrast, the views of Mill, Jevons and Marshall on natural-resource scarcity signal an important transition from the classical to the more modern analysis of the problem. Of particular importance was the recognition of the new role of exhaustible resources in an industrialized economic process and the welfare implications of essential environmental services. But most significantly, the failure of the gloomier classical prognoses on the fate of the economy from increasing scarcity of land as well as the erroneous assumptions that Jevons made in analysing the future scarcity of coal, allowed Marshall and the new neo-classical economists to adopt a far more optimistic view of natural-resource scarcity – if they bothered to think it a problem worth considering any longer. Even Marx never viewed natural-resource scarcity as a potential constraint on growth; his prime concern was in developing a labour theory value to expose the exploitative social relationships behind capitalist market production.

So it is not surprising that, up until the 1960s, the modern conventional economic perspective on natural-resource scarcity had been virtually unaltered since Marshall's views on the subject. Nor is it a surprise that modern Marxism – the major ideological challenger to neo-classical ideas over this era – has not offered an alternative view. With the momentous political and economic events that occurred between Marshall's time and the 1960s having little to do with problems of resource scarcity and environmental decline, and with this era being one of tremendous technological progress, this lack of concern with the economics of natural-resource scarcity is understandable.

Thus, the major contribution of Hotelling during this period to the economics of exhaustible resources, combined with the optimal growth theory of Ramsey, re-emerged as the starting point for many important theories of natural-resource scarcity in the 1960s and early 1970s (see Chapter 3).[91] Yet there is very little difference between Hotelling's view on exhaustible resource depletion and Marshall's, although Hotelling's theory is clearly more elaborate and fully developed. As a result, the conventional economic view of natural-resource scarcity of Marshall's time, with its rejection of the possibility of an absolute natural-resource scarcity constraint and its belief that any relative scarcity of economically useful resources would be automatically reflected in market prices, still predominates.

In the early 1960s, this view received strong support from the study by Barnett and Morse. As the basis for their empirical investigations, the authors adopted the conventional hypothesis that increasing natural-resource scarcity "would reveal itself in an increasing trend of unit cost of resource conversion as reflected in extractive production" or will show its effects in "a rise in the unit cost of extractive output *relative* to that of extractive output".[92] Examining per-unit labour-and-capital costs for extracting various raw material resources in the United States since the late nineteenth century, Barnett and Morse concluded that this data showed little evidence of increasing natural-resource scarcity, which they attributed to the "continual enlargement of the scope of substitutability – the result of man's technological ingenuity and organizational wisdom".[93]

Barnett and Morse also make it clear that only the "economically useful properties" of "selected segments of the environment" (that is, only one function of the natural environment, as supplier of the raw material and energy inputs to the economic process) is considered relevant to the phenomenon of natural-resource scarcity.[94] Thus, the conventional definition of natural resources is usually limited to those environmental resources providing economically valuable productive services. As Smith and Krutilla suggest, this "conception of resources as a source of material inputs leads one to consider the environmental side-effects of extraction and conversion activities as phenomena to be distinguished from resource utilization and depletion".[95] On the whole in the conventional literature, the environmental problems of waste generation and declining recreational, amenity, ecological and life-support services are accorded separate treatment as special cases of negative externalities, and not related to the specific economic scarcity problem arising from the depletion of "economically useful" natural resources (see Chapter 4).

Limiting the analysis of natural-resource availability to the economic scarcity of those "selected segments of the environment" that serve as productive inputs, allows the conventional view to be optimistic about the long-run effects of any potential scarcity problem. By providing useful productive services, those natural resources appropriated as raw material and energy inputs have an economic value greater than zero. As stocks of these resources become increasingly scarce, in a market economy their prices will rise relative to those of other goods. Therefore, as neo-classical general equilibrium theory predicts, the market system should respond to the increasing 'relative' scarcity of raw material and energy stock through price appreciation:

> If the past is any guide for the future, there seems to be little reason to worry about the exhaustion of resources which the market already

treats as economic goods.... The economist's initial presumption is that the market will decide in what forms to transmit wealth by the requirement that all kinds of wealth bear a comparable rate of return. Now stocks of natural resources – for example, mineral deposits – are essentially sterile. Their return to their owners is the increase in their prices relative to prices of other goods. In a properly functioning market economy, resources will be exploited at such a pace that their rate of relative price appreciation is competitive with rates of return on other kinds of capital.... Natural resources *should* grow in relative scarcity – otherwise they are an inefficient way for society to hold and transmit wealth compared to productive and physical capital. Price appreciation protects resources from premature exploitation.[96]

Although, over time, certain raw material and energy stocks may become relatively scarce, the resulting price appreciation should allow the economic system to correct any over-exploitation and thus automatically alleviate the scarcity problem. In a dynamic economy exhibiting technological innovation and productivity growth, higher relative prices will incite the necessary economic adjustments to reduce dependency on the scarce resources. In the long run, therefore, such dynamic economic responses will prevent any lasting general scarcity constraint on economic growth:

That man will face a series of particular scarcities as a result of growth is a foregone conclusion; that these will impose general scarcity – increasing cost – is not a legitimate corollary.... In short, the resource problem is one of a continual accommodation and adjustment to an ever-changing economic-resource quality spectrum. The physical properties of the natural-resource base impose a series of initial constraints on the growth and progress of mankind, but the resource spectrum undergoes kaleidoscopic change through time. Continual enlargement of the scope of substitutability – the result of man's technological ingenuity and organizational wisdom – offers those who are nimble a multitude of opportunities to escape.[97]

The increasing scarcity of certain economically valuable resources may "impose a series of initial constraints" in the form of higher relative costs in the short run, but over time such costs actually provide the incentives for the economic innovations necessary to mitigate any scarcity problem. This optimistic prediction is often supported through analogy with past innovative responses to material and energy shortages:

Modern industrial economies possess a remarkably wide range of options with respect to the exploitation of the natural-resource environment. At any one time the range of substitution possibilities among material-resource inputs is far higher than is generally recognized. From a historical point of view, these possibilities are, in large measure, the product of past technological change which has produced new substitute inputs or raised the productivity of old ones. The ways in which it has done this defy simple categorization, but they have included the following:

1. Raising output per unit of resource input – as, for example, the decline in the amount of coal required to generate a kilowatt-hour of electricity, which fell from almost seven pounds in 1900 to less than nine-tenths of a pound in the 1960s.
2. Development of totally new materials – synthetic fibres, plastics, etc.
3. Raising the productivity of the extractive process.
4. Raising the productivity of the process of exploration and resource discovery.
5. Development of techniques for the reuse of scrap or waste materials.
6. Development of techniques for the exploitation of lower-grade, or other more abundant, resources. One of the main effects of these technological developments is to reduce the economy's dependence upon any specific resource input and to widen progressively the possibilities of material substitution. As a result, although particular resources of specified quality do inevitably become increasingly scarce, the threat of a *generalized* natural resource scarcity constraint upon economic growth by no means follows from this.[98]

By limiting its analysis to the scarcity of those natural resources used as productive inputs and by assuming that the higher economic costs associated with the increasing relative scarcity of these inputs will automatically induce the appropriate mitigating innovations, the conventional view is generally optimistic about the ability of the economic system to overcome any such natural-resource scarcity constraint in the long run. As this chapter has indicated, however, this more contemporary perspective on the resource problems facing advanced industrialized economies is far removed from the early economic theories – developed by Malthus, Ricardo and others – that sought to explain the scarcity effects arising from the interactions among population growth, land availability and agricultural productivity in nascent industrial economies.

## *APPENDIX:* THE MALTHUS-RICARDO THEORY OF DIMINISHING RETURNS

The Malthus-Ricardo theory of diminishing returns and declining profits in agriculture is described in Figures 1.2–1.4.

Figure 1.2 depicts the situation in agriculture without either the

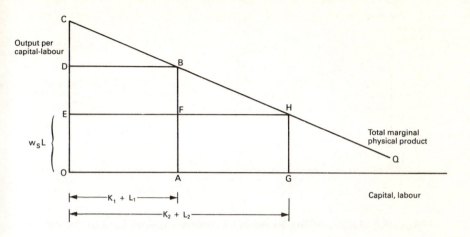

**Figure 1.2: The Basic Malthus–Ricardo Model of Diminishing Returns**

substitution of capital for labour or technological improvements to increase output; hence, it is the basic Malthus–Ricardo model of diminishing returns in agriculture. As increasing amounts of capital plus labour (OA, OG) are applied in agriculture to expand cultivation, the marginal physical product (curve CQ) declines. Assuming a minimum fixed level of subsistence maintenance per labourer ($w_s$), total subsistence-wage income for labour ($w_s L$) increases as more labour is applied to the land (i.e., $L_1 < L_2$). Since rent must also increase as cultivation is extended to less fertile lands, profits must eventually fall.

For example, in the initial phase producing output OABC, OABD represents total wages and profits income (in physical units) and DBC represents total rent. OABD is divided into subsistence income OAFE (= $w_s L_1$) and profits EFBD. In the second phase, as cultivation is expanded to produce output OGHC, the total return to capital and labour equals OGHE and rent is EHC. However, because the total return to capital and labour must go to labour (i.e., OGHE = $W_s L_2$), profits must equal zero. Therefore in this phase, as profits approach zero, capital accumulation stops and a stationary state is reached in agricultural production.

Figure 1.3 shows how the substitution of capital for labour in agriculture could postpone diminishing returns by breaking the dependency of cultivation on labour. For example, in phase one OA amount of labour is employed at subsistence wage $w_s$ to produce an agricultural output (such as corn) of OABC. Subsistence income is therefore OABD and rent is DBC. In phase two, the substitution of capital for labour reduced labour input to OE and increases labour productivity to $C^1 Q^1$.

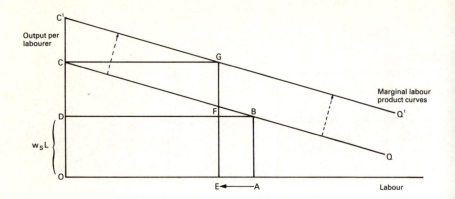

**Figure 1.3: Diminishing Returns Offset by Capital-Labour Substitution**

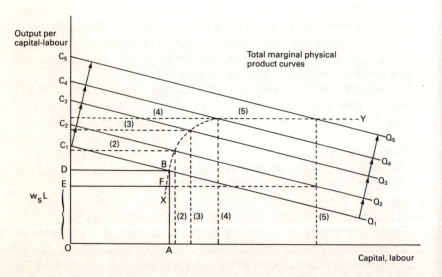

**Figure 1.4: Diminishing Returns Postponed by Technological Change**

*Source:* Morton Paglin, *Malthus and Lauderdale: The Anti-Ricardian Tradition* (Augustus M. Kelley: New York, 1961).

Assuming that the latter effect outweighs the former, the new level of output, OEGC¹, is greater than the previous level, OABC. Given the fixed wage, however, subsistence income has fallen to OEFD, and the remaining product is divided between profit and rent. For example, profits could be DFGH and rent C¹GC. Hence the substitution of capital for labour in agriculture could both increase output and generate profit to stimulate further capital accumulation.

Figure 1.4 depicts the situation, perhaps envisaged by Malthus in his *Principles of Political Economy*, where technological improvements in agriculture offset diminishing returns. Such improvements can be represented by an outward shift of the marginal physical product curve (CQ). Since this expands the total returns to capital and labour (OABD), despite the increase in total subsistence income ($w_sL$) in each period, substantial profits continue to be made (i.e., EFBD continuously expands). However, the marginal returns to capital and labour (dotted line XY) are decreasing, and eventually fall to zero in period five. As depicted in Figure 1.2, diminishing returns set in, and profits eventually decline to zero. Thus technological improvements in agriculture may postpone diminishing returns in agriculture for a significant period of time.

## NOTES

1. Harold J. Barnett and Chandler Morse, *Scarcity and Economic Growth: The Economics of Natural Resource Availability* (Johns Hopkins University Press: Baltimore, 1963). See also Herman E. Daly, *Steady-State Economics* (W.H. Freeman: San Francisco, 1977), p. 40; and Richard Lecomber, *The Economics of Natural Resources* (Macmillan: London, 1979), p. 15.
2. Barnett and Morse, op. cit., p. 51.
3. Ibid., pp. 58–60.
4. Ibid., p. 63.
5. Ibid., p. 244.
6. Hla Myint, "The classical view of the economic problem", in Joseph J. Spengler and W.R. Allen (eds), *Essays in Economic Thought: Aristotle to Marshall* (Rand-MacNally: Chicago, 1960), pp. 451–2.
7. Vivienne Brown, "Property and value in economic thought: An analysis of conceptions of scarcity in classical and neoclassical theory, with special reference to Adam Smith, David Ricardo and Walrasian Theory", unpublished PhD thesis (Birkbeck College: University of London, 1982); and H.M. Robertson and W.L. Taylor, "Adam Smith's approach to the theory of value" in Spengler and Allen, op. cit.
8. Robertson and Taylor, op. cit., p. 299. See also Adam Smith, *An Inquiry into the Significance and Causes of the Wealth of Nations* (J.M. Dent & Sons: London, 1910).
9. Brown, op. cit., p. 93; and Robertson and Taylor, op. cit., pp. 299–301.
10. William J. Barber, *A History of Economic Thought* (Penguin Books: Harmondsworth, England, 1967), p. 43.
11. See, in particular, Smith, op. cit., pp. 306–7.
12. Barber, op. cit., pp. 44–5.

13. It is worth distinguishing two editions of Malthus's thesis: Thomas R. Malthus, *An Essay on The Principle of Population* (1st edn), (J. Johnson: London, 1798) and Thomas R. Malthus, *An Essay on The Principle of Population* (2nd edn), (J. M. Dent & Sons: London, 1914).

14. Barnett and Morse, op. cit., p. 53.

15. Malthus (2nd edn), op. cit., pp. 6 and 8.

16. Malthus (1st edn), op. cit., pp. 13–14. Curiously, Malthus does not appear to have kept this oft-quoted statement in the second edition of his *Essay*.

17. Thomas R. Malthus, *Principles of Political Economy: Considered with a View to Their Practical Application* (John Murray: London, 1820).

18. Ibid., pp. 139–40. Malthus (p. 134) employed the classical definition of rent: "The rent of the land may be that portion of the value of the whole produce which remains to the owner of the land, after all the outgoings belonging to its cultivation, of whatever kind, have been paid, including the profits of the capital employed, estimated according to the usual and ordinary rate of the profits of agricultural stock at the time being." He goes on to stress (p. 140): "The quality of the soil here noticed as the primary cause of raw produce, is the gift of nature to man. It is quite unconnected with monopoly, and yet it is so absolutely essential to the existence of rent, that without it no degree of scarcity or monopoly could have occasioned an excess of the price of raw produce above what was necessary for the payment of wages and profits." However, in Chapter 3, "Of the Rent of Land" (particularly pp. 187–8), Malthus clearly indicates that he does not agree with Ricardo that the relative fertility of land is the only determinant of rent.

19. As quoted by Barber, op. cit., p. 65.

20. Malthus, *Principles of Political Economy*, op. cit., p. 295.

21. Ibid., pp. 298–9.

22. Ibid., p. 300.

23. Barber, op. cit. (p. 66), notes that Malthus's conception of the problem of diminishing returns differs from the modern "static" version: "In the hands of Malthus and his contemporaries the analysis of the tendency for returns per successive unit of input in agriculture to diminish was not developed around static conditions in which all factors, save one, are held constant. Instead the argument was constructed in a context of change – particularly of population and of the size of the capital stock.... For Malthus (and for most classical economists) this analysis was intended to refer only to agricultural production."

24. Or in Malthus's own words: "In the cultivation of land, the immediate and main cause of the necessary diminution of profits appeared to be the increased quantity of labour necessary to obtain the same produce. In manufactures and commerce, it is the fall in the exchangeable value of the products of industry in these departments, compared with corn and labour." Malthus, *Principles of Political Economy*, op. cit., p. 300.

25. See, for example, Malthus, *Principles of Political Economy*, op. cit., Chapter 2, "On the Nature and Measures of Value", especially Section One "Of the Different Sources of Value".

26. Morton Paglin, *Malthus and Lauderdale: The Anti-Ricardian Tradition* (Augustus M. Kelley: New York, 1961), pp. 45–6.

27. Malthus, *An Essay on Population* (2nd edn), op. cit., p. 11.

28. David Ricardo, *The Principles of Political Economy* (J.M. Dent & Sons: London, 1973), p. 276.

29. Ibid., p. 75.

30. Ibid., pp. 103 and 194.

31. Paglin, op. cit., pp. 61–2.

32. Ricardo, op. cit., p. 75.

33. Barnett and Morse, op. cit., p. 63.

34. Ricardo, op. cit., pp. 39–40.

35. Ibid., p. 7.
36. Brown, op. cit., pp. 179–80.
37. Paglin, op. cit.
38. Ricardo, op. cit., p. 71.
39. Malthus, *Principles of Political Economy*, op. cit.
40. Paglin, op. cit., p. 83. Thus quoting Malthus, Paglin (p. 84) argues: "Malthus further believes that increasing returns will prevail in the future as well. 'A great demand for corn of home growth must tend greatly to encourage improvements in agriculture, and a great demand for labour must stimulate the actual population to do more work.' These circumstances are 'sufficient to counterbalance the effect of taking additional land into cultivation (and) are so strong that in the actual state of most countries in the world, or in their probable state for some centuries to come, we may fairly lay our account to their operation when the occasion calls for them.'"
41. John Stuart Mill, *Principles of Political Economy With Some of Their Application to Social Philosophy* (5th edn), (Parker, Son and Bourn: London, 1862), Vol II, Book IV, Chapters 2–6.
42. Ibid., pp. 320 and 267.
43. Mill, op. cit., Vol. I, p. 216.
44. Mill, op. cit. (p. 284), distinguished between two such types of improvements in agriculture: those that "consist in a mere saving of labour, and enable a given quantity of food to be produced at less cost, but not on a smaller surface of land than before" and those that "enable a given extent of land to yield not only the same produce with less labour, but a greater produce; so that if no greater produce is required, a part of the land already under culture may be dispensed with."
45. Ibid., p. 266.
46. Mill, op. cit., Vol. I, p. 229.
47. John Stuart Mill, *Principles of Political Economy With Some of Their Application to Social Philosophy* (1909 edn), (Augustus M. Kelley: Clifton, New Jersey, 1973), p. 63.
48. Mill, op. cit. (5th edn), Vol. I, p. 217.
49. Ibid., pp. 217–18.
50. Mill, op. cit. (1909 edn), p. 475.
51. Mill, op. cit. (5th edn), Vol. II, p. 325.
52. According to Mill, the "stationary state" would be considered desirable provided that there existed "a conscientious or prudential restraint on population" and "a system of legislation favouring equality of fortunes". Hence, "under this twofold influence society would exhibit these leading features: a well-paid and affluent body of labourers; no enormous fortunes, except what were earned and accumulated during a single lifetime; but a much larger body of persons than at present, not only exempt from the coarser toils, but with sufficient leisure, both physical and mental, from mechanical details, to cultivate freely the graces of life and afford examples of them the classes less favourably circumstanced for their growth". Mill, op. cit. (1909 edn), Book IV, Chapter 6.
53. Of all the modern theorists on natural-resource scarcity, particularly those adherents to the more alternative view, Daly (op. cit.) has followed Mill's conclusion the most rigorously by arguing that a stationary economic state is the necessary condition for ensuring the preservation of essential "natural" services. On the other hand, this aspect of Mill's analysis is usually either dismissed or treated more ambiguously by more conventional modern theorists. For example, Barnett and Morse (op. cit., pp. 69–71) apparently play down Mill's belief in a stationary state as being a desirable outcome, especially with regard to preserving environmental quality, by suggesting that "Mill was asking others to share his confidence in the evolutionary direction of the world by coupling a concern for the quality of human living with the classical concern over diminishing returns." In contrast, Wilfred Beckerman, *In Defence of Economic Growth* (Jonathan Cape: London, 1974), pp. 57–8, asserts that Mill "might

have been writing some of the contemporary anti-growth literature".

54. William Stanley Jevons, *The Coal Question: An Inquiry Concerning the Progress of the Nation and the Probable Exhaustion of Our Coal-Mines* (Macmillan: London, 1909).

55. See, for example, J.W. Forrester, *World Dynamics* (Wright Allen: Cambridge, Massachusetts, 1971); and Dennis L. Meadows, Donnella H. Meadows, Jorgen Randers and William Behrens, *The Limits to Growth* (Universe Books: New York, 1972). The major difference is, of course, that the modern studies concentrate on economic growth and resource depletion rates in a global context, whereas Jevons was solely concerned with Great Britain and coal.

56. Jevons, op. cit., p. 195.

57. Ibid., p. 11.

58. Ibid., p. 74.

59. Ibid., p. 183 and Chapter 8.

60. Ibid., pp. 184–5.

61. Ibid., pp. xxxvi–xxxvii and Chapter 4.

62. Ibid., pp. 140–41 and Chapter 7.

63. Ibid., p. 291 and Chapter 13.

64. Barber, op. cit., pp. 190–91.

65. Alfred Marshall, *Principles of Economics: An Introductory Volume* (8th edn), (Macmillan: London, 1949), p. 125.

66. Ibid., p. 127. Barnett and Morse, op. cit., p. 58, note 4, argue that Marshall made the same mistake as Malthus in his conception of diminishing returns in agriculture; that is, he allowed for "'great variations in the relative amounts of labour and capital in a dose', without recognizing that this casts doubt upon the validity of the alleged 'law'."

67. Marshall, op. cit., p. 137.

68. Ibid.

69. Ibid., pp. 137–8. For Marshall, "organization" was such a significant element in production that he considered it to be a possible fourth "agent of production": "Organization ... has many forms, e.g. that of a single business, that of various businesses in the same trade, that of various trades relative to one another, and that of the State providing security for all and help for many". More importantly, "organization aids knowledge", and "knowledge is our most powerful engine of production: it enables us to subdue nature and force her to satisfy our wants" (p. 115).

70. Ibid., pp. 138–9.

71. Ibid., p. 139.

72. Ibid., pp. 138 and 364.

73. To a large extent, this view on the relationship between rent and the price of exhaustible resources is still adhered to in conventional analyses as justification of why price functions as an indicator of relative resource scarcity (see, for example, Chapter 3). Anthony C. Fisher, *Resource and Environmental Economics* (Cambridge University Press: Cambridge, 1981), pp. 111–13, does qualify this by suggesting some instances (e.g., the presence of government regulation, market imperfections and environmental externalities) in which this is not always the case.

74. Marshall, op. cit., pp. 138–9.

75. Ibid., p. 368.

76. Ibid., p. 138.

77. Nicholas Georgescu-Roegen, *The Entropy Law and the Economic Process* (Harvard University Press: Cambridge, Massachusetts, 1971), pp. 2 and 288–9.

78. Karl Marx, *Capital: A Critique of Political Economy*, Vol. I (Penguin Books: Harmondsworth, England, 1976), pp. 284–5 and 287.

79. Meghnad Desai, *Marxian Economic Theory* (Gray-Mills Publishing: London, 1974), Chapter 2.

80. Karl Marx, "Critique of the Gotha Programme" in David Fernbach (ed.), *Karl*

*Marx: The First International and After, Political Writings*, Vol. III (Penguin Books: Harmondsworth, England, 1974), p. 341.

81. John M. Gowdy, "Marx and resource scarcity: An institutional approach", *Journal of Economic Issues*, Vol. 18, June 1984.

82. Gowdy, op. cit.

83. Michael Redclift, *Sustainable Development: Exploring the Contradictions* (Methuen: London, 1987).

84. Ibid., pp. 48 and 51.

85. Piers Blaikie, *The Political Economy of Soil Erosion in Developing Countries* (Longman: London, 1985), p. 9.

86. See, for example, H. Bernstein, "Notes on capital and peasantry", *Review of African Political Economy*, Vol. 10 (1977), pp. 64–5; John Harriss, *Capitalism and Peasant Farming: Agrarian Structure and Ideology in Northern Tamil Nadu* (Oxford University Press: Bombay, 1982); and Gavin Kitching, *Class and Economic Change in Kenya: The Making of an African Petite Bourgeoisie, 1905–1970* (Yale University Press: New Haven, 1980).

87. Jack Goody, "Feudalism in Africa?", Chapter 8 in George Dalton (ed.), *Economic Development and Social Change: The Modernization of Village Communities* (The Natural History Press: Garden City, New York, 1971).

88. Kitching, op. cit., pp. 460–61.

89. Ibid.

90. See Redclift, op. cit., as an example of a neo-Marxist interpretation and Blaikie, op. cit., as an example of a non-Marxist perspective.

91. Harold Hotelling, "The economics of exhaustible resources", *Journal of Political Economy*, Vol. 39 (1931), pp. 137–75; and Frank Ramsey, "A mathematical theory of saving", *Economic Journal*, Vol. 38 (1928), pp. 543–59.

92. Barnett and Morse, op. cit., pp. 164 and 201.

93. Ibid., p. 244. The one exception proved to be forest products. "By the 1950's, relative prices of 'all forest products' had increased to two and a half times the level of the 1870s" (p. 213). These findings have been extended to include the 1957–70 period, with little or no change in the basic results. See Harold J. Barnett, "Scarcity and growth revisited" in V.K. Smith (ed.), *Scarcity and Growth Reconsidered* (Johns Hopkins University Press: Baltimore, 1979).

94. Ibid., pp. 55–6.

95. V. Kerry Smith and John V. Krutilla, "The economics of natural resources: An interpretive introduction" in V.K. Smith (ed.), op. cit., p. 4.

96. William D. Nordhaus and James Tobin, "Growth and natural resources", in R. Dorfman and N.S. Dorfman (eds), *Economics of the Environment* (2nd edn), (W.W. Norton: New York, 1977), p. 402.

97. Barnett and Morse, op. cit., p. 244.

98. Nathan Rosenberg, "Innovative responses to materials shortages," *American Economic Review*, Papers and Proceedings, vol. 63 (1973), p. 116.

# 2
# Non-Economic Influences

In the 1960s, new economic perspectives on environmental problems began to emerge that were subject to important non-economic influences such as environmentalism, thermodynamics and ecology. This chapter will explore their contribution to our knowledge and perception of human interaction with the natural environment, and how they have influenced new theories in resource and environmental economics. To the extent that these new theories have carried on the conventional approaches to analysing natural-resource scarcity, as exemplified by the 1963 Barnett and Morse study, they will be classified as "conventional". To the extent that they deviate from this tradition, they will be considered alternative theories. As the remaining chapters of this book make clear, the increasing concern over the economic threats posed by environmental and resource problems, particularly the persistent convergence of environment and development problems in the developing world, has given greater impetus to these new developments in environmental and resource economics that deviate from the more traditional theories and approaches.[1]

## CONSERVATIONISM

In tracing the historical development of the natural-resource scarcity doctrine adopted by the early American Conservation Movement (1890–1920), Barnett and Morse note that the essential postulate of this doctrine was that "the facts of ecological interdependence are physical ... Mineral depletion is a physical necessity in an industrialized society." As a result, "finite physical limits of natural resources, to the early Conservationists, constituted economic scarcity." In addition, the Conservationists argued that "nature's own ecological balance has intrinsic merit simply because of its high physical value – its 'naturalness'. The doctrine attaches positive cultural and social values to an ecological balance in which nature's biological systems are at high levels of physical output and activity, and fears or deplores radical departures from such ecological levels".[2]

An important forefather of contemporary conservationism was George Perkins Marsh.[3] According to Barnett and Morse, Marsh's views contain three contributions to the economic analysis of natural-resource scarcity.

First, Marsh rejected the way classical economics simplified the concepts of "nature" and "natural resources" to the static category of "agricultural land." He argued that the fundamental characteristic of nature is its ecological complexity and diversity, which is continually undergoing change. For Marsh, the heterogeneity of natural resources cannot be summarized or measured in terms of the declining fertility of arable land or the increased effort needed to extract less accessible mineral resources, but is an essential, irreducible and unquantifiable characteristic of nature – the result of the continuous dynamic interaction and interdependence among nature's components. Marsh considered the complexity and heterogeneity of nature to be the most significant feature determining the relationship between people and nature. Secondly, Marsh viewed nature and humanity as an inseparable, interdependent unit – the "nature-man continuum". He argued that "man changes the natural complex and nature's changes, in turn, exert their major influence on man. The interaction is continuous." Finally, this view of an inseparable "nature-man continuum" led to the assumption that economic analysis could not afford to ignore the basic physical interdependency between people and the environment. Unlike the classical economists (with perhaps the exception of Mill), Marsh believed that dependence on natural resources "is not that of a simple flow of food from agricultural land, but is much more complex. Man depends upon nature and open individual components of nature for many products, facilities, and services – material and intangible."[4]

Thus for Marsh and modern conservationists, nature's complexity and diversity and the essential fact of our dependence on nature, makes the whole environment inherently valuable to humankind. It is unthinkable to consider only one function of the environment as having value, that of supplier of useful material and energy inputs into the economic process. Only when these inputs are sufficiently scarce relative to their demand is this scarcity reflected in market prices. Nor do the conservationists accept that the value of another function of the environment, as assimilator of the waste generated by the economic process, only registers when this function is overloaded and results in a negative externality (i.e., pollution). To the conservationists, the fundamental physical dependency of the entire economic process on dynamic, heterogeneous and complex ecological systems means that the entire natural environment must have value to humanity. Moreover, by assuming that biological complexity and diversity are essential for ecological stability and resilience allows the conservationists to believe that environmental preservation must also be valuable.

Marsh and modern conservationists argue additionally that the heterogeneity of nature is the source of its weakness in its interactions with people. The physical demands that we place on nature are capable of disrupting its necessarily diverse and complex ecological relationships, which in turn threaten the material and non-material services it performs for humankind. Unlike the classical economists, Marsh did not believe that natural-resource scarcity is an inevitable natural law but is, in effect the result of our modifications of the "nature-man continuum".[5] Nature is capable of sustaining humankind indefinitely, provided that our physical demands do not seriously disrupt the ecological relationships of this continuum. Natural-resource scarcity results from these demands exceeding nature's capacity to fulfil them. Therefore, the alleviation of the threat of scarcity requires humankind to live within the physical limits dictated by a stable ecological balance between nature and the exploitation of its resources. The essentiality of this balance to human livelihood suggests that its disruption poses an absolute constraint on economic activity. Therefore, preservation is of infinite instrumental value to human welfare.

The existence of such an absolute ecological constraint on economic activity implies absolute limits to economic exploitation of the environment. Thus conservationists have argued consistently for structural changes in the economic process in order to limit ecological damage, regardless of the costs in terms of production and foregone consumption. In essence, such changes involve minimizing the material and energy throughput requirements of the economic process, investing directly in the 'improvement' of the environment, and preserving environmental quality. As summarized by Page, the basic resource-saving criteria of conservationists are:

i) The regenerative capacity or potential of renewable resources (such as forests, grazing land, cropland and water) should not be physically damaged or destroyed.

ii) Renewable resources should be used in place of minerals, in so far as is physically possible.

iii) Plentiful mineral resources should be used before less plentiful ones, in so far as is physically possible.

iv) Non-renewable resources should be recycled as much as possible.[6]

Conservationists frequently justify such criteria on the grounds that preservation of a stable ecological balance is essential in the long run to human welfare. In addition, they argue that environmental preservation is a moral obligation because of nature's intrinsic value as the source of all life. That is, as well as its instrumental value to human welfare, nature and the "nature–man continuum" is sacred because life is sacred:

One of the more important tasks for any society is to distinguish between ends and means-to-ends, and to have some sort of cohesive view and agreement about this. Is the land merely a means of production or is it something more, something that is an end in itself? And when I say "land", I include the creatures upon it.... There is no escape from this confusion as long as land and the creatures upon it are looked upon as *nothing but* "factors of production". They are, of course, factors of production, that is to say means-to-ends, but this is their secondary, not their primary, nature. Before everything else, they are ends-in-themselves; they are meta-economic, and it is therefore rationally justifiable to say, as a statement of fact, that they are in a certain sense sacred. Man has not made them, and it is irrational for him to treat things that he has not made and cannot make and cannot recreate once he has spoilt them, in the same manner and spirit as he is entitled to treat things of his own making.... It is a metaphysical error, likely to produce the gravest practical consequences, to equate "car" and "animal" on account of their utility, while failing to recognize the most fundamental difference between them, that of "level of being".[7]

In recent years, the moral and philosophical arguments and practical concerns for environmental preservation have been meshed into a holistic view of environment and development in the global biosphere.[8] In particular, the idea of an environmentally sustainable pattern of economic development is no longer seen to be just a luxury of the advanced industrialized economies who are suffering the environmental excesses of their overdevelopment, but is increasingly seen to be a necessity for developing countries seeking to industrialize and expand their economies. That is, these essentially resource-based economies require both efficient and sustainable management of their resource base in order to ensure the success of their long-run development efforts. As a result, the growing recognition that the overall goals of environmental conservation and economic development are not conflicting but can be mutually reinforcing has prompted serious policymaking interest in environmentally sustainable economic development.[9]

The 1972 United Nations Conference on the Human Environment, held in Stockholm, is usually credited with popularizing this concept of sustainable development. However, the origins of the term probably lie in the Paris Biosphere Conference and the Washington DC Conference on the Ecological Aspects of International Development, which were both held in 1968.[10] In general, the concept arose out of the conservationists' concern that:

> Few if any countries take adequate account of environmental considerations when making policy or planning development. Few allocate or regulate uses of their living resources so as to ensure that they are environmentally appropriate and sustainable. Many lack either the financial or technical resources, or the political will, or

adequate legislative, institutional, or public, support for conservation (or any combination of these) to carry out fully the conservation
measures required.[11]

Attempting to translate conservationists' concerns and criticisms into
analytical precise and rigorous recommendations for economic policymaking has not been an easy task for proponents of sustainable
development. More often than not, precision is sacrificed to the
acceptability of age-old and universal conservationist principles. For
example, the *World Conservation Strategy* emphasizes "the maintenance
of essential ecological processes and life-support systems, the preservation
of genetic diversity, and the sustainable utilization of species and
ecosystems" with the overall aim of achieving "sustainable development
through the conservation of living resources".[12] While lauding the general
underlying message, sympathetic economists have none the less criticized
the definition and objectives outlined in the *World Conservation Strategy*
as being too vague for practical application; failing to perceive the crucial
issues of trade-offs among economic and conservation goals; and for
ignoring valuation problems.[13]

Perhaps the greatest contribution that the conservation movement has
made and will continue to make to economics is that of spurring
economists on to tackle the following problems: making the concept of
sustainable development more workable; focusing economic analysis on
the value of environmental preservation; examining the economic role of
ecological relationships and environmental functions; and considering an
absolute ecological constraint under certain economic conditions.

## ECOLOGY

In seeking to understand key ecological relationships and their importance to the economic process more fully, economics has become
increasingly influenced by ecology. Ecology is a division of biology that
studies the relation or interaction of organisms with their environment.
The science of ecology is closely related to the study of genetics, evolution,
physiology and animal behaviour, yet it has emerged as a completely
independent discipline. Its distinguishing feature is the categorization of
the natural environment in terms of distinct systems, called *ecosystems*,
that share characteristic features:

> There is a natural sequence to the subject matter of ecology,
> proceeding from the inorganic to the organic world.... The climate,
> soils, bacteria, fungi, plants, and animals at any particular place
> together constitute an *ecosystem*. Thus each ecosystem has both
> abiotic (nonliving) and biotic (living) components. The biotic
> components of an ecosystem, or all the organisms living in it, taken

together, comprise an ecological *community*. The abiotic components can be separated into inorganic and organic, whereas the biotic components are usually classified as producers, consumers, and decomposers. Producers, sometimes called *autotrophs*, are the green plants that trap solar energy and convert it into chemical energy. Consumers, or *heterotrophs*, are all the animals that either eat the plants or one another; all heterotrophs are thus directly or indirectly dependent on plants for energy. Several levels of consumers are recognized (primary, secondary and tertiary) depending on whether they eat plants directly or other herbivorous or carnivorous animals. Decomposers, also heterotrophs, are often bacteria and fungi; they function in the ecosystem by breaking down plant and animal material into simpler components and thereby returning nutrients to the autotrophs. Decomposers are therefore essential in recycling matter within an ecosystem.[14]

Ecology's study of ecosystems has traditionally involved three approaches – descriptive, functional and evolutionary. "The descriptive point of view is mainly natural history and proceeds by describing the vegetation groups of the world, such as the temperate deciduous forests, tropical rain forests, grasslands, and tundra, and by describing the animals and plants and their inter-relationships for each of these ecosystems."[15] Modern ecology, however, tends to emphasize both the functional and evolutionary perspective: "Functional ecology studies *proximate* causes – the response of populations and communities to immediate factors of the environment. Evolutionary ecology studies *ultimate* causes – the historical reasons why natural selection has favoured the particular adaptions we now see."[16] This functional–evolutionary approach analyses the environment at three levels of integration: populations, communities and ecosystems.

A population is a set of organisms belonging to the same species and occupying a particular area at the same time.[17] Therefore population ecology studies the changes in size, density and other characteristics of populations. Of particular importance is the biotic potential, or intrinsic rate of natural increase, of a population, and its process of natural selection. The former has featured in many bio-economic models of optimal renewable resource management, such as of fisheries.[18]

Community ecology links up with population ecology in the study of interspecific competition (competition among two or more species). For example, predator–prey models have been used to explain both population fluctuations and the role of predator–prey relationships as an organizing force in ecosystem communities. Early theoretical models predicted well-defined oscillations in predator and prey populations due to positive and negative reinforcing feedback effects. In later models, a simple predation process has led to a stable equilibrium, oscillation, or extinction in response to a fluctuating environment.[19] Essentially, most models show that when the population of predators is low, that of prey increases. After some time lag this causes predators to increase. Eventually, however, predators over-eat their prey and the prey population declines, which, after a time lag causes predators to decrease again. This basic predator–prey model has also been adapted by economics for optimal harvesting models.[20]

Given the complexity of ecological relationships, verification of theories at the ecosystem level is particularly difficult. Nevertheless, ecology generally represents the natural development of ecosystems as a long-term process of succession, in which a more stable ecosystem emerges through improved feedback, or homeostatic, responses to changes in the physical environment:

> *Ecosystem development*, or what is more often known as *ecological succession*, may be defined in terms of the following three parameters:
> (1) It is an orderly process of community development that involves changes in species structure and community process with time; it is reasonably directional and, therefore, predictable.
> (2) It results from modification of the physical environment by the community; that is, succession is community-controlled even though the physical environment determines the pattern, the rate of change, and often sets limits as to how far development can go.
> (3) It culminates in a stabilized ecosystem in which maximum biomass (or high information content) and symbiotic function between organisms are maintained at per unit of available energy flow.... In a word, the "strategy" of succession as a short-term process is basically the same as the "strategy" of long-term evolutionary development of the biosphere, namely increased control of, or homeostasis with, the physical environment in the sense of achieving maximum protection from its perturbations.[21]

Through natural succession, ecosystems develop complex feedback mechanisms to ensure their stability. For example, "biotic controls of grazing, population density, and nutrient cycling provide the chief negative feedback mechanisms that contribute to stability in the natural system by preventing overshoots and destructive oscillations."[22] These feedback mechanisms and controls therefore represent the ecological parameters regulating the density and size of an ecosystem's community and populations.

Of course, humankind is the only population that has developed the ability to manage the environment so as to ensure survival of the species. As Odum argues, however, such extensive exploitation threatens the ecological stability crucial to human welfare:

> Man, of course, more than any other species attempts to modify the physical environment to meet his immediate needs, but in doing so he is increasingly disrupting, even destroying, the biotic components which are necessary for his physiological existence. Since man is a heterotroph and phagotroph who thrives best near the end of complex food chains, his dependency on the natural environment remains no matter how sophisticated his technology becomes. The great cities are still only parasites in the biosphere when we consider what have been aptly called the *vital resources*, namely air, water, and food. The bigger the cities the more they demand from the surrounding countryside and the greater the danger of damaging the natural environment "host". So far, man has been so busy "conquering" nature that he has yet given little thought or effort to reconciling the conflicts of his dual role, that of manipulator of and inhabitant of ecosystems.[23]

Moreover, the type of damage inflicted on natural ecosystems can be so extensive and pervasive that natural feedback mechanisms breakdown and, instead of dampening any initial disturbance, tend to amplify its effects through successive ecological interactions. This process is described for the case of human disruptions to natural hydrological cycles, soil run-off and erosion:

> Man's activities can change the nature of the land surface in ways that are quite fundamental to the operation of natural ecosystems by, for example, the removal or modification of the accumulated living and dead biomass of the natural vegetation and the disruption of the ecosystem's functional organisation.... These modifications lead to changes in the water balance of catchment areas, usually increasing the proportion of surface runoff. In addition the distribution of runoff through time is changed also, normally producing concentrations of runoff into higher peak flows. These hydrological changes in turn permit greater removal of mineral material from the land surface in the form of increased rates of erosion. In order to accommodate these increased flows of water and minerals, river channel adjustments take place. Such changes in process are normally progressive, as the negative feedback processes prevalent in natural systems are replaced by positive feedback mechanisms.[24]

So, through extensively modifying the natural environment, people often endanger the ecological stability on which they are dependent. As biological organisms, people are an integral part of the ecological functioning of their environment; as highly-advanced social animals, they are capable of organizing the means to exploit the resources of nature to satisfy their material needs on an unprecedentedly extensive and intensive scale. The result is that we have become the dominant organism in any ecosystem we utilize and so have the capacity to transform and alter radically any natural ecosystem:

> If ecosystems are defined as distinct assemblages of plant and animal life, together with their effective environment, then any heavily used ecosystem contains man as the dominant animal, and his crops as dominant flora.... To a greater or lesser degree, all ecosystems utilized by man are created or modified by man's activity.... While the inanimate and non-human elements of ecosystems have overwhelming numerical dominance, the process–response relationships which define the ecosystems are to a large degree governed by the decisions and activities of man in all those which he closely occupies. The replacement of natural ecosystems by man-modified and man-created ecosystems now extends over most of the earth, including the oceans.[25]

By altering the natural environment through modifying or creating new ecosystems (by introducing agricultural systems, urban areas or water reservoirs, for instance) we can facilitate the social activity of satisfying our material needs. At the same time, if such modifications or newly introduced systems in the environment lead to severe disruptions in its ecological functions, then the consequences for human welfare could be drastic. For example, the setting up of an intensive yet ecologically inappropriate agricultural system in a previously natural environment could cause the leaching of soil nutrients, erosion and eventual desertification.

An increasingly important question for ecologists, as well as for economists and other social scientists, is to what extent is the people–nature balance – or ecological stability and sustainability (resilience) – of managed ecosystems dependent on the resilience or adaptation of natural ecological processes to the disorder inflicted by economic and other human activity: "in an equilibrium model, adaptive processes are those that tend to maintain homeostasis in crucial variables in the face of perturbation".[26] This need for continuous ecological adjustment and adaption by the environment in response to human "perturbation" is described by Tivy and O'Hare:

> ... one of the most important attributes of the climax or mature ecosystem is that of *stability*. This is the ability of a system to maintain a relatively constant condition in terms of its species composition, biomass and productivity, with minor fluctuations around a mean value (the equilibrium point), and to return to this steady condition fairly rapidly after internal or external disturbances.... Nearly all human activities disturb "natural" ecosystems to a lesser or greater extent. And, as has already been stressed, there

are very few areas of the earth's surface unaffected by direct or indirect human influence. They can, and often do, cause disturbances such as were formerly not encountered by organisms and which are beyond the limit of tolerance of the ecosystem. They subject the ecosystem to stresses greater than would otherwise occur. These, as have already been noted, can completely destroy an ecosystem. In some cases, severe stress may inhibit its re-establishment or effect an irreversible change.[27]

An endemic problem facing all analyses of environmental change is that knowledge of human impact on ecosystems is inadequately developed. Our knowledge of evolution in general, and ecological development in particular, is limited. Perhaps what is most limited is our understanding of the diversity and complexity of ecosystems themselves.

The total energy flow of an ecosystem is defined as the portion of incoming solar radiation that is successfully converted through photosynthesis into plant matter and is thus potentially available to herbivores. As Table 2.1 shows, total energy flow per annum of most solar-powered natural ecosystems varies from 1,000 to 40,000 kilocalories per square metre (4.185–167.4 megajoules (MJ) per m²). This range covers both unsubsidized solar-powered natural ecosystems that depend largely or entirely on solar energy for their sources of energy; and naturally subsidized solar-powered ecosystems that augment solar energy by the auxiliary energy input of tides, waves, wind, rainfall or water power and/ or through the energy content of any organic matter or nutrients imported from other ecosystems.[28] For the latter ecosystems, these auxiliary energy sources reduce the unit cost of self-maintenance (in energy terms) by the ecosystem, which increases the amount of solar energy input converted to the chemical potential energy of plants. Hence, one would expect the mean energy flow for a stable naturally subsidized ecosystem (such as an estuary or a rainforest) to be higher than that for a purely solar-powered ecosystem (such as upland forest or grasslands). For the biosphere as a whole, Odum estimates that the total energy flow per annum is approximately 2,000 kcal/m² (8.37 MJ/m²), roughly .04 per cent of the total incoming solar energy flow per square metre per year.[29]

If the complexity and diversity of ecological systems and processes make it difficult enough to understand the conditions necessary for ensuring ecological stability and sustainability (resilience), our limited knowledge of evolution in general and ecological development in particular make it extremely difficult to assess the extent to which negative human impacts interfere with the normal process of evolution, or change, in ecosystems.

First, although the pattern of natural ecological development, or *succession*, may be a continuous trend towards increased stability, environmental changes do not necessarily reverse this process of suc-

**Table 2.1: Ecosystems Classified According to Source and Level of Energy**

| | Annual energy flow (power level) (kilocalories per m$^2$) |
|---|---|
| 1. *Unsubsidized Natural Solar-Powered Ecosystems* Examples: open oceans, upland forests. These systems constitute the basic life-support module for the earth. | 1,000–10,000 (2,000) |
| 2. *Naturally Subsidized Solar-Powered Ecosystems* Examples: tidal estuary, some rain forests. These are the naturally productive systems of nature that not only have high life-support capacity but also produce excess organic matter that may be exported to other systems or stored. | 10,000–40,000 (20,000) |
| 3. *Man-Subsidized Solar-Powered Ecosystems* Examples: agriculture, aquaculture. These are food and fibre-producing systems supported by auxiliary fuel or other energy supplied by man. | 10,000–40,000 (20,000) |
| 4. *Fuel-Powered Urban-Industrial Systems* Examples: cities, suburbs, industrial parks. These are man's wealth-generating systems in which terrestrial energy replaces the sun as the chief energy source. These are dependent on classes 1–3 for life support, food and fuel. | 100,000–3,000,000 (2,000,000) |

Numbers in Parentheses are estimated round-figure averages.
*Source:* E.P. Odum, *Ecology* (2nd edn), (Holt, Rinehart and Winston: London, 1975), Table 2.1.

cession by producing equally steady decreases in ecological stability. Instead they often take the form of abrupt, discontinuous shocks to the ecosystem. As a result, species diversity and population levels are distrupted, and the ecosystem is quickly transformed from one stage to another (see Figure 2.1). Thus environmental change often involves discontinuous interruptions to the normal pattern of succession rather than steady declines in ecological stability.[30]

Secondly, for each ecosystem, its fragility (that is "the ease with which an ecosystem can be disrupted") depends essentially on two factors: "first on the relative resilience of the system and, second, on the type of disturbance to which it is subjected".[31] The aggregate effects of any large-scale environmental changes involving the interacting responses of several interlinking ecosystems may be an unusual capacity for resilience and regeneration in some cases and a tendency towards rapidly reinforcing

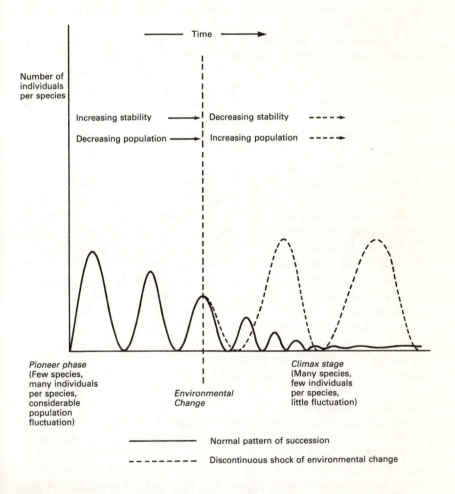

**Figure 2.1: Environmental Change as Discontinuous Shocks to the Normal Pattern of Succession**

disturbance and disruption in others. For example, interlinking grassland ecosystems are often able to absorb a high degree of physical stress from human intervention. Even if there is significant destruction of surface biomass or conversion of land for cultivation, the grassland's ability to recover and regenerate is not impaired.[32] In comparison (see further discussion in Chapter 6), the Amazonian tropical forest system is comprised of three completely distinct, interlinking ecosystems – the tropical forest ecosystem proper, the river bank swamp areas and the aquatic river ecosystems. These sub-systems are so intricately interdependent that any external disturbance to one is bound to have repercussions for the entire Amazonian region. Hence, it is difficult to make comparisons and generalizations about the resilience of different ecosystems when subjected to large-scale human disturbances and ecological destabilization.

Understanding ecological resilience in the face of external disturbances is also of importance to managed ecosystems, particularly agriculture where the purpose of human activity is to transform an ecosystem deliberately.[33] As noted above, the key question is whether or not the human modification and transformation of ecosystems affect their stability and resilience (sustainability). If the natural mechanisms of control and stabilization are replaced by increased human management and control, the application of human knowledge, and the use of both human and natural resources – all with minimal ecological disturbance – the result may be little change in ecological stability or sustainability.[34]

In Java, the process of transforming ecosystems into a complex system of paddy rice fields produced a fairly stable, managed ecosystem that persisted for centuries until this system was transformed by Dutch rule.[35] In contrast, the extensive transformation of parts of the Amazonian forest into large-scale commercial agriculture and ranching, as well as colonist shifting cultivation zones, does not appear to have established a sustainable or stable modified system since the loss of natural ecosystems of control have not been adequately compensated by proper human management (see Chapter 6). Recently, there has been growing concern that the inappropriate transformation of unsuitable areas of existing agricultural systems into more monoculture, hybrid-species systems dependent on petro-chemical based fertilizers and pesticides, has tended to increase the fragility, rather than the resilience, of these important managed ecosystems.[36]

A further problem is that ecosystems modified by people do not exist in isolation but interact with the untransformed ecosystems of the environment. Consequently, the inherent stability or resilience of the former may be linked to the stability and resilience of the latter.[37] From an anthropomorphic perspective, a stable and sustainable (resilient) people–nature balance may actually require a good mixture of early successional systems modified to suit human needs and undisturbed climax ecosystems. In assessing the stability and sustainability of such an economic–environmental system, one has to be careful to distinguish between local changes in the resilience of particular modified and natural ecosystems, and global changes in the resilience of the entire interconnected system.

The application of fertilizers and pesticides to an agricultural system may increase production from its annual cycle and appear to leave the system as stable as before. On the other hand, the surface run-off of petrochemical wastes may cause considerable disruptions to the surrounding natural ecosystems which, as a result, could become less stable and resilient. Whether the entire economic–environmental system would experience a global deterioration in stability and sustainability, however, depends upon the feedback effects between the natural and modified ecosystems. Again, these may vary according to the resilience of the ecosystems and the type of external disturbance involved.

As emphasized by Conway, precisely because agricultural systems – or agro-ecosystems – are ecological systems modified by human beings to produce fibre or other agricultural products, their capacity for sustainability and stability cannot be understood solely by examining their flows and cycles of energy and materials.[38] One consequence of this transformation is that the system boundary of an agroecosystem acquires a socioeconomic dimension (Figure 2.2). Therefore it becomes essential to analyse how the complexity and diversity of agro-ecosystems (characteristics which in turn affect the stability and sustainability of these systems) arise from the interaction between socio-economic and ecological processes.

As suggested by Holling, the basic system properties for natural populations, communities and ecosystems, are *productivity* (in terms of numbers/biomass of individuals species), *stability* (constancy) and *resilience*.[39] In contrast, a unique feature of the agro-ecosystem is that it is also geared towards the socio-economic goal of increased social value. Social value – or welfare – is defined by Conway "in terms consistent with classical welfare economics" as being

> a function of the amounts of goods and services produced by the agroecosystem, their relationship to human needs (or happiness) and their allocation among the human population.... In practice, therefore, an assessment of an agroecosystem's performance has to be made not in terms of the theoretical goal but in relation to those key system properties that contribute most directly to realizing the goal.[40]

Conway suggests four agro-ecosystem properties – productivity, stability, sustainability and equitability – that directly relate to the realization of social value, and presumably in return, are affected by

**Figure 2.2: The Ricefield as an Agro-ecosystem**

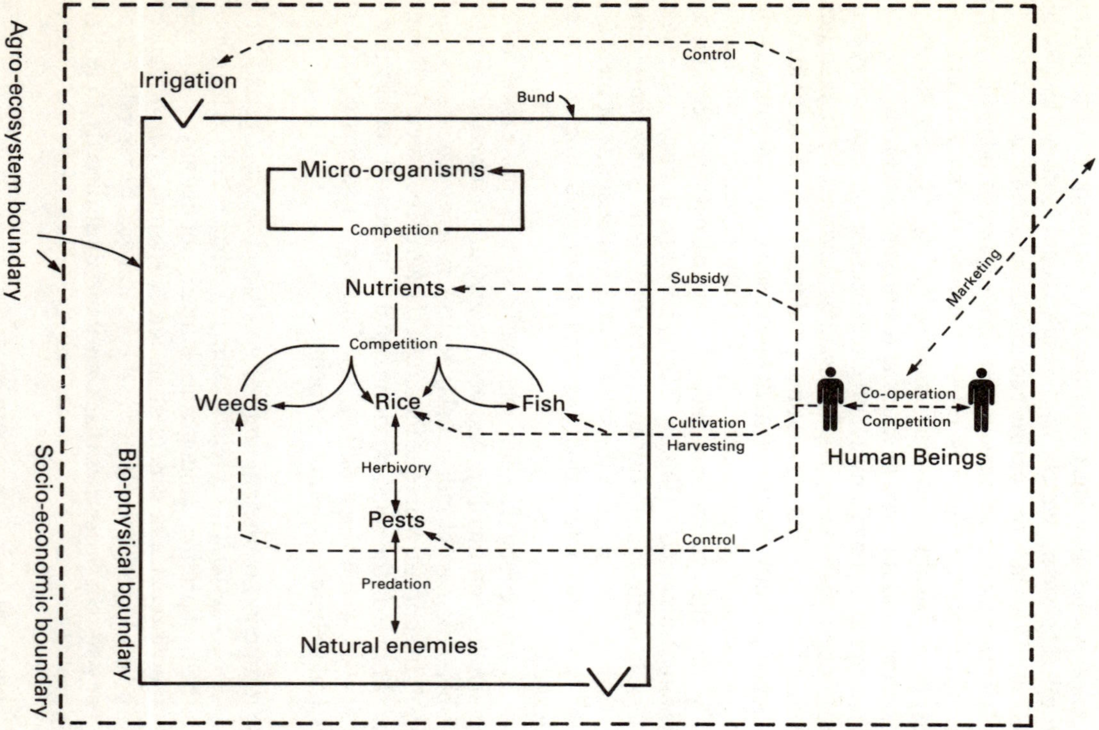

*Source:* Gordon R. Conway, "The properties of agroecosystems", *Agricultural Systems*, Vol. 24 (1987), Fig. 1, p. 97.

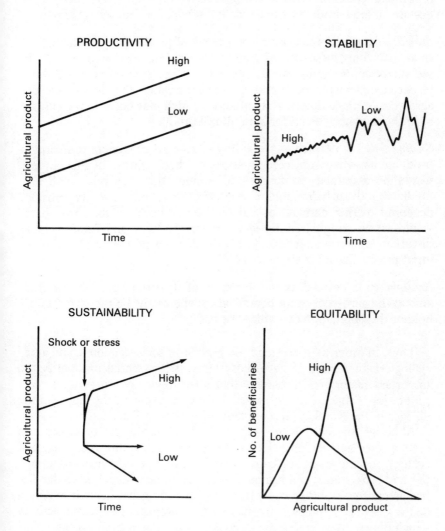

**Figure 2.3: Indicators of Agricultural Performance**

*Source:* Gordon R. Conway and Edward B. Barbier, "After the green revolution: sustainable and equitable agricultural development", *Futures*, Special Issue on Sustainable Development, Vol. 20 (1988), in press.

attempts to maximize social value through different modes of agricultural development (see Figure 2.3).[41]

*Productivity* is defined as the output of valued product per unit of resource input, with common measures of productivity being yield or income per hectare, or total production of goods and services per household or nation.

*Stability* may be defined as the constancy of productivity in the face of small disturbing forces arising from the normal fluctuations and cycles in the surrounding environment. Included in the environment are those physical, biological, social and economic variables that lie outside the agro-ecosystem, and normal fluctuations which may occur in the climate or in the market demand for agricultural products.

*Sustainability* is defined as the ability of an agro-ecosystem to maintain productivity when subjected to stress or shock. Stress in this context would be a regular, sometimes continuous but relatively small and predictable disturbance such as the effect of salinity, toxicity, erosion, declining market demand or indebtedness. Shock on the other hand would be an irregular, infrequent, relatively large and unpredictable disturbance such as a rare drought or flood, a new pest or a sudden rise in input prices (like oil in the mid-1970s).

*Equitability* is defined as the evenness of distribution of the product among the agro-ecosystem beneficiaries who might be the farm household or the population of a village or nation.

Thus, in order to understand the process of socio-economic and agro-ecological interaction in agro-ecosystems, it is essential to identify the important factors and processes that affect these four primary system properties. Table 2.2 shows one such list of impacts for the high altitude villages in the Karakoram mountains of Northern Pakistan.

Although the complexity and diversity of ecological processes and systems pose a formidable challenge to our understanding, the science of ecology has improved our knowledge of natural populations, communities and ecosystems, and human ecological impact. This knowledge has had an enormous influence on those recent approaches in environmental and resource economics concerned with the impact of economic activity – including activity within managed ecosystems such as agro-ecosystems – on environmental degradation. The effect of such activity may, in the extreme, take the form of breakdowns in natural feedback mechanisms and controls which, in turn, can accelerate change in ecosystems beyond the limits of tolerance. Thus, it is not surprising that, in the attempt to understand the interaction between socio-economic and ecological processes, the work at the frontiers of ecology and economics is converging more and more.

**Table 2.2: Key Variables and Processes Affecting the System Properties of Villages in the Northern Areas of Pakistan**

| *Positive* | *Negative* |
|---|---|
| **PRODUCTIVITY** | |
| Construction of Karakoram Highway | Shortage of cultivable land |
| Development of new land | Shortage of water |
| Inorganic fertilisers | Weeds, pests and diseases |
| New wheat and fruit varieties | Seasonal labour shortage |
| Introduction of seed potato cultivation | |
| New credit loan system | |
| **STABILITY** | |
| Integration of crops and livestock | Crop pests and diseases |
| Co-operative marketing | Livestock diseases |
| Improvement of irrigation channels | Temperature fluctuations |
| **SUSTAINABILITY** | |
| Farmyard manure | Glacier movement |
| Crop rotation (wheat, potatoes) | Mudflows, avalanches |
| Training of village livestock specialists | Earthquakes |
| | River bank erosion |
| | Virus of seed potatoes |
| | Overuse of pesticides |
| **EQUITABILITY** | |
| Traditional co-operation | Sale of land |
| Creation of village organisations | Education |
| Rotation of pasturing | Emigrant labour |
| Development of new land | |

*Source:* Gordon R. Conway, "The properties of agroecosystems", *Agricultural Systems*, Vol. 24 (1987), Table 2, p. 104.

# THERMODYNAMICS

Economics has always looked to physics for its theoretical and methodological inspiration. Consequently when, in the 1960s, economists were looking for another analogy in physics with which to characterize the basic physical relationship between the economic process and the environment, thermodynamics seemed to be appropriate. Thermodynamics developed

as a branch of physics devoted to the understanding of energy transformations, particularly the conversion of available energy into work and waste
heat. Of particular interest to economists were the first two laws of
thermodynamics, which seemed to be analogies for the material and
energy transformations of the economic process.

A formal definition of the first law of thermodynamics is usually stated
as: "The change in the internal energy of a system is equal to the net
energy flow across the boundaries of the system."[42] In general, however,
this law is interpreted as meaning that energy, like matter, can neither be
created nor destroyed and therefore must be constant during any
interaction between a system and its surroundings. Thus, the first law is
often referred to as the "law of conservation of matter and energy".[43] In
the 1960s and 1970s, this law formed the basis for material–energy balance
models of the economic process.[44]

As is suggested by the first law,

> when materials – minerals, fuels, gases, and organic materials – are
> extracted and harvested from nature and used by producers and so-
> called consumers, their mass is not altered in these processes except
> in trivial amounts. Materials and energy residuals are generated in
> production and consumption activities, and the mass of the former
> must be about equal to that initially extracted from nature.
> Accordingly, it is basically deceptive to speak of the consumption of
> goods.[45]

Consequently, if one takes the internal system as being the economic
system of production and consumption of material commodities, its
surroundings to be the natural environment, and the inflows and outflows
across the boundaries of the system to be the raw material and energy
resource inputs and waste residuals respectively, then one can deduce
from the law of conservation of matter and energy that

> each increase in the production levels of physical goods in our
> economy has two effects: (1) a corresponding increase in the amounts
> of material inputs and energy from the environment and (2) a
> corresponding increase in the waste loads placed on the absorption
> capacity of the environment.[46]

This implies that economic growth in terms of "physical goods" cannot
occur without the additional extraction of resources from the environment, and increased waste.

In its formal application in modern physics, the second law of
thermodynamics is applied to the flow of energy in a system, and entropy
is defined as a measure of the unavailable energy in that system.
Therefore, in any thermodynamic system one can distinguish the
available (free) energy from the unavailable (bound) energy. That is,
available energy is distributed unevenly in highly ordered forms, such as

the kinetic energy of a waterfall or the potential-chemical energy of coal and other fossil or biomass fuels. These qualitative properties of available energy make it useful for conversion into mechanical work. In contrast, energy that is unavailable is spread evenly or completely dissipated as waste heat in the system, which prevents it from being used for mechanical work. When coal or other fuels are burned, the heat dissipates quickly into the local atmosphere at a low temperature. This makes it virtually useless for, say, boiling water to produce steam. So in thermodynamics, entropy is a measure of the *qualitative* state of energy in a system, and the entropy of a system is said to increase as the energy contained within it dissipates from a more available to a less available state. In this sense, therefore, "entropy is a negative measure associated with utility. An increase in entropy corresponds to a decrease in utility; hence, entropy is a measure of disutility".[47]

A formal definition of the second law of thermodynamics is usually stated as: "No self-acting and cyclic device (unaided by any external agency) can make heat pass from one body to another at a higher temperature".[48] Or more simply, "heat flows by itself only from the hotter to the colder body, never in reverse".[49] The implication of the entropy law is that any conversion of the energy supplied to a system into mechanical work must invariably involve some energy waste (that is, waste heat) and the energy converted for work must also eventually dissipate. When this occurs, the entropy of the system has increased. Consequently, "even though energy is conserved in a closed system, the system tends toward an energy state corresponding to that of minimum usefulness".[50]

However, Georgescu-Roegen has consistently argued that the concept of entropy of the second law need not be confined to energy transformations.[51] In macroscopic transformations of matter and energy, such as those occurring in the economic process, matter as well as energy is being dissipated from a more available (useful) state to a less available (useless) state. By analogy, therefore, the entropy law can also be applied to this macroscopic transformation of matter. If a more general interpretation of the second law allows entropy to be regarded as an index of dissipation or disorder, then one could argue that both energy and matter are subject to entropic dissipation by the economic process.

Low entropy (highly ordered) fossil fuels enter the economic process capable of performing mechanical work, but leave the economic system having been dissipated into waste heat, smoke and residual matter. Similarly, raw materials and mineral resources can be transformed into consumer and producer durable goods. Eventually, however, these items will be used up (that is, physically depreciated) and discarded as useless items. In general, the material inputs from the environment into the economic system – timber from trees, mineral ores, foodstuffs and so on – are highly ordered, available and thus useful sources of material. On the completely or partially disordered, dissipated materials and material structures that are no longer useful to humankind.[52]

As a consequence, if the economic process is dependent on the surrounding environment for sources of material and energy, then this process irrevocably and irreversibly transforms the useful (low entropy) matter and energy available in the environment into useless (high entropy) material and energy waste. The result of the throughput of terrestrial sources of material and energy in the economic process must therefore be an increase in the entropic state of the environment:

> In fact all environmental degradation can be defined as increased environmental entropy. Entropy is a measure of unavailable energy and disorder. Thermal pollution is unavailable energy; therefore, the discharge of waste heat to water and air results in increased environmental entropy. Likewise, the emission of liquid, gaseous and solid wastes, which are the disordered by-products of industrial processes, increases environmental disorder and raises the level of environmental entropy.[53]

Hence, by analogy with the second law of thermodynamics, one could say that the increased disorder, or entropy, of the environment is a direct consequence of the appropriation of its resources as material and energy inputs by the economic system.

The economic system appropriates these low-entropy resources in order to maintain its own physical elements – the human population, consumer and producer durables and so forth, in a highly ordered (and thus useful) state. But this maintenance of order within the economic system must correspond to a loss of order by the source of the matter and energy used by the economic process – the terrestrial environment. In turn, the environment maintains its natural resources in an ordered (low entropy) state by utilizing the flow of available energy from the sun. However, if the dissipation of environmental resources by the economic process occurs at a faster rate than that at which the ecosystems can recuperate, then the increased disorder in the environment resulting from the material and energy throughput of the economic process will cause irreparable damage to the terrestrial environment:

> We have two sources of low entropy: terrestrial stocks of concentrated minerals, and the solar flow of radiant energy. The terrestrial source (minerals in the earth's crust) is obviously limited in total amount, though the rate at which we use it up is largely a matter of choice. The solar source is practically unlimited in total amount, but strictly limited in the rate at which it reaches the earth. These means are finite ... terrestrial stocks can, for a while at least, be used at a rate of man's own choosing, that is, rapidly. The use of solar energy and renewable resources is limited by the fixed solar flux, and the

rhythms of growth of plants and animals, which in turn provide a natural constraint on economic growth. But growth can be speeded beyond this constraint, for a time at least, by consuming geological capital – by using up the reserves of terrestrial low entropy.... The throughput flow maintains or increases the order within the human economy, but at the cost of creating greater disorder in the rest of the natural world, as a result of depletion and pollution.[54]

## SUMMARY AND CONCLUSION: TOWARDS AN ALTERNATIVE VIEW

Conservationism, ecology and thermodynamics have in recent decades exerted an enormous influence on environmental and resource economics – the sub-discipline in economics concerned with economic–environmental interactions. Unlike the period of rapid industrialization and long-run economic expansion from the late nineteenth century up until the 1960s, the current era is one in which problems of natural resource depletion and environmental degradation – such as pollution, the 1970s oil shock and environmentally "unsustainable" development – have once again become major policy issues. In an effort to understand these new problems, which are fundamentally different from the land–scarcity concerns of classical economists, some contemporary economists have been quick to borrow from non-economic influences.

With the renaissance of the environmental movement since the 1960s, there has been renewed interest in the moral and philosophical arguments of conservationists. As noted in this chapter, the present-day natural-resource scarcity doctrine of the conservationists has a long intellectual tradition dating back to the writings of Marsh, and emphasizes the fact that human dependence on nature, or the "nature–man continuum", makes the whole environment inherently valuable to humankind. Moreover, given that biological diversity and complexity is essential to this continuum, then environmental preservation must also have value to humankind. More recently, conservationists have argued that efficient and sustainable resource management is essential to the long-term development of Third World countries.

If conservationism has provided the moral and philosophical arguments for new approaches to environmental and resource economics, ecology has furthered our scientific understanding of ecological relationships and how they are affected by human activity. Ecologists have underlined the complexity and diversity of ecological relationships and processes, and have clarified greatly notions of ecological stability and resilience (sustainability) in the face of the human disturbance of ecosystems. Of particular interest are the managed ecosystems, such as agro-ecosystems, that have been deliberately transformed to meet human needs. Understanding the conditions for long-term stability and sustainability of these systems has led some ecologists to consider the interactions between socio-economic and agro-ecological processes. At the frontiers of both disciplines, ecology and economics are increasingly finding common ground for approaching the problems of economic-environmental interaction.

Thermodynamics has supplied some economists with the methodology for depicting the "throughput" of material and energy from the environment into the economic process and then back into the surrounding environment.[55] As a result, the first law allows the economic system and the environment to be viewed together as a closed circular system of energy and material transformation. The second law can be analogously applied to depict this process as an irreversible transformation of ordered, useful (low entropy) material and energy into disordered, dissipated and therefore useless (high entropy) waste. Moreover, as the environment is the source of the resources transformed by the economic process, and the recipient of its wastes, the net effect of this transformation is to maintain or increase the order of the economic system at the expense of increasing the disorder (degradation) of the natural environment.

The economic interpretations taken from conservationism, ecology and thermodynamics can be put together in an alternative view of natural-resource scarcity that differs substantially from the more conventional perspective that prevailed before the 1960s. At the heart of this alternative view is the recognition of a new natural-resource scarcity problem: that increasing environmental degradation (or disorder) may, under certain conditions, threaten ecological stability and sustainability. By supplying more and more resources to the economic process and by having in turn to absorb the resulting waste, the environment can no longer maintain indefinitely the same degree of ecological activity or stability. Ecosystems may eventually break down if the environment is continually disrupted and cannot maintain its resilience. Under such circumstances, the opportunity cost in environmental terms of supplying the material needs of the economic system with terrestrial resources is increasing ecological instability and unsustainability.

Borrowing an analogy from thermodynamics, as the existence of available energy and material in the environment is intrinsically related to the ordered complexity and diversity of ecosystems, the transformation by the economic process of this available material and energy into dissipated waste must represent an increase in the disorder in the ecosystems of the environment. For example, when an environmental resource (such as a tree or a coal deposit) is appropriated by the economic system, the surrounding environment has lost some usefully ordered structure or store of material and/or energy; it has become less ordered as the result of the extraction of the resource. The loss of such an ordered structure of material and energy can have an impact on the functioning and stability of ecosystems: the cutting down of a tree could exacerbate problems of soil erosion and fertility and affect hydrological cycles, as well as destroy the natural habitat for many plant and animal populations. Similarly, the extraction of a coal deposit must invariably involve some disruption to the surface area under which it is found. This affects the soils, the surface water of the area, and the local biomass.

At the other end of the economic process, the generation of dissipated waste presents a problem of assimilation for natural ecosystems. Even when this waste is non-toxic or biodegradable, ecosystems can be limited in their capacity to absorb large quantities. Thus massive run-offs of slurry – organic effluent from intensive farming of livestock – can cause the sealing of soil surfaces, which retards water and oxygen infiltration, and prevents adequate nutrient cycling. This can lead to nitrogen in the soil building up to toxic levels as well as to an increase in the uptake of toxic trace elements by plants and animals. Consequently, the absorption of the net material waste generated by the economic process represents an additional source of increased disorder in the environment, which potentially disrupts ecological functions and stability. In the long run, such pervasive disruptions can affect overall ecological sustainability.

These examples emphasize a dynamic problem of natural-resource scarcity that manifests itself primarily as a problem of environmental degradation and ecological disruption. In essence, this dynamic natural-resource scarcity problem stems from the physical dependency of the economic process on its surrounding environment – not just as a source of material and energy inputs but also as an assimilator of waste, and the provider of ecological functions crucial to the maintenance of economic activity and supportive of amenity values, welfare and life in general. The remainder of this book will focus on this alternative view of natural-resource scarcity and its potential contribution to our understanding of the contemporary problems of economic-environmental interaction. We will begin by examining how this view has influenced more conventional economic theories of resource depletion and pollution.

## NOTES

1. Some past writers on natural-resource scarcity have been closer to this contemporary alternative view. For example, John Ise, "The theory of value as applied to natural resources", *American Economic Review*, Vol. 15 (1925), pp. 284–91; Ise argued that the depletion of US natural resources is dangerously biased towards present, near-term use, at the expense of future generations. S.V. Ciriacy-Wantrup, *Resource Conservation; Economics and Policies* (University of California Press: Berkeley, 1952), approached the same problem from a more institutional perspective.
2. Harold J. Barnett and Chandler Morse, *Scarcity and Economic Growth: The Economics of Natural Resource Availability* (Johns Hopkins University Press: Baltimore, 1963),

pp. 75–8. As is discussed in the following chapter, this natural-resource scarcity doctrine is still prevalent in contemporary conservationism. Timothy O'Riordan, *Environmentalism* (2nd edn), (Pion: London, 1981), analyses the important contributions of the contemporary environment movement in many fields, including economics. Talbot Page, *Conservation and Economic Efficiency: An Approach to Materials Policy* (Johns Hopkins University Press: Baltimore, 1977), bases his "permanent livability criterion" on contemporary conservationist thinking. David W. Pearce, "Sustainable development: Ecology and economic progress", draft paper IIED/UCL Environmental Economics Centre (London: 1988), also examines the implicit contributions of conservationism to key theorists in the economics of sustainable development, whereas Edward B. Barbier, "The concept of sustainable economic development", *Environmental Conservation*, Vol. 14 (1987), pp. 101–10, explores how the concept of sustainable economic development as applied to the Third World has emerged from environmentalist concerns over development. Contemporary conservationists who have been influential in challenging modern economic ideas include Rachel Carson, *Silent Spring* (Houghton-Mifflin: Boston, 1962); Barry Commoner, *The Closing Circle: Man, Nature and Technology* (Knopf; New York, 1971); E.F. Schumacher, *Small is Beautiful: Economics as if People Mattered* (Harper & Row: New York, 1973); W. van Dieren and M.G.W. Hummelinck, *Nature's Price: The Economics of Mother Earth* (Marion Boyars: London, 1979); and Barbara Ward and Rene Dubos, *Only One Earth* (Penguin Books: Harmondsworth, 1972).

3. George P. Marsh, *Man and Nature* (Charles Scribner: New York, 1865).
4. Barnett and Morse, op. cit., pp. 91–2.
5. Marsh, op. cit.
6. Page, op. cit., p. 175.
7. Schumacher, op. cit., pp. 103–05.
8. International Union for the Conservation of Nature (IUCN), *World Conservation Strategy: Living Resource Conservation for Sustainable Development* (IUCN-UNEP-WWF: Gland, Switzerland, 1980); Schumacher, op. cit.; Ward and Dubos, op. cit.; and World Commission on Environment and Development (WCED), *Our Common Future* (Oxford University Press: Oxford, 1987).
9. Jeremy J. Warford, *Environment, Growth and Development*, Development Committee Paper No. 14 (World Bank: Washington, DC, 1987); and WCED, op. cit.
10. Lynton K. Caldwell, "Political aspects of ecologically sustainable development", *Environmental Conservation*, Vol. II (1984), pp. 299–308.
11. IUCN, op. cit., para. 8.8.
12. Ibid.
13. Clement A. Tisdell, "An economist's critique of the world conservation strategy, with examples from the Australian experience", *Environmental Conservation*, Vol. 10 (1983), pp. 43–52; and David W. Pearce, "Sustainable futures: Economics and the environment", Inaugural Lecture (University College London, 1985).
14. E.R. Pianka, *Evolutionary Ecology* (Harper & Row: New York, 1983), pp. 4–5.
15. Charles J. Krebs, *Ecology: the Experimental Analysis of Distribution and Abundance*, (3rd edn), (Harper & Row: New York, 1985), pp. 8–9.
16. Ibid., p. 9.
17. R. Brewer, *Principles of Ecology* (W.B. Saunders: Philadelphia, 1979), p. 286. For classic works in population ecology see R.H. MacArthur and E.O. Wilson, *The Theory of Island Biogeography* (Princeton University Press: Princeton, 1967); E.R. Pianka, "On r and K selection", *American Naturalists*, Vol. 104 (1970), pp. 592–7; and E.R. Pianka, "r and K selection or b and d selection", *American Naturalist*, Vol. 106 (1972), pp. 581–8.
18. See, for example, John R. Beddington and Colin W. Clark, "Allocation problems between national and foreign fisheries with a fluctuating fish resource", *Marine*

*Resource Economics*, Vol. 1 (1984), pp. 137–53; Colin W. Clark, *Mathematical Bioeconomics: The Optimal Management of Renewable Resources* (John Wiley & Sons: New York, 1976); and Partha Dasgupta, *The Control of Resources* (Basil Blackwell: Oxford, 1982).

19. See A.J. Lotka, *Elements of Physical Biology* (William & Wilkens, Baltimore, 1925); and V. Volterra, "Fluctuations in the abundance of a species considered mathematically", *Nature*, Vol. 188 (1926), pp. 558–60, as examples of the early predator–prey models. For later models see R.M. May, "Limit cycles in predator–prey communities", *Science*, Vol. 177 (1972), pp. 900–902; R.M. May, "Simple mathematical models with very complex dynamics", *Nature*, Vol. 261 (1976), pp. 459–67; and Imanuel Noy-Meir, "Stability of grazing systems: An application of predator–prey graphs", *Journal of Ecology*, Vol. 63 (1975), pp. 459–81.

20. See, for example, Clark, op. cit., and David L. Ragozin and Gardner Brown Jr, "Harvest policies and nonmarket valuation in a predator–prey system", *Journal of Environmental Economics and Management*, Vol. 12 (1985), pp. 155–68.

21. Eugene P. Odum, *Fundamentals of Ecology* (3rd edn), (W.B. Saunders: Philadelphia, 1971), p. 251.

22. Ibid., p. 257.

23. Ibid., p. 23.

24. I.D. White *et al.*, *Environmental Systems* (George Allen & Unwin: London, 1984), pp. 438–9.

25. Harold Brookfield, "On man and ecosystems", *International Social Sciences Journal*, Man in Ecosystems, Vol. 93 (1982), pp. 375 and 383.

26. Anne Whyte, "The integration of natural and social sciences in the MAB programme", *International Social Sciences Journal*, Man in Ecosystems, Vol. 93 (1982), p. 421.

27. J. Tivy and G. O'Hare, *Human Impact on the Ecosystem* (Oliver & Boyd: Edinburgh, 1981), pp. 143–5. Some ecologists distinguish the *stability* of an ecosystem from its *resilience* (sustainability). See, for example, Gordon R. Conway, "Agroecosystem analysis", *Agricultural Administration*, Vol. 20 (1985), pp. 31–55; Gordon R. Conway, "The properties of agroecosystems", *Agricultural Systems*, Vol. 24 (1987), pp. 95–117; C.S. Holling, "Resilience and stability of ecological systems", *Annual Review of Ecological Systems*, Vol. 4 (1973), pp. 1–24; and CS. Holling, "The resilience of terrestrial ecosystems: Local surprise and global change", Chapter 10 in WC. Clark and R.E. Munn (eds), *Sustainable Development of the Biosphere* (Cambridge University Press: Cambridge, 1986), pp. 292–317.
For instance:

> Stability (*sensu stricto*) is the propensity of a system to attain or retain an equilibrium condition of steady state or stable oscillation. Systems of high stability resist any departure from that condition and, if perturbed, return rapidly to it with the least fluctuation. It is a classic equilibrium-centred definition.... Resilience, on the other hand, is the ability of a system to maintain its structure and patterns of behaviour in the face of disturbance. The size of the stability domain of residence, the strength of the repulsive forces at the boundary, and the resistance of the domain to contraction are all distinct measures of resilience.... Stability, as here defined, emphasizes equilibrium, low variability, and resistance to and absorption of change. In sharp contrast, resilience emphasizes the boundary of a stability domain and events far from equilibrium, high variability, and adaptation to change. (Holling, "The resilience of terrestrial ecosystems", op. cit., pp. 296–7).

Consequently, stability is "the ability of a system to maintain a relatively constant condition in terms of its species composition, biomass and productivity, with minor fluctuations around a mean value (the equilibrium point)" whereas resilience is simply "adaption to change", that is "the ability of a system to maintain its structure and patterns of behaviour in the face of disturbance". The analogy in economics is between long-term trends (resilience) versus short-run fluctuations around these trends (stability). As will be discussed below, Conway, op. cit., also maintains this distinction between stability and resilience, although he refers to the latter as *sustainability*. From now on, this distinction between stability and resilience (sustainability) will be employed.

28. Odum, op. cit., pp. 17–18.
29. Ibid., p. 62.
30. For example, as van Dieren and Hummelinck (op. cit., pp. 102–03) note, "... if we are concerned about the disappearance of the primary rain forest" due to shifting cultivation, ranching, timber operations and so on, "it is because the transition from secondary to primary forest takes so long: thousands to tens of thousands of years." See also the discussion of Amazonian deforestion in Chapter 6.
31. Tivy and O'Hare, op. cit., p. 144.
32. Ibid., pp. 163–4.
33. Conway, op. cit.; and White *et al.*, op. cit., pp. 444–5.
34. Brookfield, op. cit.; Conway, op. cit.; Richard Norgaard, "Coevolutionary development potential", *Land Economics*, Vol. 60 (1984), pp. 160–73; and Tivy and O'Hare op. cit.
35. Clifford Geertz, *Agriculture Involution: The Process of Ecological Change in Indonesia* (University of California Press: Berkeley, 1963).
36. See, for example, Gordon K. Douglass (ed.), *Agricultural Sustainability in a Changing World Order* (Westview Press: Boulder, Colorado, 1984); KEPAS, *The Sustainability of Agricultural Intensification in Indonesia* (KEPAS, Agency for Agricultural Research and Development: Jakarta, Indonesia, 1983); and WCED, op. cit., Chapter 5.
37. See, for example, Eugene P. Odum, *Ecology* (2nd edn), (Holt Rhinehart and Winston: London, 1975), pp. 163–4.
38. Conway, op. cit.
39. See Holling, op. cit. and note 27.
40. Conway, "The properties of agroecosystems", op. cit., p. 100.
41. Ibid.
42. R. Eden *et al.*, *Energy Economics: Growth, Resources and Policies* (Cambridge University Press; Cambridge, 1981), p. 22.
43. Nicholas Georgescu-Roegen, *The Entropy Law and the Economic Process* (Harvard University Press: Cambridge, Massachusetts, 1971); and Nicholas Georgescu-Roegen, "Energy analysis and economic valuation", *Southern Economic Journal*, Vol. 45 (1979), pp. 1023–58.
44. See, for example, Gerogrescu-Roegen, op. cit.; Allen V. Kneese, Robert U. Ayres, Ralph C. d'Arge, *Economics and the Environment: A Material Balances Approach* (Johns Hopkins University Press: Baltimore, 1970); Allen V. Kneese and Blair T. Bower, *Environmental Quality and Residuals Management*; (Johns Hopkins University Press: Baltimore, 1979); Peter Nijkamp, *Theory and Application of Environmental Economics* (North-Holland: Amsterdam, 1977); and Peter A. Victor, *Pollution: Economics and the Environment* (Allen & Unwin: London, 1972).
45. Kneese and Bower, op. cit., pp. 5–6.
46. Nijkamp, op. cit., p. 12.
47. Jeremy H. Krenz, *Energy: Conversion and Utilization*, (1st edn), (Allyn & Bacon: Boston, 1976), p. 70.
48. Eden *et al.*, op. cit., p. 12.
49. Nicholas Georgescu-Roegen, *Energy and Economic Myths: Insitutional and Analytical Economic Essays* (Pergamon Press: New York, 1976), p. 7.
50. Krenz, op. cit., p. 70. A closed thermodynamic system exchanges energy with its surroundings but not matter, whereas an open system exchanges both energy and

matter. In contrast, an isolated system exchanges neither energy nor matter with its surroundings.

51. Georgescu-Roegen, op. cit. See also Kenneth E. Boulding, "The economics of the coming spaceship earth" in H. Jarrett (ed.), *Environmental Quality in a Growing Economy* (Johns Hopkins University Press: Baltimore, 1966).

52. As Kneese and Bower (op. cit., p. 6) indicate, the non-usefulness of a residual in the economic process can also depend on such factors as the state of technology and the relative costs of using the residual as a recycled input:

> A residual is a nonproduct (material or energy output), the value of which is less than the costs of collecting, processing, and transporting it for use. Thus, the definition is time dependent, that is it is a function of (1) the level of technology in the society at a point in time and (2) the relative costs of alternative inputs at that point in time. For example, manure in the United States is now a residual, whereas thirty or so years ago it was a valuable raw material.

Assuming, in the long run, that the relative scarcity of natural resources yields favourable relative costs for recycling and that the required technology is available, then it might be *theoretically* possible to recycle all residuals. Nevertheless, the point of the second law is that, even under these ideal conditions, complete recovery and recycling of all waste residuals, including material residuals, remains a *physical* impossibility. As material inputs are continuously re-used in the economic process, there is bound to be losses of gases, particulate dust, and even dry and wet solids. Moreover, even if collecting, processing and transforming potentially recoverable material residuals is economically and technologically feasible, the recycling will require new inputs of energy and material that yield other irrecoverable wastes (e.g., the carbon, hydrogen and waste heat from fossil fuels used in recycling) and result in some loss of the recycled waste (e.g., as particulate dust or gas).

53. John P.E. Coyne, "Resource analysis as an alternative basis for project evaluation", unpublished PhD thesis (Cambridge University: Cambridge, 1981), p. 27.

54. Herman E. Daly, "Entropy, growth and the political economy of scarcity" in V. Kerry Smith (ed.), *Scarcity and Growth Reconsidered* (Johns Hopkins University Press: Baltimore, 1979), pp. 74 and 76.

55. The concept of material and energy "throughput" appears to have been first coined by Boulding, op. cit.

# 3
# Conventional Theory: Optimal Rates of Depletion

As a consequence of the growing concern about the increasing scarcity of fossil fuel and other raw materials, as well as the spread of the non-economic influences described in the previous chapter, conventional theories of natural-resource scarcity were extended and modified significantly after the early 1960s. In theoretical work, the emphasis has been laid on the optimal rate of depletion of exhaustible and renewable resources, with extensions to include monopoly, uncertainty and other market imperfections. The main criticism of such approaches, however, is that they are limited to a specific class of environmental problems: the increasing scarcity of economically valuable resource inputs into production. Nevertheless, they have established an important theoretical foundation for more ambitious explorations of the economic problem of environmental degradation. This chapter will survey these theories and discuss this criticism.

## CONVENTIONAL THEORIES OF NATURAL-RESOURCE SCARCITY

As noted in Chapter One, classical and early neo-classical economists recognized long ago that the relative scarcity of those natural resources appropriated as productive inputs is linked to their rate of use, or depletion: the earth can only supply a finite amount of available energy and raw material to the economic process. At any given time, society's ability to exploit these resources is limited, among other things, by its technological capabilities and methods of production. On the other hand, the lack of evidence of any binding natural-resource scarcity constraint on modern economic growth has reinforced the emerging conventional economic wisdom that "there seems to be little reason to worry about the exhaustion of resources which the market already treats as economic goods".[1] For those environmental resources used as basic material and energy inputs, market forces should dictate the optimal rate of exploitation automatically and effectively.[2]

There is conventional optimism in the economic system's ability to successfully adapt in the long run to any natural-resouce scarcity constraint. However, most economists accept that the over-exploitation of one or more limited sources of energy and material inputs could lead to a situation of temporary scarcity. So, from a purely analytical perspective, the unique feature of natural-resource scarcity is that it arises from finite stocks being depleted by the economic process.

Theoretical approaches based on this conventional view of natural-resource scarcity tend to concentrate on the optimal rate of depletion over time of those natural resources used as energy and material inputs by the economic process. Traditionally, a distinction is made between non-renewable – or exhaustible – resources and renewable resource stocks. In addition, the problem of pollution is usually treated as a separate problem of market failure and so is not incorporated into the analysis of natural-resource scarcity problems (see Chapter 4).

The general convention is to call "extractive resources renewable or non-renewable depending on whether they exhibit economically significant rates of regeneration."[3] In the case of strictly non-renewable resources, it may be optimal to deplete the resource completely if the availability of future technologies and perfect substitutes mean that exploitation of the resource is no longer "essential" for future production.[4] That is, because the future scarcity of the resource has been mitigated, the resource is not worth holding on to compared to other income-earning assets, and the optimal choice may be to exhaust the resource quickly and invest in these other assets. Even in the case of renewable resources, such as a forest valued for its timber, exhaustion may be optimal if the resource is growing at a slow rate, harvesting costs are low and its value appreciates more slowly than the market rate of interest.[5]

## EXHAUSTIBLE RESOURCES

The classic work on the optimal rate of depletion is by Hotelling. He demonstrated that, under optimal conditions, the price of an exhaustible resource net of extraction costs must be rising at a rate equal to the rate of interest on other assets. Eventually, as extraction costs fall and the net price (i.e., rent) rises, the market price will increase and the quantity demanded will start to fall. At the optimal rate of depletion, the resource will be exhausted the instant demand falls to zero and production stops completely.[6]

In recent years, Hotelling's analysis has been combined with characterizations of the optimal path of economic growth based on Ramsey's approach which determines the pattern of investment in reproducible capital in accordance with a utilitarian social welfare function.[7] This approach has generally been used both to analyse the comparable rates of return on natural resources compared to that of other assets, and to define the optimal depletion rate of exhaustible resources under various market conditions.

A simple, but very effective, formulation of the latter problem is developed by Dasgupta and Heal, who assume economic production to be dependent on the depletion of an exhaustible resource, R, and a reproducible capital stock (i.e., capital goods), K. Economic production, Q = F(K, R), that is not used for consumption goods, C, is therefore used to reproduce and add to the capital stock over time at a rate equal to dK/dt. Consumption, C, is assumed to benefit social welfare, U, which the planners aim to maximize over time at a discounted rate, r.[8] The authors go on to demonstrate that optimal depletion policy depends crucially on whether the resource, R, is essential to the production of the consumption good, whether technological change permits the development of a substitute that makes the resource inessential, whether there is uncertainty over the probability of a new resource being discovered, and on the elasticity of substitution between the resource and the capital good, K.

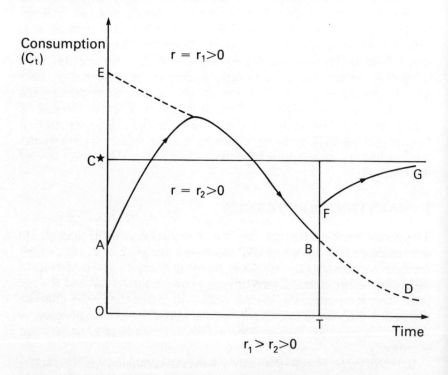

**Figure 3.1: Optimal Depletion of an Exhaustible Resource**

*Source:* Adapted from Partha Dasgupta and Geoffrey M. Heal, "The optimal depletion of exhaustible resources", Symposium on the Economics of Exhaustible Resources, *Review of Economic Studies* (1974), Figure 5, p. 22.

A typical outcome is illustrated in Figure 3.1, which shows how consumption, C, varies over time. If the exhaustible resource is essential to production (that is, the elasticity of substitution between R and K is less than one), if the discount rate (r) is positive, and if there is no technological breakthrough allowing a subsitute for the resource, then consumption will initially peak but then decline towards zero (curve ABD). With a positive rate of time preference r, future generations lose out. A utilitarian society is not concerned with accumulating sufficient capital in the early years to offset the inevitable use of declining resources later on. With an even higher discount rate ($r_1$ as opposed to $r_2$), consumption peaks in the present and declines thereafter (curve EBD). This dire situation can nevertheless be avoided by the introduction of a technological breakthrough in some future time T. The economy effectively receives a new lease of life, accumulating capital and increasing consumption again until it settles down to the long-term stationary state of $C^*$ (curve ABFG).

The conditions under which technological change and capital-resource substitution avert the scarcity constraints imposed on an economy by an exhaustible resource have been extensively explored. Using a model similar to the above, but with a Rawlsian social welfare function, and assuming an elasticity of substitution no less than unity, Solow suggests that exhaustible resources are optimally depleted if this augments the stock of reproducible capital.[9] Likewise, using a more specific Cobb-Douglas aggregate production function, Stiglitz demonstrates that technical change and capital accumulation can offset the effects of declining inputs gained from the exhaustible resource.[10]

In recent years, analysis of the problem has focused on making the approaches more robust by explicitly incorporating technological change and uncertainty. For example, Kamien and Schwartz extend the basic model of Dasgupta and Heal by allowing for endogenous technical change which relaxes any constraint imposed by the exhaustibility of a resource.[11] Such innovation is not without cost but can only occur in current periods through the diversion of economic resources from consumption or investment to research and development (R & D). As a consequence, the model shows that, along with consumption, R & D effort may eventually fall toward zero as the essential non-renewable resource is exhausted. If in the meantime the new technology is successfully implemented, then the economy avoids any constraint. Similarly, Dasgupta and Stiglitz analyse the uncertainty arising from the unknown arrival date of a new technology that allows perfect substitution for an essential but exhaustible resource. The model indicates that until the invention occurs, the optimal rate of depletion should leave the economy with a positive resource stock.[12] Finally, Dasgupta and Heal discuss in extensive detail the role of uncertainty and irreversibility of decisions with regard to the optimal depletion of a particular grade of exhaustible resource, and conclude that recognition of the technological potential for finding substitutes for a depletable resource is not the same thing as certain knowledge that perfect substitution is feasible.[13]

Most theoretical approaches to the optimal depletion rate initially assumed competitive market conditions.[14] More recent theoretical explorations have concentrated on the problem of the common exploitation of an exhaustible resource under conditions of market imperfection.[15] The basic assumptions are that with a constant elasticity of demand for the extractable resource, ownership of the resource dominated by a small number of firms, and zero marginal extraction costs, any seepage of the resource (such as oil) across fields would render it non-exclusive. That is, each owner could draw as much oil as costs would allow from the common pool of the resource. With the exception of Kemp and Long's analysis, the general conclusion is that such common resource pools will lead to over-extraction relative to the socially optimal depletion rate suggested by Hotelling's rule. This result contrasts with the exclusive ownership (i.e., monopoly) case analysed by Stiglitz, which indicates that the extraction rate can be optimal despite a monopoly market structure.[16] Moreover, Dasgupta and Heal suggest that any departure from this optimal rate under exclusive ownership rights would tend to favour excess conservation as opposed to over-exploitation.[17]

A second approach to the optimal depletion of exhaustible resources has been to examine the empirical evidence in support of Hotelling's rule: that the net-price appreciation of an exhaustible resource should equal increases in the rate of return on other assets.[18] The basic approach compares observed resource-price movements with the optimal path predicted by the theory. In general, the evidence does not overwhelmingly support Hotelling's rule. For example, in an arbitrage model that assumes traders switch funds from resource to capital markets in response to expectations about relative rates of return on the two assets, Heal and Barrow indicate that explanations of actual resource-price movements must be more complicated than Hotelling has suggested. These findings are confirmed by V.K. Smith, who evaluated several studies of resource-price trends. This discrepancy between empirical results and theoretical predictions has been explained by models incorporating rising extraction costs and production lags resulting from exploration and resource development.[19] Thus Frank and Babunovic stress the importance of slow supply responses to market shocks and technological progress in resource extraction. The latter conclusion supports the earlier findings of Barnett and Morse and the more recent follow-up by Barnett.

## RENEWABLE RESOURCES

Analysis of the optimal rate of harvesting of renewable natural-resource inputs into the economic process has had to take into account both the common property problem and the natural growth-rate of resource stocks. This has widened the scope of analysis to include characterizations of the steady-state equilibria for optimally managed resources and the socially optimal conditions leading to extinction. Initial studies concerned with the formal analysis of optimal management of common-property renewable resources concentrated on the fisheries and forest-harvesting problems.[20]

The basic renewable resource problem can be illustrated by a simple biological capital model. In the model developed by V.L. Smith, an economy produces both an ordinary commodity, $q_1$, and a harvested output from a biological resource, $q_2$. The growth rate of the renewable resource, Q, after harvest is assumed to be $dQ/dt = kG(Q) - q_2$, and the fixed labour supply, L, is allocated to both production tasks. Thus the social welfare function, $u = u_1(q_1) + u_2(q_2)$, is maximized over time at a discounted rate r.[21] As a result, the optimal rate of exploitation of a renewable resource equates the marginal value, or price, of a harvested unit net of its value as living biological capital (i.e., its unharvested value) with the marginal harvesting cost. If private property rights are well-defined (e.g., domestic animals), the value of the living resource is its going market price. In the case of competitive bidding for a common property resource (e.g., for publicly owned forest tracts), the unharvested value is the competitive bid price. Finally, if there is no such market for the common-property resource (e.g., open-access ocean fishery), this value must be an implicit price.

As in the case of exhaustible resources, the analysis of optimal exploitation of renewable resources also encounters problems over property rights and uncertainty. For example, it is often believed that the common ownership of renewable resources is the major cause of over-exploitation. That is, each user of the commonly owned resource may maximize his or her share with the possible result of degrading the shares of others and diminishing the future potential of the resource for all concerned. This may not be the case, however, where users have evolved highly organized controls over the use of common land, including sanctions by the community against individual over-exploitation. In the absence of interventions, agreements or traditional management rights, users have open access to the resource and therefore no incentive to control over-exploitation. If rapid technological and economic changes are introduced, over-exploitation may worsen and may also lead to distributional consequences:

> For marine fisheries with *free entry* the foregoing problem can arise via a seemingly convoluted process. In free waters, where *historical rights* to the traditional fishermen are not respected, it can happen that large firms enter with modern fishing vessels. For the short run unit harvesting costs are thereby dramatically reduced, thus exacer-

bating the tendency towards overfishing. Meanwhile, the traditional fishermen, unable to compete with such equipment, are left impoverished for want of any catch. But in the long run, as a consequence of continual overfishing, harvest costs increase, despite – one should say, *because* of – the use of modern harvesting techniques. Nor can one even necessarily argue that the introduction of modern harvesting techniques in the seas is at least partially blessed at the altar of intertemporal efficiency; for the market wage–rental ratio in many less-developed countries is thought to be too high.[22]

The renewable resource problem is illustrated in Figure 3.2. The upside-down, U-shaped curve represents the natural growth rate of the resource $G(Q)$ which is a function of the size of the resource stock (for instance, a fishery). If the resource stock is either too low, $Q_L$, or too high, $Q_M$, the growth rate is zero. In contrast, population level $Q^*$ leads to a maximum sustainable yield growth rate, as this is the maximum harvest level (that is, $q = G(Q^*)$) that can be sustained indefinitely without depleting the population.

In Figure 3.2, harvesting of the resource is represented by the upward-sloping curve q, which we will assume to be a properly regulated common-property fishery. Note that at stock level $Q_P$, where the

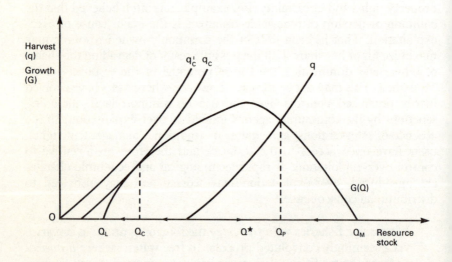

**Figure 3.2: The Optimal Depletion of a Renewable Resource**

harvesting rate just equals the growth rate of the resource (e.g., q = $G(Q_p)$), the population is at a stationary state level. Given the relationship between the harvesting rate and the resource stock as shown, this stationary state must be stable in the long run. For example, if the initial resource stock is less than the stationary state level (i.e., $Q_o < Q_p$), the natural growth rate will exceed the harvesting rate. This means that the population will grow until it reaches the stationary state level, $Q_p$, where growth is just offset by harvesting. On the other hand, if $Q_o > Q_p$ harvesting will exceed natural growth. The population will therefore decline until, once again, the stationary state level $Q_p$ is attained. So no matter what the initial resource stocks are, given the rate of harvesting represented by curve q, the population will eventually settle down to the long-run equilibrium represented by $Q_p$.

Figure 3.2 also shows what can happen if the rules governing a common-property resource break down so that users have free open access. As noted above, when this occurs, users of the resource tend to harvest more for a given stock level as they will now ignore any user and externality costs.[23] Thus curve $q_c$ now represents the new harvesting rate. The new stationary state level should now be $Q_c$ but this is not always sustainable in the long run. As the diagram shows, if the resource is initially greater than this level (i.e., $Q_o > Q_c$) then harvesting exceeds natural growth and the stock will decline to $Q_c$ as a long-run equilibrium. On the other hand, if the initial stock is much lower, i.e. $Q_o < Q_c$, then harvesting will still exceed natural growth. As a result, the resource will not increase to $Q_c$ in the long run but instead will decline towards zero. Hence, an open-access resource may be exhausted to extinction if the initial stocks of that resource are too low.

It should also be noted that if the value of the harvested resource increases, or technological change lowers per unit harvesting costs (e.g., the use of modern harvesting techniques for open-access fishing as quoted above), then users will be able to harvest even more for a given stock level. In Figure 3.2 this is represented by curve $q_c'$, which has shifted even further to the left. As a consequence, harvesting always exceeds the natural growth rate irrespective of the initial stock level, and the resource will inevitably be exhausted.

Intertemporal theories of the economics of renewable resources have further explored the conditions under which exhaustion is optimal.[24] Three important conditions appear to be:

i) If the social discount rate is high enough, or the regenerative capacity of the resource low enough, then it is economically profitable to exhaust the resource. That is, it is more profitable to harvest the resource as quickly as possible and invest the proceeds in other assets whose value will increase much faster.

ii) Equally, if the harvesting cost is low enough, or the value of a harvested unit is high enough, then it may also be economically profitable to exhaust the resource. For example, the reason why grey squirrels are not an endangered species can be attributed more to their low value as game than to either rapid growth or the high cost of hunting them.

iii) Conditions i) and ii) may hold even if society sees some value in preserving the species (i.e., for the sake of beauty, existence or biological diversity). The solution is to exhaust the resource until a minimum stock level is reached below which the population is not allowed to fall. For example, if whale populations are considered worth saving from extinction, there should be a moratorium imposed on international whaling once these populations reach a certain minimum threshold.

As in the case of exhaustible resources, uncertainty is a major problem encountered in the analysis of the optimal exploitation of renewable resources. This has been linked to the overall uncertainty about general environmental problems consequent to economic activity as well as to the specific difficulty of ecological uncertainty, where the natural rate of growth varies at random.[25]

## SUMMARY AND CONCLUSION

Given the conventional concern that exists about the availability of those natural resources extracted and used as direct productive inputs in the economic process, and the assumption that the increasing scarcity of these resources is reflected in rising relative prices, the most common theoretical approach has been to concentrate on optimal rates of depletion. Analysis of exhaustible resources has focused either on the economic conditions determining the optimal depletion rate or on the relationship between actual and optimal price movements. The analysis of renewable-resource management has had to incorporate additional features, such as the rate of biological growth and the problems of open access. Nevertheless, the fundamental economic inquiry of these conventional approaches is essentially the same: what is the optimal rate of exploitation of a natural resource whose primary value is as a productive input into the economic process?

Such an approach has been instrumental in understanding the key economic conditions governing the optimal management of particular resource stocks. It has also laid the theoretical foundations for further explorations of more complex economic–environmental interactions – including the process of environmental degradation that undermines so many economic systems dependent on natural resources. None the less, by definition, conventional theories in resource economics limit themselves to only one class of environmental problem. Even the problem of optimal pollution discharges, although related, is generally analysed separately to external costs and market failure.

If nature as a whole is considered to provide a variety of essential environmental services or functions to humankind, then the definition of economically valuable functions must be broadened to include not only the raw material and energy-resource inputs into the economic system but all the other important environmental services as well. The latter will typically include the function of the environment as the assimilator of waste by-products from the economic process and the provider of essential life-support, ecological and amenity services. Together, these environmental functions underline the physical dependency of the economic process and human welfare upon ecological processes and the sufficiency of potentially scarce environmental resources. Proper valuation of the economic consequences of resource degradation cannot be limited to examining the scarcity of just one of these functions of environmental assets. Instead, what is required is the proper valuation of each of these functions and the way they interlink with economic activity, and the subsequent use of these valuations to indicate the trade-offs that may emerge from natural-resource degradation.

Such an approach requires a broader, alternative view of natural-resource scarcity than conventional economic theories allow (see Chapter 5). Before discussing this broader view, it is first necessary to complete the review of conventional theories by examining important contributions to the economic analysis of pollution and the preservation of natural environments.

## NOTES

1. William D. Nordhaus and James Tobin, "Growth and natural resources" in R. Dorfman and N.S. Dorfman (eds), *Economics of the Environment* (2nd edn), (W.W. Norton: New York, 1977), p. 402.
2. However, Partha Dasgupta and Geoffrey Heal (*Economic Theory and Exhaustible Resources* (Cambridge University Press: Cambridge, 1979), pp. 5–7) point out, although "capital–resource substitution may be sufficient to overcome the 'drag' imposed by an essential and exhaustible resource" in theory, in practice this requires a "complete set of forward markets". This condition "is certainly not met" in actual market systems and, "as a consequence resource markets may be unstable, and will almost certainly display 'market bias' in the sense of depleting the resource at a rate different from an optimal rate." Quite clearly, the problem is "uncertainty about future resource stocks and about future technology."
3. F.M. Peterson and Anthony C. Fisher, "The exploitation of extractive resources: A survey", *Economic Journal*, Vol. 87 (1977), p. 681.
4. See, for example, Partha Dasgupta and Geoffrey Heal, "The optimal depletion of exhaustible resources", *Review of Economic Studies*, Symposium on the Economics of Exhaustible Resources, (1974), pp. 3–28; Dasgupta and Heal, *Economic Theory*, op.

cit.; Partha Dasgupta and Joseph E. Stiglitz, "Resource depletion under technological uncertainty", *Econometrica*, Vol. 49 (1981), pp. 85–104; Morton I. Kamien and Nancy L. Schwartz, "Optimal exhaustible resource depletion with endogenous technical change", *Review of Economic Studies*, Vol. 45 (1978), pp. 179–96; Robert M. Solow, "Intergenerational equity and exhaustible resources", *Review of Economic Studies*, Symposium on the Economics of Exhaustible Resources (1974), pp. 139–52; and Joseph E. Stiglitz, "Growth with exhaustible resources: Efficient and optimal growth paths", *Review of Economic Studies*, Symposium on the Economics of Exhaustible Resources (1974), pp. 123–37.

5. See Colin W. Clark, *Mathematical Bioeconomics: The Optimal Management of Renewable Resources* (John Wiley & Sons: New York, 1976); and V.L. Smith, "Control theory applied to natural and environmental resources: An exposition", *Journal of Environmental Economics and Management*, Vol. 4 (1977), pp. 1–24.

6. Harold Hotelling, "The economics of exhaustible resources", *Journal of Political Economy*, Vol. 39 (1931), pp. 137–75. See also the interesting interpretation by Robert M. Solow, "The economics of resources or the resources of economics", *American Economic Review*, Papers and Proceedings, Vol. 64 (1974), pp. 1–14.

7. Frank Ramsey, "A mathematical theory of saving", *Economic Journal* Vol. 38 (1928), pp. 543–59. Note that most modern growth models assume a positive rate of time preference, whereas the original utilitarian framework of Ramsey's model gives equal weighting to both current and future utility in the objective function to be maximized. T. Mitra ("Some results of the optimal depletion of exhaustible resources under negative discounting", *Review of Economic Studies*, Vol. 48 (1981), pp. 521–32) takes the original approach of Ramsey and adds the assumption of exponential population growth, thus generating a model of optimal resource depletion over time governed by a negative effective discount rate.

8. See Dasgupta and Heal, "The optimal depletion", op. cit. The planning problem can be formally stated as:

$$\max \quad \int_0^\infty e^{-rt}U(C)\, dt, \text{ subject to}$$
$$R\, dt \leqslant S_o,$$
$$\dot{K} = dK/dt = F(K, R) - C, \text{ where}$$
$$C, K, R \geqslant 0 \text{ and } K_o \text{ given.}$$

9. Solow, "Intergenerational equity", op. cit.
10. Stiglitz, op. cit.
11. Kamien and Schwartz, op. cit.
12. Dasgupta and Stiglitz, op. cit.
13. Dasgupta and Heal, *Economic Theory*, op. cit.
14. See, for example, Solow, "The economics of resources", op. cit., and Joseph E. Stiglitz, "Growth with exhaustible natural resources: The competitive economy", *Review of Economic Studies*, Symposium on the Economics of Exhaustible Resources (1974), pp. 139–52.
15. See, for example, Dasgupta and Heal, *Economic Theory*, op. cit.; M. Eswaran and Tracy Lewis, "Appropriability and the extraction of a common property resource", *Economica*, Vol. 51 (1984), pp. 83–96; M.C. Kemp and N.V. Long, *Exhaustible Resources, Optimality and Trade* (North-Holland: Amsterdam, 1980); F. Khalatbari, "Market imperfections and otpimal rate of depletion of an exhaustible resource", *Economica* Vol. 44 (1977), pp. 409–14; and H.W. Sinn, "Common property resources, storage facilities and ownership structures: A Cournot model of the oil market", *Economica*, Vol. 51 (1984), pp. 235–52.
16. Joseph E. Stiglitz, "Monopoly and the rate of extraction of exhaustible resources", *American Economic Review*, Vol. 66 (1976), pp. 655–61.

17. Dasgupta and Heal, *Economic Theory*, op. cit.
18. See, for example, Harold J. Barnett, "Scarcity and growth revisited" in V.K. Smith (ed.), *Scarcity and Growth Reconsidered* (Johns Hopkins University Press: Baltimore, 1979); Barnett and Morse, op. cit.; J. Frank and M. Babunovic, "An investment model of natural resource markets", *Economica*, Vol. 51 (1984), pp. 83–96; Geoffrey Heal and M. Barrow, "The relationship between interest rates and metal price movements", *Review of Economic Studies*, Vol. 47 (1980), pp. 161–81; R.S. Pindyck, "The optimal exploration and production of non-renewable resources", *Journal of Political Economy*, Vol. 86 (1978), pp. 841–61; V. Kerry Smith, "The empirical relevance of Hotelling's model for natural resources", *Resources and Energy*, Vol. 3 (1981), pp. 105–18; M.C. Weinstein and R.J. Zeckhauser, "The optimal consumption of depletable natural resources", *Quarterly Journal of Economics*, Vol. 89 (1975), pp. 371–92.
19. See, for example, Frank and Babunovic, op. cit. and Pindyck, op. cit.
20. See, for example, G. Faustmann, "On the determination of the value which forest land and immature stands possess for forestry" reprinted in English in *Oxford Institute Papers*, Vol. 42 (1968); H.S. Gordon, "Economic theory of common property resources", *Journal of Political Economy*, Vol. 62 (1954), pp. 124–42; and A.C. Scott, "The fishery: The objectives of sole ownership", *Journal of Political Economy*, Vol. 63 (1955), pp. 116–24. For an excellent historical review of forestry economics see Paul Samuelson, "Economics of forestry in an evolving society", *Economic Inquiry*, Vol. 14 (1976), pp. 466–92.
21. V.L. Smith, op. cit. The planning problem can be formally stated as:

$$\max \quad {}_0\!\int^{\infty} u e^{-rt}\, dt, \text{ subject to}$$
$$q_1 = f_1\,(L_1),$$
$$q_2 = f_2\,(L_2,\, Q),$$
$$L = L_1 + L_2,$$
$$\dot{Q} = dQ/dt = kG(Q) - q_2, \text{ where}$$
$$q_1,\, q_2,\, L_1,\, L_2,\, Q \geqslant 0 \text{ and } Q_0 \text{ given.}$$

22. Partha Dasgupta, *The Control of Resources* (Basil Blackwell: Oxford, 1982), pp. 17–18.
23. Mathematically, it can be shown that when common-property rules are enforced so that all users co-operate to behave as if they were a sole owner exploiting the resource, the industry harvesting equilibrium occurs where the price of a harvested unit p, net of user cost u, is equal to the marginal cost of harvesting, $dc/dq$:

$$p - u = dc/dq$$

On the other hand, when users can enter freely and no co-operative agreements have been reached, all profit from harvesting is competed away. This leads to a competitive equilibrium where price equals the average cost of harvesting:

$$p = c/q$$

In the latter open-access situation, yields will generally be higher for a given stock of the resource, as each user is ignoring the user cost of extracting a unit today (i.e., u) as well as the externality costs of crowding (i.e., the difference between marginal (dc/dq) and average (c/q) costs). For proof of these conditions see Dasgupta, *op. cit.* and Anthony C. Fisher, *Resource and Environmental Economics* (Cambridge University Press: Cambridge, 1981).

24. See, for example, Clark, op. cit.; Dasgupta, op. cit.; Fisher, op. cit.; and V.L. Smith, op. cit.

25. See, for example, John R. Beddington, "Harvesting and population dynamics" in R.M. Anderson (ed.), *Population Dynamics Symposium of the British Ecological Society* (Blackwells: Oxford, 1978); John R. Beddington and Colin W. Clark, "Allocation problems between national and foreign fisheries with a fluctuating fish resource", *Marine Resource Economics*, Vol. 1 (1984), pp. 137–54; Clark, op. cit.; Dasgupta, op. cit.; and R.S. Pindyck, "Uncertainty in the theory of renewable resource markets", *Review of Economic Studies*, Vol. 51 (1984), pp. 289–303.

# 4
# Conventional Theory: Pollution and Natural Environments

On the whole, conventional theories treat the problem of pollution as an externality problem separate to that of optimal resource use. Theoretical considerations of the pollution problem, however, have led to further concern about the assimilative capacity of the environment and the preservation of natural systems. This chapter will discuss these further developments and argue that the next step is to develop a more integrated approach focusing on the trade-off between resource use and environmental degradation.

## POLLUTION AS AN EXTERNALITY

The term pollution usually refers to the waste by-products, or residuals, created by the economic activities of production, its intermediate processes, and consumption. Thus by definition, a waste residual or pollutant has an important economic interpretation:

> A residual is a non-product (material or energy output), the value of which is less than the costs of collecting, processing, and transporting it for use. Thus, the definition is time dependent, that is, it is a function of (1) the level of technology in the society at a point in time and (2) the relative costs of alternative inputs at that point in time. For example, manure in the United States is now a residual, whereas thirty or so years ago it was a valuable raw material.[1]

As pointed out by Baumol and Oates, the conventional economic approach has always been to see "the problem of environmental egradation as one in which economic agents imposed external costs upon society at large in the form of pollution. With no prices to provide the proper incentives for reduction of polluting activities, the inevitable result was excessive demands on the assimilative capacity of the environment. The obvious solution to the problem was to place an appropriate price, in this case a tax, on polluting activities so as to internalize the social costs."[2] Thus, pollution is an example of a negative externality: that is when the actions of one economic agent affect the welfare of another, who is not compensated for the ensuing damages.³ No compensation takes place because the damages are not automatically reflected in market prices. The market price of a polluting activity indicates its private costs but under-estimates the full social costs.

This situation is illustrated in Figure 4.1 with the example of burning coal for industrial use. Curve S is the private supply curve of the industry, and curve D is the demand for coal. At price P, the private supply is therefore equal to the demand, and the industry will sell amount Q of coal. However, the damages inflicted on some people in society from the burning of coal (e.g., air pollution or the effects of acid rain) should be added to the schedule of private costs (represented by S) to indicate the true social cost. This leads to the social supply curve, S'. Thus the socially desirable outcome is really Q★, where demand is equal to the schedule of social, not private, costs. Consequently, society is burning too much coal because the market price P does not account for the external costs of coal pollution. In Figure 4.1, the shaded area represents the social, or welfare, loss associated with burning too much coal. As noted above, the conventional economic solution is to adjust market prices until the socially desirable output level Q★ is attained. In Figure 4.1, this is achieved by imposing a tax on the burning of coal, that would be equal to the marginal

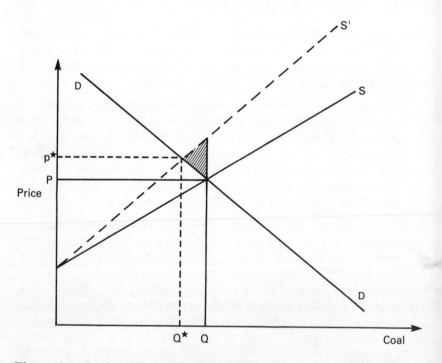

**Figure 4.1: Optimal Tax on Pollution**

social damage produced by that activity and would raise the market price to P*.

The economic analysis of externalities has a long history, dating back to Marshall and Pigou.[4] In fact, the solution depicted in Figure 4.1, of charging polluters an effluent fee equal to (net) marginal social damage, is often referred to in the literature as a "Pigouvian tax".

Similarly, most externalities have traditionally been treated as a special type of "public good" – or in the case of pollution as a "public bad". Public goods (or bads) are usually characterized by "jointness of supply" (i.e., "undepletability") and by "non-excludability". For example, the former implies that consumption of the good by one individual does not reduce the consumption by anyone else, whereas the latter indicates that it is impossible to exclude any potential consumers. Indeed, most forms of pollution have the characteristic of being undepletable. For example, if coal burning pollutes the air, it affects all who breathe it simultaneously and not just each individual incrementally. Moreover, a decrease or increase in the number of people breathing the polluted air does not reduce the level of pollution; one individual's consumption does not affect the quality of air breathed by others.[5]

Not all forms of pollution are necessarily (undepletable) public bads. For example, when trash is dumped on someone's property, it clearly affects only that person and nobody else. This is an example of a depletable externality: by one person receiving all the trash on his or her property, the amount received by others is clearly reduced. Nevertheless, except for some special cases, the basic policy perscription for both depletable and undepletable pollution externalities is the same: the imposition of a Pigouvian tax.[6]

In the conventional analysis of a pollution problem, the determination of the optimal level of the (Pigouvian) tax to be levied is a crucial issue. As noted above, and discussed with reference to Figure 4.1, this tax must ultimately be equal to the marginal social damage caused by the effluent discharge. In calculating this tax, however, it is important to weigh the benefits of reducing social damage against the additional abatement costs imposed on the polluters as they attempt to control waste outflows. At some level of effluent discharge, it may cost more to abate the pollution further than it is worth (in terms of the additional gains from reducing damage). This is therefore the optimal level of pollution, and the tax should be set to equal marginal social damage at this point.

This theory can be illustrated simply (see Figure 4.2). In Figure 4.2, the curve AB represents marginal abatement costs which increase as the level of pollution is reduced. In the case of coal burning as discussed above, industries are producing OY of uncontrolled pollution. Curve CD represents the marginal damage costs incurred by society for each pollution level. At OY of effluent discharge, these social damages are clearly positive, whereas the costs to industry of controlling coal pollution are zero. OY is therefore not the optimal level of pollution. This is level OX, where the marginal abatement costs just equal the marginal damage costs. So in order to maintain this optimal level of pollution, a per unit tax must be levied of EX equal to the marginal social costs of pollution at OX. Although a higher tax could be imposed to reduce pollution even further, say to OZ, this is also not optimal, as at this discharge level the additional abatement costs imposed on the industry more than exceed the reduction in social damage.

## OPTIMAL POLLUTION CONTROL: CHARGES VERSUS STANDARDS

Although, in theory, the imposition of (Pigouvian) effluent charges appears fairly straightforward, in practice it is neither simple nor cost free. Equally, the alternative method of legislating a maximum ceiling on pollution (for example, equal to OX in Figure 4.2) is difficult to implement. In general, the process of monitoring and evaluating effluent discharge rates, formulating and legislating various methods of pollution

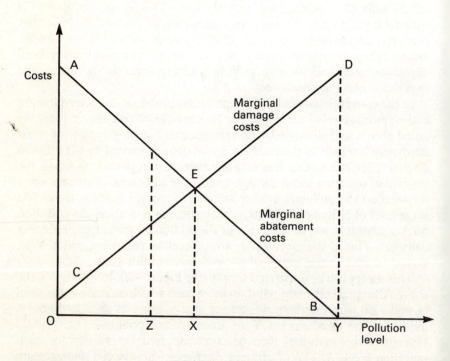

**Figure 4.2: Determining the Optimal Pollution Tax**

control and attempting to estimate the appropriate "market equilibrium" to be approximated, is extremely complicated. It is not surprising that a mixed bag of pollution control policies – including environmental standards, pollution taxes, dumping licences and charges, marketable permits, abatement subsidies and planning zones – is resorted to. The mix depends on the institutional framework of the economy and the circumstances under which pollution occurs.

Nevertheless, there is a substantial body of economic literature about the optimal policies for pollution control – particularly on the relative merits of indirect controls (such as Pigouvian charges and subsidies) compared to direct controls (such as standards). In some cases, both approaches have been rejected altogether in favour of alternative methods of reaching socially optimal levels of waste emission.

One of the classic challenges to the orthodox tax versus standards approach was the so-called "Coase theorem".[7] Coase argued that, first, the direction of a pollution externality depends on property rights, and secondly, where there is a small number of victims and an equally small number of polluters, voluntary bargaining between the two parties – rather than a Pigouvian tax – will lead to the optimal solution. For instance, in the coal-burning case described in Figure 4.2, if the number of polluting industries is small and the number of victims suffering from emissions is equally small, then negotiations between these two parties will be relatively cost free. Through bargaining, the victims may be willing to pay the polluters to reduce their emission levels from OY to OX (see Figure 4.2). As the number of generators and victims are small, introducing a Pigouvian tax may be unfeasible and even distorting.[8]

Coasian bargaining clearly only works when the numbers of victims and polluters are small. As these numbers increase, bargaining is no longer cost free, and both individual and group interests tend to diverge. Moreover, when the numbers are small, there may be circumstances when Coasian bargaining breaks down or when certain forms of strategic behaviour emerge which make Pigouvian taxes optimal. Finally, if only one firm is burning coal, then it essentially has "monopoly power" in the bargaining over pollution reduction. Consequently, it is likely to bargain for a higher price from the victims for less of a reduction in emissions. On the other hand, if the firm monopolizes the product market, it may have already restricted output, such as below Q* in Figure 4.1, in order to maximize profits. Therefore, the firm would actually be producing a sub-optimal level of output and thus pollution. To reach the optimal level, the monopolist has to be compensated, but it is unreasonable to expect the victims to agree to this as they would be incurring the ensuing damage.[9]

As the most frequent and serious pollution problems involve *large* numbers of victims and/or polluters, the major focus has been on the relative merits of charges compared to standards.

Although a system of standards is easier to administer, there is no guarantee that these will yield the socially optimal level of pollution (i.e., OX in Figure 4.2). These are usually selected on the basis of environmental impact with no consideration given to abatement costs. Moreover, the cost-minimizing polluter has little incentive to use new abatement technologies to reduce effluents but will instead tend to discharge at the maximum permissible levels. In contrast, with emission fees, there is an incentive to use new technologies to reduce the level of effluents in order to minimize the charges.[10]

One major drawback in imposing a Pigouvian tax, or charge, on polluters is that this must be equal to the marginal social damage of pollution. Estimating the latter is extremely difficult, given the need to know the environmental impacts of the pollutants, their damage in terms of health, aesthetic, amenity and other costs, and their monetary value. In addition, the optimal tax is not equal to the marginal damage at the initial level of pollution generation (e.g., OY in Figure 4.2) but rather to the damage that would be caused if pollution were adjusted to its optimal level (e.g., OX). As argued by Baumol and Oates, "if there is little hope of estimating the damage that is currently generated, how much less likely it is that we can evaluate the damage that would occur in an optimal world that we have never experienced or even described in quantitative terms".[11] Whereas the calculation of a Pigouvian tax only requires knowledge of marginal social damage and allows the polluters to adjust their private abatement costs accordingly, this does not always imply that a system of charges is superior to direct regulatory controls. Charges are only unequivocally preferable where the pollution control agency is able to identify polluter groups among which there are differences in environmental impact and within which there are significant variations in abatement costs. Obtaining this information and establishing differential charges is, once again, a costly approach.[12]

Establishing effluent charges is also difficult for reciprocal and non-separable pollution externalities. The example of coal burning discussed so far is a *unidirectional* externality; that is, the industry is imposing the costs of coal pollution on the rest of society and not the other way around. On the other hand, if a pollution externality is *reciprocal*, party A and party B mutually impose an externality on each other. For example, coal burning by one industry may increase corrosion in the installations of another type of industry, while at the same time the chemical waste discharged by the latter may affect the quality of water used in the coal burning industry. Such a reciprocal pollution externality is also *non-separable*, in that each industry's cost function is dependent on the other's. A system of optimal pollution charges has therefore to deal with the additional obstacle of determining these cost interdependencies.[13]

Given the tremendous uncertainty surrounding the design of optimal pollution control policies, more recent theoretical explorations of such policies have explicitly tried to incorporate the problem posed by uncertainty. For example, given uncertainty over abatement costs, the general conclusion is that neither a linear tax schedule (i.e., a marginal tax rate that does not vary with the quantity of emissions discharged) nor a pollution quota (i.e., a maximum level of permissible discharge) is optimal. Instead, the best policy is to use tax rates that vary with the quantity of pollutants discharged. One way in which this can be approximated is through a system of marketable (i.e., transferable) emission permits, where the pollution control authority determines the aggregate quantity of emissions and then issues a limited number of permits corresponding to shares in this aggregate emission level. The authority then allows polluters to trade freely for these permits in an open market. Not only will the market price for these permits reflect the true social costs of pollution, and eventually cause marginal abatement costs to be equalized among competitive polluters, but it also means that the emission fee will now most likely vary with the quantity of emissions discharged by each polluter. Nevertheless, just as there are a range of special circumstances in which uncertainty dictates that administrative standards are preferable to an effluent charge, there are also circumstances where uncertainty over costs favour charges over marketable permits.[14]

In the conventional approach to the pollution problem, which is to treat it as a special example of market failure, there is a distinct predilection for the use of (Pigouvian) taxes to correct the price mechanism. In practice, however, economists are more resigned to the difficulty of implementing such an ideal solution and instead accept a more mixed policy of standards, charges, zoning, dumping fees, marketable permits, abatement subsidies, and so on. These seem more feasible given the constraints that exist on information and administration. One such frequently advocated mixed approach involves the selection of desired environmental standards for the control of pollution levels but then uses a combination of specific charges, marketable permits and even moral persuasion to achieve them. This is in preference to any attempt to base them on the unknown, and difficult to estimate, value of marginal social damage.[15] Both the standards and the various systems of charges could be adjusted as more information on pollution and individuals' preferences becomes available.


## THE PRESERVATION OF NATURAL ENVIRONMENTS OVER TIME

In recent years, conventional economic theory has stretched its horizons in order to consider another particular problem of the public good – the preservation of natural environments. As with pollution, uncertainty is an important aspect of this problem, although in the case of environmental preservation, uncertainty is a special feature of the decision whether or not to develop a given natural area.

There have generally been two approaches to the problem of environmental preservation. Some studies have emphasized the environmental costs of irreversible economic activity, such as "the transformation and loss of whole environments as would result, for example, from clear cutting a redwood forest, or developing a hydroelectric project in the Grand Canyon."[16] Others have stressed the essential utility-yielding role of natural ecosystems and their environmental functions.[17] The general conclusion deduced from both approaches is that "too few resources are likely to be devoted to the preservation of non-producible environmental assets that provide amenity services". This is the result of two factors:

i)  There are few adequate substitutes for rare natural environments. While the value of these areas appreciates with increased demand, their fixed (and in some cases, diminishing) supply precludes an increase in their availability. Thus the economic value of natural areas is expected to increase over time.

ii) There is often asymmetry between alternative uses of scarce natural wonders. A natural resource can either be preserved in its current state or developed. The development decision is irreversible, whereas if the resource is preserved in its natural state, both preservation and development remain open as options. Irreversible conversion entails an opportunity cost – the loss of the value of retaining an option to consume the services of the gift of nature under conditions of uncertain future demand for its services.[18]

As noted in Chapter 1, John Stuart Mill is usually credited as the first economist who considered the need to preserve natural environments as an economic problem. In more recent times, however, analysis of this problem has clearly moved beyond Mill's concern with the scarcity of natural beauty and solitude. Nevertheless, as modern approaches make clear, the basic supposition underlying Mill's concern still holds namely that as long as development of a natural environment is irreversible, some account must be taken of the behaviour of future costs and benefits. In fact, under certain conditions it may even be worthwhile to have too little development in the present to avoid future and greater losses from too much development. These conditions include assuming that:

i)   the natural environment that is to be irreversibly developed is *unique*; i.e., that technology can do little to replicate its ecological, physical and geographical characteristics;

ii)  the *amenity services* of this environment *enter directly into the utility functions of consumers* with no intervening production technology;

iii) *perfect substitution* (in consumption) between this and other environments *is not possible; and*

iv) *that technical change is asymmetric*; that is, it results in expanded capacity to produce ordinary goods and services, but not natural environments.[19]

As long as these conditions hold, unique natural environments and the services they yield are likely to appreciate in value relative to the ordinary goods and services produced by the irreversible development of these environments. Moreover, because the natural services provided by these common property resources do not exchange on organized markets, the option value of preservation is not accurately taken into account when the resources are exploited economically. So although natural environments and their essential services may be growing increasingly scarce, allocative choices based on market criteria are biased towards appropriating these resources for development. Only the costs of preservation – the opportunity cost of foregoing the development option – are seen as being "real".

Such a bias obscures the fact that the irreversible conversion of natural areas in fixed supply may have a high opportunity cost by foreclosing the future option of deriving environmental services from these areas. "When a tract of wildland is being considered for a use that irreversibly changes the landscape or ecology, the values which are lost by foreclosing future options must be taken into account."[20] These option values may take the form of the loss of future genetic material of scientific, education or cultural significance, the loss of future recreational values, and even the loss of important ecological functions. Thus, option values arise out of the uncertainty of irreversible change. Moreover, they may exist "not only among persons currently or prospectively in the market, but among others who place a value on the mere existence of biological diversity and natural landscape variety."[21]

Economic approaches to the conservation of biological diversity are in some respects an extension of the environmental preservation approach. For example, it has long been recognized that reducing biological diversity results in uncertain, irreversible effects. This led Ciriacy-Wantrup, more than thirty years ago, to argue that as a result of irreversible extinction of a species, future societies may discover that they have foregone significant benefits. If there were close substitutes for the goods and services of the threatened species, and if there was a technological bias favouring these substitute goods, then the costs of preserving a minimum viable population of the species and its required supporting habitat would be small.[22]

Although the value placed on biological diversity reflects the full range of option, quasi-option and existence values for moral, ecological or aesthetic reasons,[23] the primary economic argument invoked in favour of preserving species has been their potential use directly or indirectly in obtaining improved agricultural, medical, or manufactured goods. As pointed out by Brown and Goldstein, the minimum information required for determining whether or not to preserve a species is "to know the probabilities of discovering improved products and how these probabilities are changed by deleting particular species embodying a particular genetic mosaic".[24] It is doubtful whether sufficient knowledge can ever be attained to estimate these probabilities. Moreover, there are likely to be cases where previously economically insignificant species are discovered to have great value, or where completely unknown species are destroyed. The process of valuation becomes even more complex when considering the ecological feedbacks associated with the extinction of a species, let alone the destruction of entire habitats.

Faced with uncertainty, irreversible effects and imperfect knowledge, the problem of conserving biological diversity often brings us back to the problem of preserving natural environments – in this case the optimal maintenance of wildlife habitats. The issue is a particularly difficult one in developing countries where, on the one hand, most of the world's species are to be found and, on the other, the most rapid rate of land conversion – and therefore of habitat destruction – is occurring. Given that land conversion in these countries is perceived as part of long-term agricultural and other economic development efforts, the costs of maintaining biological diversity – the direct cost of maintaining wildlife reserves and the opportunity cost of the next best use for reserve land – may not be considered small.[25] At the same time, developing countries often face various social and administrative lags in implementing conservation policies. These include "a perception lag, a lag in convincing individuals of the need of collective action, a lag in devising alternative possible policies and a delay in selecting a policy from amongst the alternatives and obtaining its social acceptance."[26] As a consequence, neither the economic incentives discouraging local populations from conversion of, or intrusion into, wildlife reserves, nor the appropriate policing methods, are adequate.

Many observers remain hopeful that some of these problems can be overcome by further aid from multilateral and bilateral donor agencies, specifically for the conservation of biological diversity and even as direct compensation for creating reserves, such as the so-called "debt–nature" swaps.[27]

## SUMMARY AND CONCLUSION

This chapter has examined conventional approaches to the problems of pollution and the preservation of natural environments. The former is usually considered an externality problem whereby the social damage, or costs, of pollution are not reflected in private-market decisions governing the allocation of the activity generating the pollutant. Similarly, the decision as to whether or not to develop a unique natural area, to convert a wildlife habitat, or to drive a species to extinction may arise from uncertainty over the values of the various options, and over the impacts of such irreversible effects. Recent approaches to these problems are pushing environmental and resource economists into considering the proper valuation of environmental functions other than simply considering them as sources of material and energy inputs for the economic process.

Such approaches have also indicated the difficulty in assessing the values of these more obscure environmental functions and values, particularly as they are not revealed through market choices. In addition, individuals may have varying perceptions of how changes in the state of the environment may affect their welfare. For example, some individuals may feel strongly about any appreciable deterioration in a landscape of natural beauty, whereas others may be more indifferent. In the absence of markets for these non-marketed, common-property environmental resources and functions, assessment of their value has involved the application of certain techniques to determine individuals' willingness to pay. These include cost-benefit analysis and direct assessment through surveys. Unfortunately, both methods are limited by the same problem that prevents *in situ* environmental resources and the services they yield from having a distinct market-price in the first place.

The essential feature of cost-benefit analysis is that the concept of price is extended to shadow price which incorporates the valuation of non-marketed resources and services, or the discrepancies between social and private costs. However, the difficulty of applying such an approach to environmental problems is that "the level of the shadow price of environmental functions is largely indeterminate because insufficient information is available on the preferences for environmental functions".[28] For instance, in order to determine the social costs and benefits of a decision to develop a previously undeveloped wilderness area, it is necessary to know both the preferences of present generations and those of future generations who may be affected by the loss of a wilderness area but who may not necessarily benefit from its current economic exploitation. As discussed above, this problem is compounded by the fact that environmental destruction is often irreversible, and knowledge about the extent and degree of loss in environmental functions is often incomplete.[29]

A related technique is obtaining information about subjective preferences and individuals' willingness to pay directly through surveying methods. In this way, monetary measures of the value of non-marketed environmental resources and functions can be estimated.[30] As well as sharing many of the problems that limit the estimates of the shadow price of these resources and functions, the survey method involves additional complications.

For example, "if an individual is asked a hypothetical question about his willingness to pay for the public good, he does not have to act on his response or live with its consequences. He incurs no actual utility loss for an inaccurate response. There is no incentive to be correct."[31] Secondly, there is a potential free-rider problem, where "persons questioned may state low amounts on the assumption that others will 'bid' sufficiently high to restore the environmental function." Similarly, "respondents may feel that individuals may not be asked to make a contribution for the environment for in their opinion this is a task for the government or because the polluter should pay."[32] Thirdly, in response to willingness-to-pay surveys, individuals may express one value for use of an environmental resource or amenity service when considering the cost or allocative implications for himself or herself, and express a different value when considering the implications for society as a whole.[33] Finally, "since the consequences of the disturbances of ecosystems are difficult to gauge", non-specialist individuals "have inadequate insight into the importance of the environmental functions", the surveying method is "pointless except in special cases (eg., noise, nuisance and stench) in which the loss of function is suffered directly by individuals".[34]

The inability to assess fully the social damage of pollution or option price of a natural environment is not an indictment of conventional economic approaches to environmental problems. A more serious concern is whether these approaches are sufficient to deal with the problems of environmental degradation that undermine the sustainability of ecological processes and therefore of entire economic–environmental systems.

Even if the external environmental costs imposed by resource depletion are estimated, as Pearce has argued, "there is nothing in the conventional concept of an external cost to account for the decay of ecological processes themselves". As a result, "in the absence of perfect information and both perfect and instantaneous response to ecological disequilibrium, the system can be unsustainable."[35] Accounting for the decay of, say, the waste assimilative capacity of the environment, is theoretically not difficult to do – as the models developed by Forster indicate.[36] Very little has been done, however, to extend this approach either methodologically or analytically so as to consider the sustainability of entire economic-environmental systems under the threat of environmental degradation.

Part of the problem has been the failure to consider adequately the productive function of environment in contrast to its role in providing consumer utility. As discussed in Chapter 2, the sustainability of entire resource-based systems, such as agro-ecosystems, may be totally dependent upon ecological processes and functions. Yet the majority of conventional approaches focus on the direct amenity and aesthetic value of natural environments for individuals, or only discuss the potential productive worth in terms of genetic material, rather than their ecological importance in terms of maintaining ecological processes and functions essential to economic activity. It is this latter aspect that may be of particular importance to resource and environmental problems in the Third World, where so much economic activity is still directly dependent on the resource base.

These limitations suggest the need to consider together the role of environment as a provider of materials/energy, an assimilator of waste, and as a provider of essential consumptive *and* productive services. Integrating these two aspects – the physical dependence of the economic process on the environment and the environmental costs of economic activity – would be an essential feature of a model of economic–environmental interaction involving all the potential functions of the environment. Again, theoretically the task is not too difficult. For example, Krautkraemer has broadened the conventional approach to optimal resource depletion to incorporate the conditions that allow the preservation of natural environments containing resources used as productive inputs.[37] In this way, the analysis takes into account the competing uses of natural resources as potential productive inputs and as providers of essential environmental services, and indicates that the real value of natural services depends on the level of consumption over time.

The analysis of optimal choice over time among consumption, accumulation and environmental quality has been the focus of a number of studies.[38]

Over all, there has been little development of a comprehensive approach examining the trade-offs of environmental functions and the implications for the sustainability of economic-environmental systems of environmental degradation. The next chapter describes the basic nature of such an approach.

NOTES

1. Allen V. Kneese and Blair T. Bower, *Environmental Quality and Residuals Management* (Johns Hopkins University Press: Baltimore, 1979), p. 6.
2. See William J. Baumol and Wallace E. Oates, *The Theory of Environmental Policy* (2nd edn), (Cambridge University Press: Cambridge, 1988), p. 1.
3. More formally, Baumol and Oates, op. cit., pp. 17–18, state that "an externality is present whenever some individual's (say A's) *utility* or *production* relationships include real (that is, non-monetary) variables, whose values are chosen by others (persons, corporations, governments) without particular attention to the effects on A's welfare." Although in the opinion of these authors, this condition is sufficient for determining whether an activity can be classified as an externality, they note that it is often suggested that the activity must also satisfy a second condition: "The decision maker, whose activity affects others' utility levels or enters their production functions, does not receive (pay) in compensation for this activity in an amount equal in value to the resulting benefits (or costs) to others." Similar definitions of an externality, using one or both of these conditions, can be found in James E. Buchanan and W.C. Stubblebine, "Externality", *Economica*, Vol. 29 (1962), pp. 371–84; E.J. Mishan,

"The relationship between joint products, collective goods and external effects", *Journal of Political Economy*, Vol. 77 (1969), pp. 329–48; E.J. Mishan, "The postwar literature on externalities: An interpretative essay", *Journal of Economic Literature*, Vol. 9 (1971); and S.K. Nath, *A Reappraisal of Welfare Economics* (Routledge and Kegan Paul; London), 1969.

4. In fact the solution depicted in Figure 4.1 was first suggested by A.C. Pigou, *The Economics of Welfare* (4th edn), (Macmillan; London, 1962). See also Alfred Marshall, *Principles of Economics: An Introductory Volume* (8th edn), (Macmillan: London, 1949).

5. The classic works on the relationship between public goods and externalities are by F.M. Bator, "The anatomy of market failure", *Quarterly Journal of Economics*, Vol. 72 (1958), pp. 351–79; and J. G. Head, "Public goods and public policy", *Public Finance*, Vol. 17 (1962), pp. 197–219. See also the discussion in Baumol and Oates, op. cit., pp. 18–21, and Mishan, "The Relationship", op. cit.

6. See, for example, Baumol and Oates, op. cit., pp. 21–3 and A. Myrick Freeman III, "Depletable externalities and Pigouvian taxation", *Journal of Environmental Economics and Management*, Vol. 11 (1984), pp. 173–9. One special case that involves a modification of the straightforward Pigouvian tax is a shiftable externality. See Peter J.W.N. Bird, "The transferability and depletability of externalities", *Journal of Environmental Economics and Management*, Vol. 14 (1987), pp. 54–7, and Baumol and Oates, op. cit., pp. 25–6. That is, in the example of trash dumping, the initial victim manages to avoid the detrimental impacts of the externality by dumping it on another's property in turn. In this case, the first victim who is shifting the externality must also be taxed on his or her re-dumping, with the tax again being equal to the marginal social damage of this activity. Nevertheless, such an approach is clearly in keeping with Pigouvian taxation.

7. See R.H. Coase, "The Problem of Social Cost", *Journal of Law and Economics*, Vol. 3 (1960), pp. 1–44; and R. Turvey, "On divergences between social cost and private cost", *Economica*, Vol. 30 (1963), pp. 309–13.

8. For example, the victims may get away with strategies that capitalize on the potential gains from reducing pollution below the socially optimal level. As shown in Figure 4.2, this optimum for coal pollution is OX, which can be achieved by imposing a Pigouvian per unit tax equal to EX. However, through Coasian bargaining, one outcome might be that the victims agree to pay polluters to reduce pollution even further to OZ, which is clearly sub-optimal from society's point of view. Thus, if a tax is imposed on polluters, a tax on victims may also be required to discourage such strategic behaviour. See, for example, Coase, op. cit. and Turvey, op. cit.

9. For further discussion of the limitations to Coasian bargaining, see Baumol and Oates, op. cit.; Peter A. Victor, *Economics of Pollution* (Macmillan: London, 1972); and Donald Wittman, "Pigovian taxes which work in the small-number case", *Journal of Environmental Economics and Management*, Vol. 12 (1985), pp. 144–54.

10. These orthodox arguments are summarized nicely by Peter Nijkamp, *Theory and Application of Environmental Economics* (North-Holland: Amsterdam, 1977), Chapter 3.

11. Baumol and Oates, op. cit., p. 161.

12. See the discussion in Paul Burrows, *The Economic Theory of Pollution Control* (MIT Press: Cambridge, Massachusetts, 1980), Chapter 4.

13. See, for example, Nijkamp, op. cit., Chapter 3, and Victor, op. cit.

14. See Zvi Adar and James M. Griffin, "Uncertainty and the choice of pollution control instruments", *Journal of Environmental Economics and Management*, Vol. 3 (1976), pp. 178–88; Baumol and Oates, op. cit., Chapter 5 and 12; J.H. Dales, *Pollution, Property and Prices* (University of Toronto Press; Toronto, 1968); Partha Dasgupta, *The Control of Resources* (Basil Blackwell: Oxford, 1982), Chapter 4; and Martin L. Weitzman, "Prices vs. quantities", *The Review of Economic Studies*, Vol. 41 (1974),

pp. 477–91. For example, Dasgupta (op. cit., p. 89) notes that "to the extent that environmental resources display threshold effects, the optimal tax schedule designed to limit their use resembles regulations governing amount of emission, and if for administrative reasons a choice has to be made solely between the optimum linear tax schedule and the optimum quota, the latter should be chosen." Similarly, for a good discussion as to the various conditions involving uncertainty under which marketable permits are preferred to emission charges and vice versa, see Baumol and Oates, op. cit., Chapter 5.

15. For example, this 'second best' approach is cogently advocated by Baumol and Oates, op. cit.

16. Anthony C. Fisher, John V. Krutilla and Charles J. Cicchetti, "The economics of environmental preservation, a theoretical and empirical analysis", *American Economic Review*, Vol. 62 (1972), p. 605. See also John V. Krutilla, "Conservation reconsidered", *American Economic Review* Vol. 47 (1967); and John V. Krutilla and Anthony C. Fisher, *The Economics of Natural Environments: Studies in the Valuation of Commodity and Amenity Resources* (2nd edn), Resources for the Future, Washington, DC, 1985.

17. See, for example, E.G. Farnworth *et al.*, "The value of natural ecosystems: An economic and ecological framework", *Environmental Conservation*, Vol. 8 (1981), pp. 275–82; A. Myrick Freeman III, *The Benefits of Environmental Improvement* (Johns Hopkins University Press: Baltimore, 1979); Roefie Hueting, *New Scarcity and Economic Growth: More Welfare Through Less Production?* (North-Holland: Amsterdam, 1980); and S.H. Pearsall III, "In absentia benefits of nature preserves: A review", *Environmental Conservation*, Vol. II (1984), pp. 3–10.

18. See Jon R. Miller and F.C. Menz, "Some economic considerations for wildlife preservation", *Southern Economic Journal*, Vol. 45 (1979), pp. 719–20.

19. See, for example, Fisher, op. cit., Chapter 5; and Krutilla and Fisher, op. cit.

20. Krutilla and Fisher, op. cit., p. 15.

21. Ibid. See also Richard C. Bishop, "Option value: An exposition and extension", *Land Economics*, Vol. 58 (1982), pp. 1–15; and A. Myrick Freeman III, "The sign and size of option value", *Land Economics*, Vol. 60 (1984), pp. 1–13; and A. Myrick Freeman III, "Supply uncertainty, option price, and option value", *Land Economics*, Vol. 61 (1985), pp. 176–181. Sometimes the term "existence value" is used to denote those option values expressed by persons who do not currently use a resource nor plan to use it in the future but none the less place a value on its mere existence. See, for example, D.S. Brookshire, L.S. Eubanks and A. Randall, "Estimating option price and existence values for wildlife resources", *Land Economics*, Vol. 59 (1983), pp. 1–15; and the discussion in David W. Pearce, *Economic Values and the Natural Environment*, The 1987 Denman Lecture at the University of Cambridge (Granta Publications: Cambridge, 1987). In addition, the term "quasi-option value" is also used to denote a situation in which uncertainties over the effects of development or the potential loss of environmental values from development are likely to diminish over time. There may be a value in learning more about these potentially lost future benefits by postponing development. See, for example, Anthony C. Fisher and W.M. Hanemann, "Quasi-option value: Some misconceptions dispelled", *Journal of Environmental Economics and Management*, Vol. 14 (1987), pp. 183–90.

22. S.V. Ciriacy-Wantrup, *Resources Conservation: Economics and Policies* (University of California Press: Berkeley, 1952). The reader should compare this conclusion with the three conditions under which exhaustion of renewable resources appears optimal discussed on pp. 69–70. That is, unless society establishes and maintains a minimum stock of an endangered species, a high discount rate and value of the harvested species coupled with low regenerative capacity and harvesting costs may irrevocably drive the species to extinction. Bishop, op. cit., has more recently developed and extended this analysis.

23. See note 21 on the distinctions among option, quasi-option and existence values for environmental preservation.

24. Gardner Brown, Jr and Jon H. Goldstein, "A model for valuing endangered species", *Journal of Environmental Economics and Management*, Vol. 11 (1984), pp. 303–309.

25. For an excellent discussion of the issues surrounding the economics of biological diversity in developing countries, see Scott Barrett, "Economic guidelines for the conservation of biological diversity" (Economics Workshop – IUCN General Assembly, San Jose, Costa Rica, 3–4 February, 1988). For example, Barrett notes that, given the optimal policy is likely to involve setting aside some land for wildlife reserves and production forest, then the appropriate approach is to consider the provision of wildlife reserves and the rate of deforestation jointly rather than separately. This is, in fact, the approach taken by more recent forest-policy reviews in developing countries. See, for example, International Institute for Environment and Development and Government of Indonesia, *Forest Policies in Indonesia: The Sustainable Development of Forest Lands*, 4 vols (Jakarta, Indonesia, 30 November 1985).

26. Clement A. Tisdell, "Conserving living resources in Third World countries: Economic and social issues", *International Journal of Environmental Studies*, Vol. 22 (1983), pp. 11–24.

27. On debt-nature swaps and other options, particularly for the World Bank, in assisting environmental preservation in developing countries, see Stein Hansen, *Debt for Nature Swaps: Overview and Discussion of Key Issues* (Environment Department Working Paper No. 1, World Bank: Washington DC, February 1988).

28. Hueting, op. cit., p. 141.

29. For an interesting approach to project analysis under conditions of risk from the irreversible loss of environmental functions, see Anil Markandya and David Pearce, *Environmental Considerations and the Choice of the Discount Rate in Developing Countries* (Environment Department Working Paper No. 3, World Bank: Washington DC, May 1988).

30. See, for example, Peter Bohm, "Estimating demand for public goods: An experiment", *European Economic Review*, Vol. 3 (1972), pp. 111–30; D.S. Brookshire, B.C. Ives and W.D. Schultze, "The valuation of aesthetic preferences", *Journal of Environmental Economics and Management*, Vol. 3 (1976), pp. 325–46; and T. Wansbbeck and A. Kapetyn, "Tackling hard questions by means of soft methods: The use of individual welfare functions in socio-economic policy", *Kyklos*, Vol. 36 (1983), pp. 249–69.

31. Freeman, *The Benefits*, op. cit., p. 97.

32. Hueting, op. cit., p. 132.

33. T.C. Brown, "The concept of value in resource allocation", *Land Economics*, Vol. 60 (1984), pp. 231–46; Michael Sagoff, "Economic theory and environmental law", *Michigan Law Review*, Vol. 79 (1981), pp. 1393–1419; and Michael Sagoff, "Ethics and economics in environmental policy planning", paper presented at a seminar by the Office of Environmental Affairs, Projects Policy Department (World Bank: Washington DC, 1983).

34. Hueting, op. cit., pp. 131–2.

35. David W. Pearce, "Sustainable futures: Economics and the environment" (Inaugural Lecture: University College London, 5 December, 1985).

36. See, for example, B.A. Forster, "Optimal consumption planning in a polluted environment", *Economic Record*, Vol. 49 (1973), pp. 534–45, and B.A. Forster, "Optimal pollution control with a non-constant exponential rate of decay", *Journal of Environmental Economics and Management*, Vol. 2 (1975), pp. 1–6.

37. J.A. Krautkraemer, "Optimal growth, resource amenities and the preservation of natural environments", *Review of Economic Studies*, Vol. 52 (1985), pp. 153–70.

38. R.A. Becker, "Intergenerational equity: the capital environment trade-off", *Journal of Environmental Economics and Management*, Vol. 9 (1982), pp. 165–85; Forster, op. cit.; Karl-Göran Mäler, *Environmental Economics: A Theoretical Inquiry* (Johns Hopkins University Press: Baltimore, 1974); and Neil Vousden, "Basic theoretical issues of resource depletion", *Journal of Economic Theory*, Vol. 6 (1973), pp. 126–43.

# 5
# An Alternative View of Natural-Resource Scarcity

The previous chapters have examined the historical background to modern economic theories of natural-resource scarcity, have noted the most significant non-economic influences on these theories in recent times, and have summarized conventional economic approaches to problems of resource depletion, pollution and environmental preservation. As noted in the Introduction, however, increasing attention has been called to a new class of environmental problems that require a different kind of theoretical approach from that used to deal with the more conventional problems. In general, this new class of problems is characterized by a process of cumulative environmental degradation resulting from economic activity that may lead to severe ecological disruption and the collapse of human livelihoods. The problem of natural-resource scarcity is therefore one of trade-offs – controlling environmental degradation in the long run versus increasing economic activity in the short run. Thus a new, or alternative, theoretical approach is required in order to analyse the phenomenon of this special type of natural-resource scarcity; to allow explicit consideration of the irreversible qualitiative change typified by environmental degradation; to incorporate the economic impacts of ecological disturbances; to examine the trade-offs among all the functions of the environment; and to consider the intertemporal implications of these trade-offs.

It must be stressed that this alternative approach is hardly a replacement for conventional environmental and resource economic theory. Rather, the alternative approach should be seen as a necessary extension of environmental and resource economics into the explicit analysis of environmental degradation and the economic consequences of ecological disruption. Thus conventional approaches to resource depletion, pollution and environmental preservation serve as the point of departure for the analysis required.

The so-called alternative and conventional approaches differ in one important respect. With the emphasis on irreversible environmental degradation and the possibility of ecological collapse, an alternative approach resurrects the notion of absolute natural-resource scarcity, which seemed to have been so successfully buried by the classical and early neo-classical theorists. As emphasized in Chapter 1, however, the distinctions between the contemporary conventional and alternative approaches are not merely a replay of the absolute versus relative natural-scarcity views of the early economists. Instead, the non-economic influences of conservationism, ecology and thermodynamics on the contemporary alternative view have evolved a notion of absolute scarcity more in line with the environmental problems of the late twentieth century. Not surprisingly, such problems (involving wide-scale environmental degradation and the transformation of natural environments leading to ecological collapse) are less evident in advanced industrialized countries, whereas they are increasingly a major phenomenon of scarcity in the developing world. If the conclusion of an alternative theory of natural-resource scarcity is the need for more environmentally sustainable development, it is a message that now has global significance.

The preceding discussion seems to imply that a coherent alternative theory of natural-resource scarcity already exists. In fact, it is only just emerging. Although there is now a growing body of work analysing the physical dependence of the economic process on ecological relationships and the environmental costs of economic activity, these two aspects have not so far been well-integrated into a comprehensive model of economic–environmental interaction. This chapter will begin such an effort by first summarizing one interpretation of what an alternative economic view of natural-resource scarcity implies, and then by capturing the essence of this view in a simple model of economic–environmental interaction. To complete the theoretical discussion, this chapter will also suggest the implications of such an approach for environmentally sustainable economic development. It will be left to subsequent chapters to discuss specific examples – at the global, regional and national level – that illustrate such unique scarcity effects.

## AN ALTERNATIVE VIEW OF NATURAL-RESOURCE SCARCITY

As discussed in the previous two chapters, the major weakness of conventional theoretical approaches to environmental problems actually lies in their strength. By analysing separately each type of environmental problem – e.g., resource depletion, optimal pollution and environmental preservation – conventional approaches have contributed significantly to our understanding of the economic implications of each of these discrete sets of problems. Yet such approaches tell us very little about the over all economic significance of physical dependency on an entire environment that is inevitably being used for more than one function; or about the economic consequences of various trade-offs among these functions; or what might be the economic implications of the loss of some or all of these functions as the environment deteriorates.

The analysis of such "global" problems of economic–environmental interaction requires stepping back from the conventional approach of analysing discrete environmental and resource problems, and instead treating such problems together as part of a wider problem of cumulative environmental degradation in an integrated economic–environmental system. There is an analogy here with the relationship between micro-economics (the study of firms and consumers in individual markets) and macro-economics (the study of how overall output, employment and prices arise in the entire economic system, across all markets, and how they are influenced by government policies). Similarly, conventional analysis of a specific problem of resource depletion, optimal pollution control, environmental preservation and so on deals with a "micro" aspect of economic–environmental interactions, whereas an alternative view that focuses on the process of environmental degradation that may be potentially destabilizing to an entire economic–environmental system can be considered a more "macro" approach. Both approaches are comple-mentary, require the same analytical tools of economics and together provide a comprehensive picture of economic interactions with the environment.[1] Whatever the size of the economic–environmental system – whether it exists on the local, regional, national, international or global level – the more macro perspective of the alternative view is appropriate for analysing the economic consequences of environmental degradation for the entire system.[2]

The key to this alternative economic view is therefore an extremely comprehensive conception of the natural-resource problem. In turn, this conception stems from a rather general definition of natural resources that emphasizes the entire spectrum of utility-yielding functions of the environment. This definition is best summarized by Krutilla and Smith:

> Natural resources are all the original endowments of the earth and, thus, in a general sense must be considered to be all of the resources comprising the life support system. Past theoretical and empirical studies have considered only industrial raw materials using arguably challengeable assumptions and, in so doing, implicitly ignored the services of environmental common property resources that are used in economic activity. This use may take the form of serving as receptacles for the residuals from production or consumption activities or in providing hospitable environments for living orga-nisms. In many cases, economic activites will usurp one or more of these services that are available without market exchanges.[3]

This definition stresses that the natural environment is inherently *multi-functional* – it provides numerous economic functions, or "ser-vices", for humankind. Some of these functions require the extraction and conversion of natural resources (e.g., the productive services of raw material and energy inputs), whereas other beneficial services are optimally provided when the environment and its resources are left relatively undisturbed (e.g., life-support and amenity services). Thus the environment is analogous to a store of natural capital that yields streams of multi-purpose services that are essential to economic activity and human welfare. As a result, in any given economic–environmental system, these essential environmental functions are competing economic uses of finite – and thus scarce – environmental assets.

In general, one can distinguish among three important economic functions performed by scarce environmental assets: first, the environment provides useful material and energy inputs for the economic process; secondly, it assimilates the waste by-products generated by this process; and thirdly, the environment provides a stream of natural services that are essential for supporting economic production and human welfare.[4] The latter range from recreational, health, cultural, educational, scientific and aesthetic services to the maintenance of essential climatic and ecological cycles and functions.[5] It is worth elaborating briefly on each of these:

1. *The environment provides resources that become the material and energy inputs into the economic process.* As noted in Chapter 3, only this function of the environment is conventionally considered relevant to the phenomenon of natural-resource scarcity. Conventionally defined, this function includes providing economically valuable non-renewable resource stocks (such as fossil fuels and mineral resources), renewable resources (such as commercial forests, fisheries and water supply systems), and semi-renewables (such as soils). In a market economy, one would expect that the extracted resources and privately-owned resource stocks would exchange through markets and that there would be a price for their productive services.

2. *The environment assimilates the emitted wastes of the economic process.* Over time, the processes of energy and material extraction and conversion, production and consumption associated with economic activity must generate waste residuals. These by-products, such as particulate matter, inorganic and organic waste, waste heat and junk, must be absorbed by the environment through its biological chains and material cycles. As noted in Chapter 4, conventional approaches to pollution problems tend to focus on the social costs of pollution as an externality and the optimal level of pollution control. They do not generally consider the decay of ecological processes themselves as the assimilative capacity of natural environments becomes overloaded. Moreover, this assimilative function of many common-property land, air and water resources usually occurs outside of market exchange relationships, despite the fact that the limited carrying capacity of these resources would indicate that such a

function is potentially relatively scarce.[6]

3. *The environment provides a flow of "natural", or "environmental", services to individuals and production systems.* Unlike the first two roles, which involve the direct physical interchange of materials and energy between the environment and the economic process, this function relies on the preservation of the environment and the maintenance of *in situ* natural resources and stable ecological relationships. As noted above, it involves a wide range of services, some of which directly benefit individuals' welfare (e.g., recreational benefits, health and life-support amenities) and others that support the production and general economic activity (e.g., ecological and climatic maintenance, materials cycling and energy flow, preservation of genetic diversity, scientific and educational benefits). These are all mainly non-marketable services; that is, although they have important welfare implications these services are largely provided by common-property resources directly to individuals or economic processes and so lie outside the market mechanism. Moreover, as in the case of the environment's waste-absorbing role, this function is really the product of many interlinking ecosystems and natural resources. Consequently, it is crucially dependent on the overall state of *environmental quality*.

Together, these three economic functions of the environment underline the physical dependency of the economic process and human welfare on ecological processes and on the sufficiency of potentially scarce environmental resources. The fundamental scarcity problem, therefore, is that as the environment is increasingly being exploited for one set of uses (e.g., to provide sources of raw material and energy, and to assimilate additional waste), the quality of the environment may deteriorate. The consequence is an increasing *relative scarcity* of essential natural services and ecological functions. This is the *short-run natural-resource scarcity* problem as identified by the alternative view. It arises because of the environmental degradation inflicted by economic activity in the economic-environmental system. An environment that is providing resources as material and energy in excess of their regeneration and is continuously absorbing waste in excess of assimilative capacity must be experiencing some ecological damage and deterioration. This increase in environmental stress, or disorder, must ultimately affect the provision of natural services. For example, clear-cutting a tropical forest for timber means the loss of a wilderness preserve; of a climax ecosystem; of the maintenance of hydrological and materials cycles; and of a store of genetic information. Similarly, the pollution of a river system not only damages other economic activities such as fishing, but may disrupt aquatic and surrounding ecosystems, endanger the health of living organisms (including humans) and destroy natural beauty.

Although the loss of these essential natural services as a result of environmental degradation is not directly reflected in market outcomes, it nevertheless has a major effect in the form of economic scarcity. In other words, if "the environment is regarded as a scarce resource", then the "deterioration of the environment is also an economic problem."[7] Unfortunately, if "we cannot rely on procedures based on the attributes of existing markets to furnish information on marginal costs and valuation of alternative use profiles through time because there are direct physical interdependencies of economic activities and natural systems which are not reflected in market outcomes", then markets cannot be relied on alone to allocate scarce environmental resources efficiently among its three competing economic functions.[8] This means that resource-dependent economic growth will tend to bias natural-resource allocation towards meeting the physical needs of the expanding economic process – in terms of the provision of raw materials and the assimilation of waste. This would be to the detriment of the provision of environmental services, unless economic policy explicitly corrects this allocation process by taking into account the growing relative scarcity of these natural services.[9]

In the long run, if pervasive environmental degradation continues unchecked, it may permanently disrupt ecological stability and resilience and thus lead to an *absolute scarcity constraint* on the sustainability of economic activity and growth.[10] This is the *long-term scarcity* effect suggested by the alternative view. In the 1960s and 1970s, initial concern with global resource problems led some analysts to argue that this constraint may be the eventual depletion of certain economically valuable raw material and energy inputs, such as fossil fuels and mineral resources.[11] More recently, it has been maintained that long before such resources are completely exhausted, the cumulative ecological impact of economic activity on the biosphere may feed back to destabilize the economic process and disrupt human welfare. This perspective is emphasized by Daly:

> The whole biosphere has evolved as a complex system around the fixed point of a given solar flux. Modern man is the only species that has broken the solar income budget. The fact that man has supplemented his fixed solar income by rapidly consuming terrestrial capital has thrown him out of balance with the rest of the biosphere.... There are limits as to how much disorder can be produced in the rest of the biosphere and still allow it to function well enough to continue supporting the human subsystem.... The difficulty is twofold. First we will eventually run out of accessible terrestrial sources. Second, even if we never run out we would still face problems of ecological breakdown caused by a growing throughput of matter-energy.[12]

This is clearly a very pessimistic perspective and one that contrasts sharply with the more optimistic conventional view of natural-resource scarcity, which assumes that the economic system will automatically adjust to counteract resource scarcity through technological innovation, conservation and resource substitution (see Chapter 3). In contrast, this alternative view is less optimistic as it assumes that an absolute *ecological* scarcity constraint cannot be automatically alleviated by self-correcting adaptive innovations within the economic system.

As noted above, the resulting deterioration in environmental quality leading up to such an "ecological breakdown" represents disruptions to non-marketable common-property resources and ecosystems; hence, there are no accurate price signals for conveying the costs. Furthermore, severe ecological disruptions imposed by environmental degradation are not likely to resemble the "normal" Ricardian scarcity effect of well-behaved, gradually decreasing environmental quality but rather take the form of sudden, often discontinuous and less predictable threshold effects.

On the other hand, analogies with the laws of thermodynamics have been used by some analysts to describe the process of resource depletion and waste generation by the economic system as an irreversible and irrevocable "entropic" process of material and energy "throughput" (see Chapter 2). As no amount of technological change can allow the economic process to recycle material waste completely or to recycle energy at all, technological innovation cannot prevent the economic process from requiring additional environmental resources as material and energy inputs or from converting them into waste. The best it can do "is to prevent any unnecessary deterioration of the environment".[13]

Is it therefore inevitable that the "entropic" nature of an economic–environmental system must inevitably lead to its own ecological collapse? Perhaps more important, is the present pattern of man's exploitation of the biosphere so precariously unstable that global "ecological breakdown" is the ultimate conclusion? This interpretation of the alternative view of natural-resource scarcity – which can be called the *strong hypothesis* – may indeed turn out to be the most important economic question raised in recent years. However, it may be empirically unverifiable unless of course, unfortunately for the human race, such a day of reckoning actually does dawn! Perhaps less important in terms of our ultimate fate but more immediately verifiable, is the *weak hypothesis* suggested by the alternative view. That is, the assumption of a potential absolute ecological constraint means that in any economic–environmental system where cumulative resource depletion and waste generation leads to unchecked environmental degradation, severe ecological disruption and the collapse of human livelihoods *might* ensue. It is this weak hypothesis that we will be concerned with from now on.

This hypothesis may be particularly relevant to the developing regions of the world, where large segments of the population depend directly on resource-based economic activities in forestry, fishing, agriculture, and hunting and gathering. In some cases in these regions, cumulative resource degradation through economic over-exploitation can lead to the collapse of economic-environmental systems. As we shall see in Chapter 6, the Amazonian region, which is suffering continuous tropical deforestation, may be subject to local and inter-regional ecological disturbances that radically alter rainfall patterns, climate and species diversity. The result may be a catastrophic decline in the ability of the forest area and neighbouring regions to support dependent economic systems and human populations. Similarly, extensive agricultural production on marginal lands in semi-arid and arid zones can lead to accelerating problems of soil erosion and long-term desertification.[14] Using the case of the uplands of Java, Chapter 8 will highlight the need for substantial changes in agricultural systems, in economic incentives, and in the pattern of investment required to ensure the long-run sustainability of agricultural production under fragile dryland ecological conditions.

In advanced industrialized economics, largely located in the more favourable ecological conditions provided by temperate zones, there may appear to be less risk of such an absolute ecological constraint on economic activity. However, this may have less to do with favourable ecological conditions than with the fact that these economic systems, with only 30 % of the world's population, are "sustained" by consuming around 70 % of global resources. As the resource depletion and waste generation associated with the high level of economic activity of advanced industrialized countries are not completely contained within their boundaries, the resulting environmental degradation is effectively spread over the entire biosphere.[15] On the other hand, the high resource consumption of these economies may be beginning to have some global, or at least transfrontier, repercussions. As will be discussed further in Chapter 6, climatic changes resulting from the excess emission of greenhouse gases from industrial activity may significantly affect global agricultural productivity and thus the ability of some regions of the world to feed their populations. An even more dramatic constraint on world economic activity would be the threat of a rise in sea-level associated with global warming thermal expansion of the oceans and perhaps even excessive melting of the polar ice-caps. Similarly, combustion of fossil fuels emitting $SO_x$ and $NO_x$ pollution in the long run may increase acid rain to levels intolerable for forest and freshwater ecosystems, thus destabilizing livelihoods dependent on fishing and forestry activities.[16]

The greenhouse effect and Amazonian deforestation are examples of disturbances to the environment caused by human activity that may have important consequences for human welfare within the next 50 years – if not sooner. However, complete ecological destabilization of the biosphere may not occur for centuries – if ever. This does not necessarily invalidate the "alternative" economic view of natural-resource scarcity nor does it denigrate its contribution to our understanding of the economics of environmental degradation.

In some areas of the world where ecosystems are particularly fragile – such as sub-Saharan Africa, marginal lands and tropical forest zones – the concept of an absolute ecological constraint on economic activity and welfare may be very relevant. It may be equally relevant to certain types of agricultural activity – such as irrigated semi-arid agriculture and erodable croplands – in advanced industrialized economies. Even in those regions with more favourable ecological conditions, and types of economic activity that do not seem susceptible to any absolute ecological constraint, there still remains the problem of environmental degradation and the relative scarcity of essential environmental services. Thus, the type of relative and absolute scarcity effects suggested by the alternative view cannot be dismissed easily; they also indicate another approach to analysing the problem of optimal use of environmental resources over time.

## A THEORETICAL MODEL

It would be wrong to infer from this discussion that such a coherent approach actually exists. There are two key aspects of the alternative view of natural-resource scarcity: the physical dependence of the economic process on the environment, and the environmental costs of economic activity. They have yet to be well integrated into a comprehensive model illustrating these effects of relative and absolute scarcity. Nevertheless, there are a growing number of studies and theoretical models emphasizing these environmental costs and physical dependencies. All these efforts have provided a foundation upon which it may be possible to build a more complete analysis of the type of scarcity effects indicated by the alternative view.

Chapter 2 noted the progress that has been made in presenting a thermodynamic-based approach to the process of economic–environmental interaction. Although the analogous application of the second, or "entropy", law to this process has had a great influence on the alternative view, it is difficult to illustrate the entropy analogy in formal economic models. In contrast, the more accessible first law of thermodynamics and the corollary law of matter conservation have been extensively adapted to input–output models. These models have usefully detailed the flow of energy and material inputs through the process of extraction and conversion, production, and final consumption into waste residuals.[17] As some theoretical explorations have shown, the materials-balance approach can be used to construct a model of an economic system that, by virtue of its resource appropriation, produces both utility-yielding goods and useless waste. Under various conditions (e.g., the presence of recycling), such a model can simultaneously depict the optimal rate of depletion of natural resources and corresponding waste generation.[18] As Page has demonstrated, this approach can usefully be extended to discuss the role of conservation and efficiency in materials policy, and to establish a rationale for considering the preservation of the resource base as an explicit policy issue.[19]

Similarly (see Chapter 4), many studies have concentrated on the environmental costs of economic activity. For example, the irreversible conversion of natural areas in fixed supply may have a high opportunity-cost in the form of foreclosing the future option of deriving environmental services from them. Other studies have stressed the essential utility-yielding role of natural ecosystems and their environmental functions.[20] The conventional approach to optimal resource depletion has also been broadened to incorporate the conditions that allow the preservation of natural environments containing resources, or to embrace an integrated approach to a variety of problems of environmental resource allocation.[21] In addition, the analysis of optimal choice over time between consumption, accumulation and environmental quality has been the focus of a number of studies.[22] On a broader front still, Norgaard discusses the co-evolutionary development of ongoing feedback and interaction between social and ecological systems, whereby the feedback mechanisms previously maintaining the ecosystem are assumed by, or shifted to, the social system.[23]

The alternative economic view of natural-resource scarcity can be described by a model that attempts to synthesize these theories. One such model is constructed in the appendix to this chapter. Figure 5.1 summarizes the model in a simple flow diagram depicting the inter-relationships among the economic process, the natural environment and human welfare (utility). As this model is concerned with those uses by the economic system of natural resources that lead to increasing environmental degradation, Figure 5.1 only indicates the transformation of material and energy from *terrestrial* sources (i.e., forests, coal deposits, mineral ores, etc.). The direct use of solar radiation and the indirect use of solar energy through wind, water, tidal and geothermal energy are not shown in the diagram. It is important to note, however, that increased direct and indirect use of solar energy by the economic process can reduce environmental degradation by substituting for the use of terrestrial resources.

According to Figure 5.1, at any time terrestrial resources, $R_t$, are appropriated by the economic system to produce output $Q_t$. This output is then either allocated for consumption $C_t$, environmental improvement services $V_t$, or investment $I_t$. Consumption leads directly to increases in social welfare, which is represented by a utility box. Environmental improvement services generally assist environmental quality $X_t$ (and thus the provision of the utility-yielding and productive services provided by

**Figure 5.1: A Flow Diagram of Economic-Environmental Interaction**

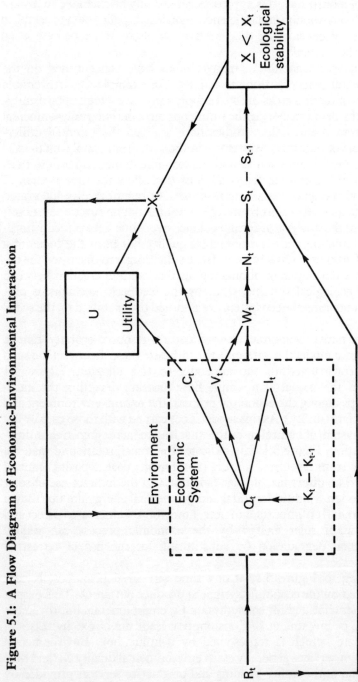

the environment), and also assist the recycling of some of the total waste emitted by the economic system, $W_t$.[24] The recycled waste effectively re-enters the economic system as a productive input (not shown). Investment can lead to capital accumulation from one period to the next, $K_t$ - $K_{t-1}$, which in turn stimulates further expansion in output capacity. Through the processes of production, consumption and saving, the economic system gradually transforms terrestrial resources into various utility-yielding purposes.

However, the extraction of resources from the environment, $R_t$, and the generation of net waste, $N_t$, by the economic system must eventually lead to increased environmental degradation, $S_t$ - $S_{t-1}$. In turn, increased environmental degradation can affect ecological stability and resilience.[25] If overall environmental quality can be kept above some minimum level, $\underline{X}$, then over all ecological stability and resilience can be said to be still maintained. Even before complete ecological instability and collapse set in, any increase in environmental degradation is bound to lower environmental quality, and thus have a negative impact on social welfare.

Economic growth may improve social welfare by increasing consumption and allowing for some improvements in environmental quality (via V). At the same time, the costs of growth, in terms of increasing environmental degradation could have a negative impact on environmental quality and so on welfare. Consequently, in the short run at least, the problem is one of balancing these various costs and benefits of growth in order to maximize the generation of utility over time. This is the relative natural-resource scarcity problem as identified by the alternative view.

There is the additional problem that eventually increased environmental degradation could permanently disrupt ecological functions and thus the overall sustainability of the economic–environmental process. As shown in Figure 5.2, at a future time T, environmental degradation may reach some maximum level $\bar{S}$, at which ecological stability and resilience is disrupted (i.e., $X_T < \underline{X}$). As a consequence, social welfare would be severely constrained (i.e., $U \rightarrow 0$). This long-term threat of ecological disruption to the overall sustainability of economic development represents the absolute natural-resource scarcity constraint of the alternative view.

Figures 5.1 and 5.2 indicate very simply the process of economic-environmental interaction by which the relative and asbsolute scarcity implied by the alternative view might arise. In the appendix to this chapter, a formal model of this interaction illustrates the optimal allocation of economic and environmental resources that may result from scarcity.

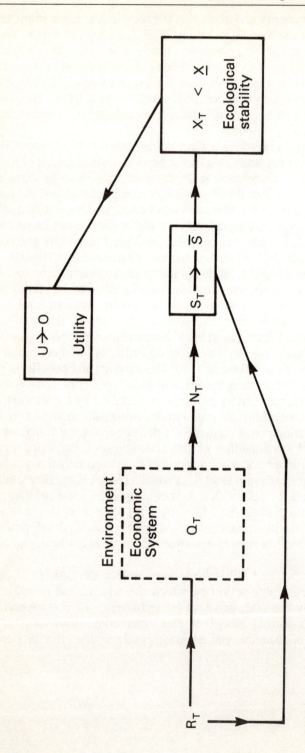

Figure 5.2: The Long-Term Ecological Constraint

## WIDER IMPLICATIONS: TECHNOLOGY, TASTES AND TIME

As noted in Chapter 3, conventional theories of natural-resource scarcity often indicate that technological innovation, substitution and improvements in resource management can be mitigating factors in overcoming increasing relative scarcity. The crucial question is whether the type of scarcity effects envisioned by the alternative view can also be mitigated by technological innovations and proper environmental management. The answer must be yes, albeit with some qualifications.

One key is, of course, slowing down the rate of environmental degradation to a level low enough to ensure that there is little appreciable or significant deterioration in vital ecological functions or natural-resource systems. This invariably calls for innovations that can slow down the rate of resource throughput in the economy by reducing the inflows of material and energy resources required from the environment and the outflows of waste. There are essentially two broad types of resource-saving innovations that can be applied to economic activity. These are

i)  innovations in the process of production; that is,
    a) *factor substitution* (e.g., labour power for energy, resource-saving capital for energy and materials, and the indirect and direct use of solar energy for terrestrial energy); b) *the re-use of scrap and waste materials* (i.e., improvements in the recovery and recycling of producer and consumer waste); and c) *the increased efficiency of resource conversion and utilization* (i.e., obtaining the maximum amount of end-use energy and material for production from the primary inflows of resources into the economic system).
ii) other innovations such as
    a) *improved organizational techniques* (i.e., better organization of production, distribution and consumption in order to reduce resource inefficiencies and resource use); b) *changes in the composition of output* (e.g., from non-durables to durables, or from resource-using goods to services); and c) *changes in product quality and/or design* (e.g., reducing sizes and weights of vehicles, eliminating built-in-obsolescence, re-designing throwaway packages and containers, and improving energy-efficiency in appliances).

The technology necessary to achieve these resource-saving innovations may already exist, or is easily achievable, in the advanced industrialized countries. As a recent report from the US Office for Technical Assessment has indicated, thanks to the mushrooming revolution in information technology, resource savings of 40–60 % of current use could be *feasible* in the near future for the United States *without* any sacrifice in economic growth.[26] However, as Page has emphasized, what is technologically feasible in terms of resource saving may not actually be realized unless the conservation criterion of keeping the resource base intact for future generations is accepted as a valid macro-economic policy goal.[27] In turn, this depends upon policymakers accepting that the type of scarcity effects stressed by the alternative view pose real constraints to the economic process, and that it is necessary to balance short-term conventional objectives of macro-economic performance with the more long-term considerations of future economic security and welfare. These and other policy implications of the alternative view will discussed further in Chapter 8.

In addition to resource-saving innovations, better techniques of environmental improvement and management could also alleviate any decline in environmental quality. The results may include an increase in productivity, particularly in the case of agricultural and other resource-based systems that are directly dependent upon ecological relationships for production. For example, in the Sahel small farmers have struggled for generations against drought, high temperature and marginal soil fertility to establish a predominantly millet-based cropping system. With the introduction of improved multicropping techniques, new drought and pest-resistant varieties of cow peas, and no-tillage mulching, water run-off and soil erosion have been reduced and yields have increased.[28] Chapter 7 discusses a similar example of how improved land-management techniques and cropping systems – accompanied by appropriate economic policies, incentives and investment strategies – might reduce upper watershed degradation in Java.

In numerous circumstances, the quality of the environment can benefit from a variety of techniques ranging from improvements in resource, land and water management; to ecologically appropriate tourist facilities, conservation areas and environmental policies; to the dissemination of new conservation skills and training. Again, the political will to design economic policies, incentives and investment strategies to implement these techniques is all that is lacking.

Despite optimism that the combination of resource-saving and environmental management techniques could indefinitely postpone binding ecological constraints, there are a number of reasons – in addition to the problem of political will – why such innovations may not be automatically or effectively implemented in response to declining environmental quality.

In the conventional case of increasing scarcity of raw materials, the existence of identifiable markets for these resources means that the price system can automatically respond to this scarcity and so induce the appropriate innovative response. However, as stressed throughout this chapter, many environmental resources exist outside the economic system, as integral components of complex resource and ecological systems, and are thus non-market common-property resources. As noted in Chapter 4, although "markets indirectly and other institutions directly influence the allocation of these resources" for use as resource inputs and waste assimilation as opposed to preservation, "unfortunately none of these can be relied upon to provide the information on the marginal valuations of the resources involved in these allocations".[29] Nor can markets or other institutions be expected to convey information accurately on the economic impacts of environmental degradation and the decline in ecological processes. Without a mechanism for conveying this information, the appropriate technological response is not assured.

The appropriateness and effectiveness of technological innovation in halting environmental deterioration depend on a clear understanding of the ecological impacts of pollution and resource depletion. However, changes in the state of the environment and its resources usually involve substantial qualitative changes and interactions. The aggregate effects on ecological functions and systems may, in some cases, be an unusual capacity for resilience and regenerative capacity. In other cases, this may lead to a tendency towards rapidly reinforcing disturbance and disruption (see Chapter 2). Because such changes are rarely stable, frequently irreversible and often cumulative and discontinuous, environmental systems almost never settle to an equilibrium state in response to perturbations and disturbances. Even in the relatively simple case of a constant input of pollution into a stream ecosystem, the environmental system may or may not reach an equilibrium for years, as the pollutant may differentially affect the survival rate, and perhaps even the course of evolution of species. In the case of multiple pollutants, the combined changes rarely equal the sum of the separate effects.[30]

There may be physical limits to the extent to which resource-saving innovations can reduce resource throughput in the economic process. It may be possible, as noted above, to reduce current US resource used by 40–60 % and still have reasonable economic growth, but any further reductions may not be feasible under even the most optimistic technological assumptions. The source of these restrictions stem from the first and second law of thermodynamics as analogously applied to the economic process (see Chapter 2):

i) from the first law, as material and energy can neither be created nor destroyed, production and consumption must require some inputs of material and energy from the environment and generate some waste;

ii) from the second law, as material and energy used in transformation must irrevocably dissipate or decay, some degradation of material and energy from a useful to a useless state by the economic process is inevitable and irreversible.[32]

In other words, resource-saving innovations may minimize, but cannot eliminate, resource throughput from the economic process. Given uncertainty over ecological processes and environmental change, even the minimum resource-throughput level required to sustain an economic process may continue to damage the environment, particularly if it has been subject to stress from past resource-using technologies for a significant period of time.

Just as the optimal allocation of output between consumption, environmental improvement services and investment is influenced by the relative preferences of consumption to environmental quality and changes in the social value of capital accumulation (see the appendix to this chapter), choices of resource-saving and environmental management innovations over other possible technological mixes will be dictated by individual tastes and preferences. The classic problem here, of course, is that choice of innovations today will affect both future consumption and environmental quality, yet future preferences and the preferences of future generations are as yet unknown. For example, very little of the yield-enhancing technical progress in US agriculture during the post-war period was induced by concern about the cumulative effects on soil erosion, and has thus contributed to the current problems of soil degradation in erodible croplands, now an urgent and pressing concern.[32] In assessing both future and present reactions to environmental degradation, the crucial problem remains that "the level of the shadow price of environmental functions is largely indeterminate because insufficient information is available on the preferences for environmental functions".[33]

In principle, resource-saving innovations in technology and environmental management should be capable of overcoming the type of scarcity effects depicted by the model in the appendix to this chapter. However, the main indicator of these scarcity effects – the relative decline in the quality of the environment and in ecological functions – occurs largely outside the institutional mechanisms of the economic system. At best, it is only indirectly and partially reflected in the market through its impact on productivity, human health, resource-management costs and so on. Therefore, the appropriate innovative responses may not be automatically forthcoming. Moreover, given the complexity of ecological relationships, their often unstable responses to stresses and shocks, the uncertainty over future and even current preferences for environmental functions and resources, and the physical limits to resource-saving techniques, the effectiveness of innovations in ameliorating environmental deterioration may be constrained. If this is the case, then the trade-off between consumption and environmental improvement services, and between more growth and increased environmental preservation may be unavoidable.

## SUMMARY AND CONCLUSION

This chapter has explored an alternative view of natural-resource scarcity that considers the trade-off between environmental quality on the one hand, and resource depletion and waste generation by the economic process on the other. For the economic–environmental system as a whole, the result of such a trade-off may be the following two scarcity effects: the short-term consequence is the increasing relative scarcity of essential environmental services and ecological functions important to economic activity and human welfare; in the long run, pervasive and cumulative environmental degradation may lead to an absolute constraint if ecosystems are destabilized and essentially collapse. Although the strict application of such an approach may be limited, it has wider implications for the role of technological change and the value of the environment in any system experiencing deteriorating environmental quality.

This more macro view of economic–environmental interaction contrasts sharply with conventional economic approaches that deal with more specific, or micro, environmental and resource problems (such as the optimal depletion of certain types of exhaustible resources, the optimal control of waste effluents, and the preservation of unique natural environments). Nevertheless, the alternative and conventional approaches are more complementary than mutually exclusive; both are necessary for improving our understanding of the complex interaction between economic and environmental systems.

The model presented in the appendix to this chapter formally illustrates this alternative view. It also confirms the general conclusion that if individuals express preferences for essential environmental resources and functions which are perceived to be deteriorating, then it may be optimal to consider trade-offs between more consumption through resource-using growth on the one hand and environmental preservation and more sustainable development on the other. With its strong assumption of increasing environmental degradation leading to ecological collapse, the model may only be strictly applicable to a limited number of economic–environmental systems. Its general insights, however, are more widely applicable to any situation where economic activity leads to declining environmental quality and the loss of ecological functions.

The following chapters explore some examples of a slightly weaker hypothesis. These are examples of economic–environmental interaction at the global, transnational and regional level where the unchecked environmental degradation from cumulative resource depletion and/or waste generation *might* lead to severe ecological disruption and the collapse of human livelihoods. The next chapter looks at the problems of Amazonian deforestation and global warming as illustrations of the short- and long-term scarcity effects depicted by the alternative view. Chapter 7 uses the example of upper watershed degradation in Java to examine the economic policies, incentives and investment strategies that might be required to tackle a specific problem of pervasive environmental degradation. Chapter 8 will discuss more generally the policy implications of reconciling trade-offs between conservation and development goals in order to achieve environmentally sustainable development.

### *APPENDIX:* A MODEL OF ECONOMIC-ENVIRONMENTAL INTERACTION[34]

Figures 5.1 and 5.2 summarize the process by which the relative and absolute scarcity effects implied by the alternative view might arise in an economic–environmental system. The relationships depicted in these figures can be adapted into a more formal analysis of the optimal allocation of economic and environmental resources over time resulting from these scarcity effects.

The following model analyses the prospect of irreversible damage to the natural environment, arising from resource depletion and waste generation. The outcome is a steady decline in environmental quality potentially leading to the long-term disruption of important ecological functions and systems. In order to capture these relative and absolute scarcity impacts of increasing environmental degradation over time, several assumptions are adopted.

First, in order to indicate the dependency of human welfare on essential environmental services and ecological functions, a stock variable representing environmental quality $X_t$ is included along with consumption $C_t$ as arguments in the social welfare function U:

$$U = U(C_t, X_t),\tag{1}$$

with $U_c(C_t) > 0$, $U_{cc}(C_t) < 0$, $U_x(X_t) > 0$, $U_{xx}(X_t) < 0$. Equation (1) indicates that at any time t social welfare is a concave, increasing function of consumption and environmental quality. To simplify analysis, the welfare function is additively separable, that is, $U_{cx} = U_{xc} = 0$.

Secondly, it is assumed that at any time t any output $Q_t$ produced by the economic system and not used for consumption, or for providing environmental improvement services $V_t$, or for replacing depreciated capital $wK_t$, leads to a net accumulation in the capital stock, $K_t - K_{t-1}$:

$$K_t - K_{t-1} = Q_t - (C_t + V_t) - wK_t.\tag{2}$$

Capital depreciates at the constant rate w. Environmental improvement services can be divided between those that directly improve environmental quality through, say, conservation practices, resource management, pollution clean-ups etc.; and those that indirectly improve $X_t$ by increased recycling and the abatement of waste residuals otherwise emitted into the environment.

Thirdly, following the relative scarcity argument of the alternative view, it is assumed that at any time t as the economic process extracts resources $R_t$ from the environment and generates (net) waste $N_t$, increasing environmental degradation $S_t - S_{t-1}$ occurs causing environmental quality to decline:

$$S_t - S_{t-1} = f(R_t, N_t) \quad , \tag{3}$$

$$X_t = X (S_t, V_t) \quad , \tag{4}$$

$$X_t < X_{t-1} \quad , \tag{5}$$

with $f_r(R_t) > 0$, $f_n(N_t) > 0$, $X_s(S_t) < 0$ and $X_v(V_t) > 0$. Equation (4) shows that environmental quality is a decreasing function of environmental degradation $S_t$, and an increasing function of environmental improvement services $V_t$. A crucial assumption is that, since $S_t - S_{t-1} > 0$ throughout any time period t, then $X_t$ must also be declining (conditions 3 and 5).[35]

Fourthly, in order to incorporate the absolute ecological constraint discussed above, the life of the economic-environmental system is assumed to be finite, where terminal time T is that period at the end of which environmental degradation reaches some maximum level $\bar{S}$, driving environmental quality to some minimum level $\underline{X}$, and thus irrevocably destabilizing the entire economic–environmental system. This constraint on the system can be summarized as:

$$t_o \leq t < T, \quad \underline{X} < X_t \text{ and } U = U(C_t, X_t) \quad , \tag{6}$$

$$\lim_{t \to T} t, \quad \lim_{S_t \to \bar{S}} X(S_t) \to \underline{X} \text{ and } \lim U \to 0.$$

Assuming population growth is constant, the remaining functional relationships of the model can be simplified to;

$$Q_t = Q(K_t) \quad , \tag{7}$$

with $Q_k(K_t) > 0$ and $Q_{kk}(K_t) < 0$.[36]

$$R_t = R(Q_t) \quad , \tag{8}$$

with $R_q(Q_t) > 0$.

$$N_t = W(Q_t) - B(V_t) \quad , \tag{9}$$

with $B_v(V_t) > 0$, $B_{vv}(V_t) < 0$ and $W_q(Q_t) > 0$. That is, production is a function of the capital stock; resource use and waste generation $W_t$ are functions of total output; and net waste generation is $W_t$ less any recycling $B_t$.

Finally, the initial and terminal conditions of the model are respectively:

$$K_o = \underline{K} \quad , \quad S_o = \underline{S} \quad , \tag{10}$$

$$K_T \geq \bar{K} \geq 0 \quad , \quad S_T \geq \bar{S} \quad . \tag{11}$$

The planning problem suggested by the model is how best to allocate economic and environmental resources over time given the current relative scarcity problem of declining environmental quality and the threat of a future ecological constraint on the entire system. A dynamic discrete-time optimization problem can be constructed from the model with the aid of a few substitutions.

Substituting (7)–(9) into (3) yields:

$$S_t - S_{t-1} = f(R(Q(K_t)), W(Q(K_t)) - B(V_t)) = g(K_t, V_t) \quad , \qquad (12)$$

with $g_k(K_t) > 0$ and $g_v(V_t) < 0$. That is, as capital accumulation leads to growth and – in the absence of technological change – more resource throughput, whereas environmental improvement services reduce waste through recycling, then environmental degradation is essentially an increasing function of $K_t$ and a decreasing function of $V_t$ at time t.

Expressions (12) and (4) can be substituted for $X_t$ in the social welfare function (1), which is now summed over the finite planning period [t, T] and discounted at the rate $0 < r < 1$:

$$U = \sum_{t=1}^{T} \frac{1}{(1+r)^{t-1}} U(C_t, X(S_{t-1} + g(K_t, V_t), V_t)) \qquad (13)$$

A Lagrangean function, $L^\star$, can now be formed from (13), (2), (10) and (11):

$$L^\star = \sum_{t=1}^{T} \frac{1}{(1+r)^{t-1}} U(C_t, X(S_{t-1} + g(K_t, V_t), V_t)) \qquad (14)$$

$$+ \sum_{t=1}^{T} p_t (K_{t-1} + Q_t(K_t) - (C_t + V_t) - wK_t - K_t)$$

$$+ p_o(\underline{K} - K_o) + p_{T+1}(K_T - \bar{K}) + u(\underline{S} - S_o) + a(S_T - \bar{S}).$$

The Lagrangean multiplier $p_t$ can be interpreted as the utility value of an additional unit of capital, that is the social value of capital accumulation that becomes available in period t.

Similarly, the multiplier u represents the social value of an increase in the initial level of environmental degradation, $S_o$, whereas a indicates the social value of a relaxation in the binding terminal constraint, as represented by an increase in $\bar{S}$.

Thus the dynamic optimization problem is to maximize (14) by optimal choice of $C_t$, $V_t$ and $K_t$. Assuming $C_t$, $V_t$, $K_t$ and $S_t > 0$, the first-order conditions are:

$$\frac{dL^\star}{dC_t} = \frac{1}{(1+r)^{t-1}} U_c(C_t) - p_t = 0 \quad , \qquad\qquad t = 1,...,T \qquad (15)$$

$$\frac{dL^\star}{dV_t} = \frac{1}{(1 + r)^{t-1}} U_x(X_t) (X_s(S_t)g_v(V_t)) = 0 \quad,$$
$$t = 1,...,T \qquad (16)$$

$$\frac{dL^\star}{dK_t} = \frac{1}{(1 + r)^{t-1}} U_x(X_t) (X_s(S_t)g_k(K_t) + p_{t+1} - p_t + p_t(Q_k(K_t) - w)$$
$$= 0, \qquad\qquad t = 1,...,T \qquad (17)$$

$$\frac{dL^\star}{dK_o} = p_1 - p_o = 0, \qquad (18)$$

$$\frac{dL^\star}{dS_0} = U_x(X_1)X_s(S_1)(1 + g(K_1, V_1)) - u = 0 \quad, \qquad (19)$$

$$\frac{dL^\star}{dS_T} = \frac{1}{(1 + r)^{T-1}} U_x(X_T)X_s(S_T) + a = O \quad. \qquad (20)$$

As has been specified, the complexity of the model prevents the characterization of a final solution to these equations. Interpretation of these conditions does however provide some useful insight into society's allocative choices when faced with the unique relative and absolute scarcity constraints of the model. For example, condition (15) can be substituted into condition (16) to yield:

$$\frac{U_c(C_t)}{U_x(X_t)} = X_s(S_t)g_v(V_t) + X_v(V_t) \quad, \qquad t = 1,...,T \quad. \qquad (21)$$

This suggests that the marginal rate of substitution of $X_t$ for $C_t$ is equated in each period with the impacts on the environment of a marginal increase in environmental improvement services. These services either protect the environment directly, $X_v(V_t)$, or indirectly by recycling waste and thus reducing some of the negative impact of the economic process on the environment, $X_s(S_t)g_v(V_t)$. Thus condition (21) defines the optimal trade-off between increased consumption and provision of services to improve the environment. That is, at any time $t = 1,...,T$ any allocation of output between $C_t$ and $V_t$ must obey this rule.

Condition (17) can be rearranged as:

$$p_{t+1} - p_t = p_t(Q_k(K_t) - w) + \frac{1}{(1 + r)^{t-1}} U_x(X_t)X_s(S_t)g_k(K_t) \quad,$$
$$t = 1,...,T \qquad (22)$$

which indicates that the social value of capital is changing in each period according to the benefits of marginal capital productivity net of depreciation $p_t(Q_k(K_t) - w)$, less the discounted marginal damage of the environmental degradation accompanying this increased productivity $U_x(X_t)X_s(S_t)g_k(K_t)$. Capital accumulation that is not replacing depreciated stock leads to increased output and thus socially valuable consumption and environmental improvement services. At the same time, however, the increased output requires a greater use of resources by the economic system, which in turn increases environmental degradation. The former can be considered the benefits of capital accumulation and the latter, the costs. If in any period the costs exceed the benefits of capital accumulation, then its social value will decline. If the costs equal the benefits, the value remains constant, that is:

$$\text{if} \quad p_t(Q_k(K_t) - w) = \frac{1}{(1 + r)^{t-1}} U_x(X_t)X_s(S_t)g_k(K_t) \quad ,$$

$$\text{then} \quad p_{t+1} - p_t = 0. \qquad\qquad t = 1,...,T \qquad (23)$$

Therefore, expressions (22) and (23) are the rules governing the optimal rate of capital accumulation, and thus growth, in the economy.

Condition (18) states that the social value of additional capital in the first planning period and the period before are equal (i.e., the social value of capital is unchanged up to the first period). Condition (19) shows that the negative social value of a decline in the initial state of the environment must be equal to the marginal damage of an increase in environment degradation in the first period. Any such increase in $S_o$ must be a social cost, for it both lowers initial environmental quality, $X_1$, and it brings the system that much closer to the level of environmental degradation that causes its "collapse", $\bar{S}$. In contrast, an increase in $\bar{S}$ would prolong the life of the economic–environmental system and is therefore beneficial to society. From condition (20), this benefit is equivalent to the marginal utility of a decrease in environmental degradation in the last period.

This model has derived the optimal conditions for allocating economic and environmental resources in an interdependent economic–environmental system where any resource depletion and waste generation by the economic process leads to deteriorating environmental quality and an eventual ecological collapse. As the model has stressed that the state, or quality, of the environment is an essential determinant of social welfare, environmental improvement services are recognized as a socially valuable component of economic output and, in every period, society must optimally allocate output between consumption and services to improve the environment. Although the key to expanding output is capital accumulation, the cost of capital accumulation and growth is increased environmental degradation. If this cost exceeds the benefits of economic expansion, then the social value of capital accumulation, and thus growth, declines. Under certain conditions determining the social welfare function (e.g., individuals' giving more weight to environmental quality than consumption, in their utility considerations), society may opt for slower or even for no growth and the allocation of an increasing share of output to environmental improvement services. Such allocative choices are clearly consistent with a preference for ecological preservation over increased aggregate consumption, a preference that is perhaps spurred by apprehension over the type of future absolute ecological constraint included in this model.

# NOTES

1. Recent surveys of environmental and resource economics, such as those by Partha Dasgupta, *The Control of Resources* (Basil Blackwell: Oxford, 1982) and Anthony C. Fisher, *Resource and Environmental Economics* (Cambridge University Press: Cambridge, 1981), have already demonstrated how specific conventional theories of optimal resource depletion, environmental preservation and pollution control all share a common analytical approach. The point made here is that these same analytical tools, suitably modified, can and should be applied to the more macro problem of environmental degradation and the destabilization of an entire economic-environmental system. Indeed, elements of this more global problem can be found in these eclectic works by Dasgupta and Fisher.

   An even more important point in stressing this macro–micro analogy is that the alternative and conventional views of natural-resource scarcity are not mutually exclusive but complementary. Both levels of analysis are needed to obtain a better understanding of environmental and resource problems and to design appropriate policy measures. Ther same micro–macro analogy was used by Talbot Page (*Conservation and Economic Efficiency: An Approach to Materials Policy* (Johns Hopkins University Press: Baltimore, 1977), p. 205) to reconcile the conservation criterion of keeping the resource base in tact with the present value criterion of intertemporal efficiency: "The conservation criterion functions at the macro-economic level establishing a context for markets; the present value criterion functions at the micro-economic level of market efficiency. For policy analysis and prescription both levels are needed."

2. The fact that economic–environmental systems exist on all different scales, or hierarchical levels, breaks the analogy between the macro aspect of the alternative view of natural-resource scarcity and macro-economics, which by definition is more or less confined to the analysis of the *national* economic system. As subsequent chapters will demonstrate, the economic consequences of environmental degradation is a problem for *all* economic–environmental systems, whether at the local, regional or global level. As discussed in Chapter 2, this point is also emphasized by Gordon R. Conway, "The properties of agroecosystems", *Agricultural Systems*, Vol. 24 (1987) in his analysis of the sustainability and other properties of agro-ecosystems – one specific type of economic-environmental system. Note, however, that as one reduces the "scale" of the economic–environmental system, or decreases its "elements" to a simpler problem of interaction between one type of economic activity and one type of environmental function, the environmental degradation problem may resemble more conventional resource problems. In an extreme case, one such reduced economic-environmental system is the classic renewable resource problem of an open-access fishery (see Chapter 3). In such a simple system, analysis of environmental degradation is the same thing as the conventional analysis of optimal harvesting, and the sustainability of the system is in turn determined by the long-term potential of the resource stock for regeneration in response to harvesting. As this chapter will discuss, the value of the alternative view lies in illuminating scarcity effects in more robust economic–environmental systems, with more than one environmental function and where these functions are potentially threatened by ecological disruption.

3. V. Kerry Smith and John V. Krutilla, "Resource and environmental constraints to growth", *American Journal of Agricultural Economics*, Vol. 61 (1979), pp. 395–408.

4. Ralph C. d'Arge, "Economic growth and the natural environment" in A.V. Kneese and B.T. Bower (eds), *Environmental Quality Analysis* (Johns Hopkins University Press: Baltimore, 1972) provides an alternative classification of these functions into four categories:

   i) a source of raw materials;
   ii) space for waste accumulation and storage;
   iii) The provision of assimilation–regeneration capacity for chemically or biologically active wastes; *and*
   iv) the determinant of health and life style, and of aesthetic satisfactions.

5. See, for example, E.G. Farnworth, *et al.*, "The value of natural ecosystems: An economic and ecological framework", *Environmental Conservation*, Vol. 8 (1981), pp. 275–82; A. Myrick Freeman III, *The Benefits of Environmental Improvement* (Johns Hopkins University Press: Baltimore, 1979); and S.H. Pearsall III, "In absentia benefits of nature preserves: A review", *Environmental Conservation*, Vol. 11 (1984), pp. 3–10.

6. The interpretation of common property used in describing this function and the following is similar to the definition outlined by V. Kerry Smith and John V. Krutilla in "Summary and research issues" in V.K. Smith (ed.), *Scarcity and Growth Reconsidered* (Johns Hopkins University Press: Baltimore, 1979), pp. 294–5: "a common property resource is one which is equally accessible to all members of society. The allocation of these resources does not take place through market mechanisms, and so the market is not available to provide incentives for individual agents to limit their patterns of consumption or rate of utilization of the resource's services."

7. Roefie Hueting, *New Scarcity and Economic Growth: More Welfare Through Less Production?* (North-Holland: Amsterdam, 1980), pp. 1 and 3.

8. Smith and Krutilla, op. cit., p. 286.

9. As will be discussed below, both the increasing relative scarcity of environmental services and the degree of resource dependency of economic growth may be mitigated by technological change. Note also that this view of the relationship between economic growth and the increasing relative scarcity of environmental services is analogous to the view of the "development versus environmental preservation option" with respect to a specific unique natural environment discussed in Chapter 4.

10. The terms ecological "stability" and "resilience" should be interpreted as defined by C.S. Holling, "Resilience and stability of ecological systems", *Annual Review of Ecological Systems*, Vol. 4 (1973), pp. 1–24; C.S. Holling, "The resilience of terrestrial ecosystems: Local surprise and global change" in W.C. Clark and R.E. Munn (eds), *Sustainable Development of the Biosphere* (Cambridge University Press: Cambridge, 1986); and G.R. Conway, op. cit. See also the discussion in Chapter 2. Note that the expression "the sustainability of economic activity and growth" could be analogously interpreted as "the ability of a system to maintain its structure and patterns of behaviour in the face of disturbance" (Holling, op. cit., pp. 296–7), where the system in question is now an economic system. Thus, the claim being made is that, given the fundamental physical dependency of any economic system on ecological processes, the sustainability of that system is not possible if a cataclysmic disturbance such as the collapse of ecological stability and resilience occurs. As will be discussed further in Chapter 8, there are different views on the ingredients necessary to make an economic system more or less sustainable in the long run; that is, there is yet to be a consensus on what actually constitutes truly sustainable economic development.

11. See, for example, J.W. Forrester, *World Dynamics* (Wright Allen: Cambridge, Massachusetts, 1971) and Dennis L. Meadows, Donnella H. Meadows, Jorgen Randers and William Behrens, *The Limits to Growth: A Report for the Club of Rome's Project on the Predicament of Man* (Universe Books: New York, 1972).

12. Herman E. Daly, "Entropy, growth and the political economy of scarcity" in V.K. Smith, op. cit., pp. 75–6.

13. Nicholas Georgescu-Roegen, *Energy and Economic Myths: Institutional and Analytical Economic Essays* (Pergamon: New York, 1976), p. 19. See the references cited in Chapter 2 for other classic works on this 'entropy' analogy. Note that the conclusion that Daly, op. cit., draws from this analogy is to argue for a steady-state economy that minimizes resource throughput. In contrast, Georgescu-Roegen, op. cit., has argued that this offers no final solution to the absolute scarcity problem as even a steady-state process at a high level of output is potentially ecologically unstable over the long run.

14. See, for example, the evidence presented in Jack A. Mabbutt, "A new global assessment of the status and trends of desertification", *Environmental Conservation*, Vol. 11 (1984), pp. 103–13; and World Bank, *Desertification in the Sahelian and Sudanian Zones of West Africa* (World Bank: Washington DC, 1985).

15. For example, not only are most of the basic sources of extractive resources consumed in advanced economies (such as mineral ores, oil and gas and forest products) obtained from the developing regions of the world but also much of the basic manufacturing (the so-called "dirty" industries of iron and steel, ship building, vehicle manufacture, chemicals, resource processing, etc.) are increasingly being transferred from advanced economies to developing countries so as to exploit financial advantages, particularly in labour. See Edward B. Barbier, "The potential for reviving economic growth: The political economy of resource misallocation", paper presented at The Other Economic Summit, London, 6–9 June 1984. Nevertheless, the majority of the output of these industries is being consumed and used as intermediate goods by advanced economies. This is one way in which the environmental costs of high resource consumption by these economies are transferred, or dissipated, from their own economic–environmental systems to that of the biosphere.

16. For an interesting overview of this problem, see World Resources Institute and International Institute for Environment and Development, *World Resources 1986* (Basic Books: New York, 1986), Chapter 10.

17. See the discussion and the references cited in Chapter 2.

18. See, for example, Ralph C. d'Arge, op. cit.; Ralph C. d'Arge and K.C. Kogiku, "Economic growth and the environment", *Review of Economic Studies*, Vol. 40 (1973), pp. 61–78; Karl-Göran Mäler, *Environmental Economics* (Johns Hopkins University Press: Baltimore, 1974); and Peter Nijkamp, *Theory and Application of Environmental Economics* (North-Holland: Amsterdam, 1977).

19. See Talbot Page, *Conservation and Economic Efficiency: An Approach to Materials Policy* (Johns Hopkins University Press: Baltimore, 1977). See also the discussion of the policy implications of sustainable economic development in Chapter 8.

20. See, for example, Edward B. Barbier, "'Alternative' economic approaches to natural-resource scarcity", PhD thesis (Economics Department, Birkbeck College: University of London, 1986); Edward B. Barbier, "Alternative approaches to economic-environmental interaction", paper presented to the 13th Annual Eastern Economics Association Conference, Washington DC, 5–7 March 1987 forthcoming in *Ecological Economics*; Farnworth *et al.*, op. cit.; Freeman, op. cit.; Hueting, op. cit.; David W. Pearce, "The limits to cost-benefit analysis as a guide to environmental policy", *Kyklos*, Vol. 29 (1976), pp. 97–112; David W. Pearce, "Efficiency and distribution in corrective mechanisms for environmental externality" in A. Schnaiber, N. Watts and K. Zimmerman (eds), *Distributional Conflicts in Environmental Policy* (WZB–Publi-

cations: Berlin, 1985); David W. Pearce, "Optimal prices for Sustainable development" in D. Collard, D.W. Pearce and D. Ulph (eds), *Economics, Growth and Sustainable Development* (Macmillan: London, 1988); and Pearsall, op. cit.

21. See, for example, Dasgupta, op. cit., and Jeffrey A. Krautkraemer, "Optimal growth, resource amenties and the preservation of natural environments", *Review of Economic Studies*, Vol. 52 (1985), pp. 153–70.

22. See, for example, Barbier, op. cit.; Robert A. Becker, "Intergenerational equity: The capital-environment trade-off", *Journal of Environmental Economics and Management*, Vol. 9 (1982), pp. 165–85; Bruce A. Forster, "Optimal consumption planning in a polluted environment", *Economic Record*, Vol. 49 (1973), pp. 534–45; Bruce A. Forster, "Optimal pollution control with a non-constant exponential rate of decay", *Journal of Environmental Economics and Management*, Vol. 2 (1975), pp. 1–6; Mäler, op. cit.; and Neil Vousden, "Basic theoretical issues of resource depletion", *Journal of Economic Theory*, Vol. 6 (1973), pp. 126–43.

23. Richard Norgaard, "Coevolutionary development potential", *Land Economics*, Vol. 60 (1984), pp. 160–73; and Richard Norgaard, "Environmental economics: An evolutionary critique and a plea for pluralism", *Journal of Environmental Economics and Management*, Vol. 12 (1985), pp. 382–94..

24. Following Becker, op. cit., and Mäler, op. cit., it is assumed that environmental quality is measured by a stock of environmental goods that yield a flow of services proportional to that stock in each time period. However, Becker, op. cit., defines this stock variable as "the differences between the level of pollution for which life ceases and the current level of pollution." Similarly, Mäler, op. cit., in his intertemporal models considers that only the quality and flow of waste residuals and recycling have an impact on environmental quality. Here, it is assumed that environmental quality may be affected not only by (net) waste generation but also by resource depletion and services to improve the environment, such as conservation and resource management. For a given type of ecosystem with its associated energy flow, a measure of environmental quality may include, in addition to Becker's definition, the ecosystem's biomass (i.e., the volume or weight of total living material found above or below ground) plus some measure of the distribution of nutrients and other materials between the biotic (living) and abiotic (non-living) components of the ecosystem. Such a measure is discussed in more detail in (Barbier, 1986, Chapter 8), and is more consistent with this model's broader concept of environmental degradation, which "comprises not just the loss of environmental quality that impinges on the senses, but also the damage to the natural purification and regenerative processes of the environmental itself" (Pearce, 1985b, p. 21).

25. See note 10 above and Chapter 2 on the distinctions between ecological stability and resilience.

26. U.S. Office for Technical Assessment, *Technology and the American Economic Transition* (OTA: Washington, DC, 1988).

27. See Page, op. cit., and Chapter 8.

28. International Institute of Tropical Agriculture, *Research Highlights for 1984* (IITA: Ibadan, Nigeria, 1985), pp. 22–6.

29. Smith and Krutilla, op. cit., p. 281.

30. Norgaard, "Environmental Economics", op. cit., p. 384.

31. For further discussion of these "limits" see Herman E. Daly, *Steady-State Economics* (W.H. Freeman; San Francisco, 1977); Herman E. Daly, "Entropy", op. cit.; Nicholas Georgescu-Roegen, *The Entropy Law and the Economic Process* (Harvard University Press: Cambridge, Massachusetts, 1971); and Nicholas Georgescu-Roegen, "Energy analysis and economic valuation", *Southern Economic Journal*, Vol. 45 (1979), pp. 1023–58.

32. Pierre R. Crosson and A.T. Stout, *Productivity Effects of Cropland Erosion in the United States* (Johns Hopkins University Press: Baltimore, 1983).

33. Hueting, op. cit., p. 141.
34. An earlier version of this model appeared in Barbier, "'Alternative' economic approaches to natural-resource scarcity", op. cit., Chapter 11; and in Barbier, "Alternative approaches to economic–environmental interaction", op. cit.
35. For this economic–environmental system, environmental degradation (or 'disorder') is assumed to occur in each period because the economic process must require some resource inputs $R_t$, for production and generate some net waste $N_t$. In fact, it may be possible to construct an index of environmental degradation that is proportional to some measure of $R_t$ and $N_t$. See Barbier, "'Alternative' economic approaches to natural-resource scarcity", op. cit., Chapter 8. However, the additional assumption that the result of environmental degradation is lower environmental quality in each period implies that: a) the level of environmental improvement services $V_t$, is insufficient to counteract the increased environmental degradation, and b) that ecosystems are unable to repair the resulting damage to crucial functions, cycles and resources, through converting the energy flow from the sun or utilizing any inputs of material and energy from neighbouring ecosystems. These are clearly strong assumptions that may not hold for all economic–environmental systems.
36. Note that, as discussed above and shown in Figire 5.1, some beneficial services of the environment (such as the maintenance of soil, air and water quality, or of climatic stability) directly aid economic production. This would suggest that environmental quality $X_t$ should also be included in the production function for economic output $Q_t$. However, to simplify analysis in this model, the more traditional production function for the economy is employed. Instead, the stream of benefits provided by environmental quality to production activities are included as part of the overall contribution of $X_t$ to welfare. Hence, $X_t$ in equation (1) can be interpreted as representing both the direct utility–yielding impacts of environmental quality on individuals and the indirect impacts on overall social welfare through assisting production and other intermediate economic activities. In any case, this may be a more appropriate way of accounting for these latter services, as their benefits are often externalities to private production and consumption allocation decisions.

# 6
# Two Examples: Deforestation in Amazonia and the Global Greenhouse Effect

In this chapter, Amazonian deforestation and the global greenhouse warming will be discussed as examples of the type of scarcity effects suggested by the alternative view. In looking at these two cases we are interested in two things: first, any evidence to support the alternative view and to indicate that its short- and long-term scarcity effects are real concerns; secondly, the potential impact of these effects on economic activity and a discussion of appropriate policy responses.

For the Brazilian Amazon, current economic policies, incentives and investment strategies have played a significant role in accelerating deforestation and forest degradation. Ameliorating the scarcity effects caused by Amazonian deforestation will mean modifying these policies. Similarly, there are a number of adaptive and preventive policy and investment strategies that should be considered if the consequences of a global warming are to be counteracted. The purpose of this chapter is to illustrate that the alternative view provides a logical framework for analysing the economic impacts of these scarcity effects, and thus for discussing the policy options available for combatting them.

## DEFORESTATION IN AMAZONIA

In the Amazon region of South America, increased economic exploitation is blamed for widespread deforestation and the degradation of the region's tropical forests.[1] This is leading to further ecological disruptions through changes in soil quality and erosion, water run-off, rainfall patterns and local climate. There may also be important consequences for the biosphere if excessive Amazonian deforestation continues. To understand the reasons for these concerns, it is necessary to appreciate the complexity of the Amazonian ecosystem.

## The Amazonian ecosystem

The Amazon River Basin covers an area of approximately 5.8 million km². It is shaped like a horseshoe and lies along the 6,500-km Amazon River and its tributaries. Roughly 70 % of this surface area is covered by tropical forest which extends into six South American countries – Brazil, Columbia, Peru, Venezuela, Ecuador and Bolivia. The Amazonian forest represents a significant proportion of the world's tropical forests; for example, Brazil – which contains around 67 % of the Amazonian tropical forest – accounts for one third of the global tropical moist forest.[2]

Together, its tropical forest and river system make Amazonia the wettest region of its size in the world, containing two-thirds of the earth's surface fresh water. Although the Amazon River system discharges one-fifth of all the river water that flows into the world's oceans and seas, more than half of the region's moisture remains within the ecosystem.[3] This is due to high rates of rainfall, and equally high rates of solar evaporation and tropical forest evapo-transpiration.

The vast Amazonian ecosystem can actually be classified into three distinct types: the *terra firme* (solid or dry ground) of the tropical forest proper; the *varzea* (swampy areas and flood lands) along the river banks flooded during rainy season and rich in nutrients; and the *igapos* (submerged areas) that are basically aquatic ecosystems fed by the various "black", "white" and "clear" water rivers. As these three ecosystems are closely linked, it is possible to view Amazonia as "a system that has achieved a steady state in its water cycle, nutrients, and energy balance ... presently a system in equilibrium."[4] Thus, the Amazon River Basin can be classified as an extensive, subsidized climax solar-powered ecosystem (see Table 2.1) which is virtually self-sufficient in material cycling and energy balance except for continuous inflows of solar radiation and a major influx of atmospheric water from the trade winds of the northern hemisphere.

In the past, the vastness of the Amazonian forests has allowed a balance between the use of forest resources for economic activity and sufficient preservation to ensure ecological stability and sustainability. For centuries, traditional forest dwellers have developed sustainable productive systems that minimize deforestation and degradation. Their economic activities have included hunting, fishing, crop growing, food gathering, and the use of trees to build homes and canoes. Important cultural mechanisms have been employed to prevent this livelihood being threatened by overpopulation. In Brazil, the forest-dwelling Indian population was estimated to be as high as six to nine million people in 1500.[5]

Similarly, traditional shifting cultivation – which involves clearing a small area of forest, burning some of the felled vegetation and leaving the remainder to decompose and gradually leach nutrients to the soil – can be a sustainable and self-contained system that minimizes deforestation. As long as the population density remains at two or three people per km², and the land is left fallow for at least ten years, then farmers need only clear the secondary forest that has grown on the fallow land. Often, the secondary forest is seeded with fruit or timber trees that make it valuable even when lying fallow. Thus many of these traditional systems have tremendous potential for not only meeting subsistence needs but also for generating marketable surpluses of valuable crops. Realizing this potential, however, requires a commitment to improving and encouraging the sustainable development of these systems.[6]

Appropriate agro-ecosystems for the fertile, alluvial flood plains have also been successfully developed. Although the *varzeas* cover only 2 % of Amazonia, with proper flood control, small-farmer production of irrigated rice, tree crops, food crops and jute – as well as water buffalo and fish – could be substantially improved without damaging the environment. Assuming a generous allocation of ten hectares (ha) per farmer, the flood plains could support up to one million farming household, or more than five million people. However, the successful development of the *varzeas* would depend upon controlling the clearance of the natural ground cover, drainage of the swamps and the excessive use of agro-chemicals.[7]

As Figure 6.1 shows, forest products from Amazonia can contribute to a number of important modern industries with minimum deforestation and environmental disruption, provided that the trees of the forest are properly harvested in order to limit unnecessary extraction and ecological damage. The phyto-chemicals derived from some forest products may prove to be ideal renewable substitutes as the price of petroleum-based synthetics increases. Although 400 of Amazonia's identified tree species are known to have commercial value, only 50 of them are being exploited, usually on an extensive scale without any regard for environmental destruction.[8] Because of the complex and highly specialized species interdependence, some forest products cannot be exploited unless the plants are allowed to remain fully integrated in their natural tropical environment.[9]

A preserved tropical forest ecosystem is also a source of genetic material for agriculture, industry, medicine and science. Although the world's tropical moist forests contain some 40 to 50 % of the earth's estimated five to ten million species, only 1 % have been subjected to intensive screening for their potential benefits to humankind. The Amazon is believed to contain at least 30,000 plant species – three times as much as in all of temperate South America. Some species have already been identified as possible sources of drugs to combat cancer, heart disorders, high blood pressure and other illnesses, and as safe contraceptives and fertility compounds. New industrial uses of forest genetic materials are being discovered, such as the development of new hybrids for boosting crop productivity and/or increasing resistance to pests.[10]

| | Catchment protection: | water supply, irrigation, soil fertility, controlled runoff. |
|---|---|---|
| *Ecological Functions* | Ecology and wildlife conservation: | recreation, national parks protection of flora and fauna. |
| | Soil erosion control: | windbreaks, reclamation of eroded lands, dune fixation. |
| | Fuelwood and charcoal: | cooking and heating. |
| | Agricultural uses: | forest grazing, fruit and nuts nitrogen fixation on mulches, shifting cultivation. |
| | Building poles: | housing, fencing, furniture. |
| *Indigenous Consumption* | Pit sawing and sawmilling: | furniture, farm buildings, joinery. |
| | Weaving materials: | ropes and strings, baskets, furniture and furnishings. |
| | Sericulture, apiculture and ericulture: | silk, honey, wax. |
| | Special woods and ashes: | carving, glassmaking, incense. |
| | Gums, resins and oils: | tannin, turpentine, distillates, resins and essential oils. |
| | Charcoal: | steelmaking, PVC, dry cells. |
| | Poles: | transmission poles, pitprops. |
| *Industrial Uses* | Sawlogs: | lumber, packing, furniture, mining, construction, sleepers. |
| | Veneer logs: | plywood, veneer, containers, construction. |
| | Pulpwood: | newsprint, paperboard, printing and writing paper, containers, packaging, distillates, textiles and clothing. |
| | Residues: | fibreboard, wastepaper. |
| | Industrial uses: | phyto-chemical substitutes for petroleum products, new forest products. |
| *Future Uses* | Agricultural uses: | new hybrids and crops. |
| | Medical and scientific uses: | drugs, contraceptives, fertility compounds, new sources of genetic material. |

## Figure 6.1:  Functions and Uses of a Tropical Forest

This diagram shows the kinds of ecological functions and sustainable economic activities that a relatively undisturbed Amazonian tropical forest system can provide.

Amazonia has traditionally existed, and could continue to exist, as a highly diverse and stable ecosystem capable of yielding essential environmental services and supporting a number of important economic activities. Exploitation of forest resources could increase even further provided that deforestation and environmental degradation is minimized. On a human timescale, the loss of such a highly developed ecosystem is tantamount to the loss of an irreplaceable asset; even if favourable conditions allow for it the regeneration of an integrated tropical ecosystem approaching the complexity and diversity of Amazonia would take tens if not hundreds of thousands of years.

### Increasing deforestation and degradation

Only rough estimates of the total amount of deforestation in Amazonia exist. For the Brazilian Amazon, official estimates from LANDSAT imagery indicate that by 1980, about 124,000 km$^2$ of tropical forest had been altered. This represents 2.47 % of the total area of the "Legal Amazon" region of Brazil, or 4.27 % of the original forest area.[11] Other estimates suggest that deforestation is proceeding at the rate of about 23,000 km$^2$ per year, and that some 290,000 km$^2$ – or about 10 % of the original forest – has been altered. Of the non-Brazilian forest in the Amazonian region, a total of 113,000 km$^2$ – about 9 % of the original forest – is also estimated to have disappeared. Thus a total of 403,000 km$^2$ of Amazonian forest has been deforested or degraded, which is almost 9.6 % of the original 4.2 million km$^2$. The deforestation rates seem to be accelerating in all the Amazonian countries, with the possible exception of Venezuela.[12]

The pattern of deforestation in Amazonia is highly concentrated and consists of two stages: road building, new settlements and the expansion of cattle-ranching to secure speculative claims come first; clearing these areas increases once they are established.[13] For example, forest areas undergoing major conversion at rapid rates include parts of Colombia's lowland rain forests, especially along the Caqueta and Putumayo Rivers, and parts of Brazil's eastern and southern sectors of Amazonian lowland rain forests, notably in Para, Mato Grasso and Rondonia. Both are due to cattle-raising colonist settlement and forest farming. There are additional areas of Amazonia undergoing moderate conversion at intermediate rates, such as much of Ecuador's Amazonian lowland and upland rain forest. Here the causes are colonist settlement, forest farming, some planned agriculture and oil exploration. Much of Peru's Amazonian lowland and upland rain forest is being converted by colonist settlement, forest farming and some planned agriculture. Other parts of Brazil's Amazonian lowland rain forests (notably in Amapa, Acre and sections along the Trans-American Highway system, the *varzea* flood plains and the Tapajas River area) have been converted by colonist settlement, forest farming, cattle raising and timber exploitation. Only after settlement has been well-established with surveyed plots and boundaries (as in the older official settlement areas in Rondonia), does the rate of forest clearing show any sign of slowing.[14]

Cattle ranching assisted by generous official subsidies is probably the greatest single factor behind this increasingly rapid deforestation. Estimates of the contribution of pasture formation to the total altered area of forest range from 38 to 73 %.[15] As population growth in the Brazilian Amazon has been increasing by 6.13 % per year – compared to a national rate of 2.78 % – small-farmer settlements are considered the second major cause of deforestation. Small farmers are thought to have been both directly and indirectly responsible for about 11 % of the Brazilian Amazon's deforestation by 1983.[16] Yet despite extensive settlement, the Brazilian Amazon still contains only about 5 % of the country's 147 million people.[17] Non-Brazilian regions of Amazonia are also suffering high deforestation rates as a consequence of small-farmer settlement; in Peru it has been estimated that some 3,000 new settlers destroy 20,000 ha of natural forest each year.[18]

Although the Amazon's share in national roundwood production doubled between 1975 and 1980, and the number of its saw mills increased from 194 in 1965 to 1,639 by 1982, the forest sector is more vital for the regional than for the national economy.[19] Most of Brazil's timber exports consist of mahogany, which is being heavily logged in Rondonia and south of Santaren. Given that only a few species of tree are commercially exploited and that the population density of any particular species is extremely low, vast areas of tropical forest must be covered in order to make logging feasible. There are other species of wood that either serve or could serve as substitutes for mahogany including virola, pau marfim, jacareuba, and jatoba or jutal. However, because there are adequate supplies of mahogany to meet current demands, there is little immediate incentive to commercially exploit other tree species.[20] Thus, extensive damage to the forest, in order to exploit a limited number of trees, is likely to continue. Further potential timber earnings are also frequently wasted when forest land is cleared for agriculture, ranching, road building, mining, hydro-electric schemes and other large-scale operations without any attempt to salvage commercially valuable trees.

The recent opening up of Amazonian areas to extensive economic exploitation has been highly destructive to the region's tropical forests. Yet the benefits, either in terms of increased national economic growth or of providing sustainable livelihoods for growing populations, seem to be far from dramatic. For example, the Brazilian Amazon contributes only 5 % to the country's GNP (gross national product), and the region's forests account for only 10 % of the national output of industrial timber.[21] These benefits look even less impressive when one examines the costs of the current pattern of Amazonian exploitation – both in terms of the relative and absolute scarcity effects caused by deforestation, and the economic distortions caused by policies to promote this pattern.

### Short-term effects: Declining environmental quality

Amazonian deforestation represents a significant increase in environmental degradation and ecological instability, which has two important scarcity impacts. First, as environmental quality declines, many natural services essential to human welfare and economic activity start to deteriorate or are lost. Secondly, extensive deforestation may eventually disrupt the crucial water, energy and nutrient cycles that link the integrated Amazonian ecosystem. This potential destabilization can be considered the long-term, absolute ecological constraint facing current economic exploitation of Amazonia. This second impact is discussed in the next section.

General environmental quality losses occurring in Amazonia include:

  i) the loss of the potentially useful genetic material of unique Amazonian species;
 ii) the decline of unique natural habitats and ecosystems that are the source of cultural, aesthetic and recreational benefits;[22]
iii) The disruption of the culture and livelihoods, and a decline in the population of traditional forest dwellers;[23]
 iv) the spread of endemic diseases and pests;[24] *and*
  v) The loss of productivity and other economic damage due to the water run-off, soil degradation and erosion accompanying deforestation. This often undermines the productivity of shifting cultivation, commercial cropping and ranching operations.[25] For example, after converted pasture is worked for two or three years, rainfall easily leaches nutrients from the thin surface soil (see Table 6.1). Soil run-off leads to the siltation of waterways and increased flooding, which affects cultivation and fishing in the flood plains.[26]

These losses in environmental quality are difficult to translate into monetary costs and few attempts have been made to estimate them in this way. This means that they are routinely ignored by those who decide on the policy for developing the Amazon. As a result, development projects, programmes and strategies do not consider the full costs of the ensuing environmental degradation, and hence fail to adequately compensate for them. Allocation of the region's scarce natural resources is thus automatically biased towards economic development that is less rather than more environmentally sustainable.

### Long-term effects: Climate change and destabilization

In the long term, deforestation may cause major disturbances in the

**Table 6.1: Changes with Time in the Composition of an Amazonian Forest Soil Converted to Pasture (Paragominas Region, Para State)**

| Sample | Organic Matter (%) | Nitrogen (%) | pH (a) | Ca²⁺ + Mg²⁺ (b) | Al³⁺ (b) | K⁺ (ppm) | Phos- (ppm) | Aluminium Saturation (%) |
|---|---|---|---|---|---|---|---|---|
| Forest soil before clearing | 2.79 | 0.16 | 4.4 | 1.47 | 1.8 | 23 | 1 | 53 |
| 1 yr of pasture | 2.04 | 0.09 | 6.5 | 7.53 | 0.0 | 31 | 10 | 0 |
| 3 yrs of pasture | 3.09 | 0.18 | 6.9 | 7.80 | 0.0 | 78 | 11 | 0 |
| 4 yrs of pasture | 2.20 | 0.11 | 5.4 | 3.02 | 0.2 | 62 | 2 | 6 |
| 5 yrs of pasture | 1.90 | 0.10 | 5.7 | 2.81 | 0.2 | 66 | 3 | 6 |
| 6 yrs of pasture | 1.90 | 0.09 | 6.0 | 3.84 | 0.0 | 74 | 7 | 0 |
| 7 yrs of pasture | 1.77 | 0.08 | 5.7 | 2.61 | 0.0 | 47 | 1 | 0 |

*Notes:* No additional application of fertilizer of legumes to land.
  (a) (H₂0)
  (b) (meq per 100 g)

*Source:* Enos Salati and P.B. Vose, "Amazon Basin: A system in equilibrium", *Science*, Vol. 225 (1984), pp. 129–38.

climate of Amazonia and its neighbouring regions. There is a danger that, as a whole, it may be pushed beyond the limits of its ecological tolerance. Such ecological destabilization would severely constrain any economic activity in Amazonia and would also affect human welfare.

The threat of adverse climatic change in Amazonia arises from the permanent loss of water from the region's hydrological cycle as deforestation spreads.[27] The increased water run-off and reduction in water absorption and retention by the disturbed soil means not only less evapotranspiration because of the eradication of vegetation, but less water stored in the soils as well. A 10–20 % reduction in the amount of recycled water would be sufficient to cause major alterations to the entire Amazonian ecosystem.[28] As this system relies on the extra energy input of frequent rainfall in order to recycle vital nutrients, even relatively small declines in precipitation could disrupt nutrient cycles and energy flows, and cause fluctuations in surface temperature.[29]

The complex interdependence of Amazonian ecosystems means that climatic change in one part of the Amazon will affect the stability of other areas. For example, as half the rain falling in Central and Western Amazonia is generated by water recycled from the Central and Eastern forests, deforestation in these areas would decrease rainfall in the West. Climatic change and ecological destabilization in Amazonia may therefore occur long before the region is completely deforested – perhaps even before 20 % of forest land is intensively altered.[30]

Disturbances in the local climate of the Amazon River Basin are likely to affect other South American regions. Although the South American climate is largely determined by the general circulation of hemispheric atmosphere and oceans, there is a degree of continentality dependent on the Amazonian climate and temperature. A net loss of water in Amazonia could reduce precipitation in the Chaco Paraguayo and in Central Brazil, shifting the climate towards increased continentality and affecting agriculture in south-central Brazil and other South American regions. For example, increased continentality could either extend the winter period or induce lower winter temperatures. This could result in the loss of valuable export earnings from sugar, oranges, soya beans and coffee production and cause major setbacks to Brazil's import-saving biomass fuel programme.[31]

The effect of Amazonian deforestation on the global climate is less clear. As the Amazonian forests have a significant impact on the global latent heat flux, in the early 1970s Newell argued that their destruction should have major repercussions on the general atmospheric circulation on earth.[32] Essentially, this would involve the expansion of the albedo effect to a global level, as Amazonian deforestation would expose a large portion of the earth's land surface, increasing the amount of solar reflection and generally causing worldwide temperature fluctuations. The second impact would be a major shift in hemispheric, and even global, rainfall patterns that could affect agricultural regions in North America and Europe.

Deforestation in Amazonia may contribute significantly to the global climatic changes associated with the greenhouse effect (see p. 133). Approximately 115 trillion tons of carbon are retained in the forest matter of Amazonia. Converting all of this forest biomass to pasture or annual crops would mean that, at most, 20 % of the carbon content of the former forest matter would remain fixed in the new vegetation. There would consequently be a net increase of about 8 % in the carbon dioxide ($CO_2$) content of the global atmosphere. Given that the 16 % increase in atmospheric $CO_2$ since the last century may have already caused some global warming, the additional contribution from Amazonian deforestation may be highly significant. Moreover, destroying the Amazonian forests may also further the global greenhouse effect by releasing important trace gases (e.g., methane, nitrous oxide, etc.) into the atmosphere.[33]

## Economic policy and the misuse of Amazonian resources

If the current pattern of economic development in Amazonia is leading to these environmental effects, as well as to increased social conflicts among smallholder squatters, larger commercial farmers, ranchers, and other developers and indigenous peoples, then clearly economic policies have not fully taken into account their cost. In the case of the Brazilian Amazon, this appears to have been a deliberate strategy:

> During the past 20 years official development strategy for the region has been, except for a brief interlude in the early 1970s, almost exclusively directed at the expansion of corporate forestry, agricultural and, more recently, mining interests virtually irrespective of any negative social and environmental side-effects.... Thus, the increased level of state intervention in Amazonia has served to attract cheap labour to the region (to prepare the rainforest for agricultural use by later incoming livestock and other farmers, as well as to supply temporary wage labour on estates) without allowing substantial small-scale ownership to take hold in a "pre-emptive" process of settlement by government and allied business interests.[34]

Such a strategy is exemplified by the recently launched US$ 1.18 billion Grande Carajas Program in the Eastern Amazon region of Brazil. Based around development of the world's largest high-grade iron ore deposit at Carajas, the 840,000 km$^2$ Program zone would include the development of 238,000 ha of mechanized soya beans, 12,600 ha of sugar cane, 417,000 ha of cattle pasture, and "enough rice to feed all of northeast Brazil". As a result, most of the money and land will go to large landholders for mechanized agriculture, cattle ranching and even silviculture; they will also receive the bulk of rural credit and an infrastructure aimed at facilitating the export of agricultural products, and the import of farm machinery and other inputs.[35]

Throughout the Brazilian Amazon, deliberate measures to promote this kind of economic development are estimated to have accounted for at least 35 % of all the forest area altered by 1980. Such policies include:

i) private capital investment in the Amazon region through tax incentives;
ii) agricultural production through rural credits;
iii) small-farmer settlement in the Amazon region through directed and semi-directed colonization; *and*
iv) exports of Brazilian products through export subsidies.[36]

Over the past two decades, the Superintendency for the Development of the Amazon (SUDAM), along with its sister organization Fundo de Investimento da Amazonia (FINAM), has been responsible for establishing incentive programmes for attracting private investment to the Brazilian Amazon. Over the period 1965 to 1983, direct tax credit subsidies worth U.S.$ 1.4 billion were granted to 808 existing and new private investment projects. Of these, around 35 % went to 59 industrial wood producers (mainly saw mills), and over 42 % went to 469 livestock projects (virtually all beef cattle production). Other tax incentives administered by SUDAM included tax holidays and deductions for operating losses.[37] Such tax breaks have clearly accelerated deforestation by subsidizing both the initial project development and the on-going operations of cattle ranchers, as well as the forest-products industry in Amazonia.

The cattle projects subsidized by SUDAM are estimated to have caused over 26 % of all forest-cover alteration from 1972 to 1980. Not only have SUDAM-financed livestock projects enjoyed generous long-term financing but, at 49,500 ha, the average size of the projects is substantially larger than the average non-SUDAM ones (9,300 ha). Thus SUDAM projects not only have a greater financial capacity to clear forest, but they also cover larger areas. Yet because SUDAM tax-credit funds are not allocated for maintenance, much clearing is not to increase the total net area in actual production but to replace already degraded fields. Perhaps 20–25 % of the forest area of the Legal Amazon that has been cleared for pasture is economically inactive.[38]

Without such generous subsidies, it is doubtful whether large-scale ranching in Amazonia would be economically viable. In fact, recent findings suggest that such projects are increasingly plagued by a low rate of implementation and with a high abandonment of pasture, attributed to the following economic factors:

i) Without any real appreciation of the land, no form of traditional ranching has a positive real rate of return in the Eastern Amazon – unless of course they receive the SUDAM incentives.

ii) Without over-grazing, real land values must appreciate at the rate of 30 % before the investments become economically viable.

iii) Even with improved pasture technologies, a real appreciation of land of between 15 and 30 % a year is required to make the rate of return to overall investment resources positive.

iv) Investors can maximize their private returns by overgrazing. They cannot improve their returns by investing in pasture improvement.[39]

The financial analysis of a typical SUDAM–financed ranch reveals that the discounted present value of net returns to the investor is US$ 1.87 million, nearly 2.5 times the investment outlay. If all subsidies were removed, however, the project would produce a net loss to the investor of US$ 0.65 million.[40]

Since 1970, the Brazilian government has subsidized directed and semi-directed programmes for small-farmer settlement in Amazonia. In general, this approach has been portrayed as a politically more acceptable option than the reform of traditional agricultural lands elsewhere in Brazil. While there are substantial differences in subsidy rates among such programmes – for example, a directed programme might spend US$ 13,000 per family in direct benefits compared to US$ 3,900 per family in a semi-directed programme – there appears to be a positive correlation between the consumption of subsidized financing and the area of forest cleared. Moreover, the impact on reducing rural population pressure in the rest of Brazil has been largely superficial; the two largest programmes are in Rondonia where, by 1980, only 48,417 families had been given either permanent or temporary land titles. Yet these two programmes were responsible for an estimated 6.6 % of the forest area altered in the Legal Amazon.[41]

Most of the extensive deforestation of the Amazon – over 15 million ha, by 1987 – can be directly related to government-financed programmes and subsidies, particularly for ranching and colonization. In addition, certain general macro-economic policies – such as the income tax, the land tax, and land titling regulations – are providing economic incentives for deforestation.

For example, a claimant who lives on an area of land has first preference to title for three times the area which he or she has cleared. This right is obtained if the claimant has used and lived on unclaimed public land for more than five years or has squatted on private land for a sufficiently long time without being challenged by the owner. Contrary to popular belief, as there are no vast areas of unclaimed land available for settlement in the Amazon, small farmers have difficulty in finding "free" land for squatting. Only corporations and large ranchers have the capital to build their own access roads into the forest, whereas squatters need to stick close to public roads in order to reach health, education and marketing facilities. So not only do the rules of land allocation encourage rapid deforestation by ranchers, as the final amount of land given legal title is a multiple of the area of forest converted to pasture, but clearing land also provides protection against squatters. This "first come first served" titling also ensures a rush to claim large tracts of land; plots of up to 3,000 ha are not uncommon. An unintended result of such land allocation procedures is that squatters are more likely to invade small forest reserves, which the forest service is finding increasingly difficult to guard.[42]

Similarly, as the land tax can be legally reduced by a factor of up to 90 % by converting unused forest land for a more productive "use", a farm containing forests is therefore taxed at a higher rate than one containing only pastures or cropland. Consequently, the land-tax system provides an incentive to larger farms which are liable for the progressive tax to convert their forests.[43]

As agriculture is virtually exempt from Brazil's income tax laws, these laws provide additional incentive for land acquisition in Amazonia by wealthy individuals and corporations – in addition to the already high demand for land as a hedge against inflation and risky financial markets. However, because small farmers or other poor individuals do not benefit from this tax break but do have to face the higher land prices that result from it, they are increasingly squeezed out of the land markets. Consequently, those without land have to resort to squatting on the Amazonian frontier, and those who do own land are tempted to sell out to larger landowners. As a result, the income tax

i) tends to increase the demand for land in Amazonia, to speed up conversion of land for agricultural uses, and to raise the price of land;

ii) tends to increase inequality in land ownership holdings; *and*

iii) increases the pace of migration of poor people to the frontier areas in search of land.[44]

## SUMMARY AND CONCLUSION

How soon, if ever, are we likely to see an ecological collapse in the Amazon? This is, of course, extremely difficult to predict. At current rates of deforestation, it may take 165 to 190 years before the remaining 3.8 million km$^2$ of Amazonian forest is completely altered or deforested. This cannot be considered a reliable estimate given the geographical concentration of deforestation – which has meant some areas experiencing an exponential growth in the rate of deforestation – and the unpredictable economic and social forces underlying Amazonian exploitation.

More alarming, however, is the prospect that any major environmental breakdown affecting Amazonia as a whole may be preceded by a series of severe, small-scale ecological disruptions in the heavily deforested areas. "The consequence will be that total annual rainfall will decrease considerably when a certain percentage of Amazon forest has been destroyed, and the seasonality of rainfall will become more pronounced."[45] Given that, at current rates of deforestation, another 15 % of the Amazonian forest will have disappeared within the next 25 years, the ecological and climatic threshold effects of rapid deforestation may already start manifesting themselves during the next two decades.

Certainly, for the Brazilian Amazon at least, current economic policies, incentives and investment strategies are accelerating the pace of deforestation and forest degradation. The two major sources of Amazonian deforestation – cattle ranching and small-farmer settlement – can be traced to direct government subsidy programmes. The same can be said for the new phase of Amazonian deforestation: large-scale agricultural development based around increased mineral exploitation. At the heart of this, however, is a whole economic strategy that is biased towards large landholdings and commercial developments at the expense of small-scale ownership. It is these complex economic and social roots that need to be tackled if the resulting short- and long-term scarcity effects are to be avoided.

## THE GLOBAL GREENHOUSE EFFECT[46]

The deforestation of Amazonia may involve irrevocable disruptions that could well be catastrophic to the local ecosystem and perhaps to many interregional ecosystems, but not necessarily to the entire global biosphere. In contrast, this section focuses on what may be a globally catastrophic ecological disturbance – the so-called "greenhouse effect". This effect is believed to result from an accumulation of carbon dioxide ($CO_2$) and trace gases in the atmosphere that trap the sun's radiation, thus slowly causing the earth's temperature to rise.

Most scientists seem to agree that, of the total annual emission rate of 5.5 to 7.0 billion (giga) tonnes of carbon, fossil fuels are the major source – accounting for approximately 5 to 5.2 gigatons.[47] Land-use changes in the tropics are a net source of at least 0.4 gigatonnes but not more than 1.6 gigatonnes, with tropical deforestation accounting for 0.3 to 1.3 gigatonnes and decreases in soil organic matter for 0.1 to 0.3 gigatonnes. Perhaps 0.1 gigatonnes is released from the kilning of limestone and 0 to 0.1 gigatonnes from land-use change in non-tropical ecosystems.[48]

As a result, atmospheric $CO_2$ concentration has increased exponentially from the pre-industrial level of about 280 parts per million by volume (ppmv) *circa* 1750, to about 315 ppmv in 1958, and about 346 ppmv in

1985. An upper estimate suggests that the $CO_2$ concentration might be double the pre-industrial level by the middle of the next century, whereas a lower estimate implies that this will not occur until after 2100.

Recent evidence suggests that the increased emission of trace gases will significantly add to any $CO_2$ greenhouse effect. Although their contribution is still relatively small, the atmospheric trace gases that currently have the largest radiative effects are methane $(CH_4)$, nitrous oxide $(N_2O)$, tropospheric ozone $(O_3)$ and the chloroflurocarbons (CFCs). Emissions of $CH_4$ and $N_2O$ are clearly linked to the growth of human populations and agricultural development, whereas the emissions of CFCs (as well as $O_3$) are largely a by-product of certain industrial processes and products. As a result of increases in these economic activities, the atmospheric concentrations of these trace gases are expected to increase quickly. Thus within the next 50 years, the radiative effect of the trace gases may exceed that of the increasing $CO_2$ concentration. CFCs, in particular, will have an increasingly important impact (second only to $CO_2$) on the greenhouse effect.[49]

By including the warming effect of trace gases, the equivalent of a doubling in $CO_2$ could occur as early as 2030. By then, most estimates suggest that we could experience an actual increase in present temperatures of between 1.0 to 2.1°C, and because the thermal inertia of the ocean delays the full warming effect, we could be subject to an eventual increase in temperatures of 1.5 to 3.1°C.[50]

### The greenhouse effect and climatic change: Two scenarios

Any global warming resulting from the greenhouse effect will probably be uneven, with an increase of only 0.5–1°C at the equator, 2–3⁰ at temperate latitudes, and as much as 4–7°C in the polar regions.[51] The result of such a distribution may be to shift climatic zones and rainfall patterns. Changes in the seasonal distribution of precipitation within regions could also be significant.[52] The polar regions could experience the greatest changes in the long run, and there is the possibility that the polar ice-caps may melt sufficiently to raise world sea levels. It is worth distinguishing two potential scenarios: the most likely scenario in the short term, of changes in regional precipitation and climatic zones; and a more dramatic long-term scenario of a global sea-level rise.

Table 6.2 shows that, as a result of global warming, the most extreme temperature changes would probably occur during winter in the high latitudes of the northern hemisphere. In contrast, temperature changes in the lower latitudes will probably be less drastic and less seasonally variable. Although forecasting regional precipitation is full of uncertainties, the most likely outcome is increased winter precipitation in the high latitudes, intensified rains in the low latitudes – except in semi-arid regions – and a decrease in summer rainfall in the mid-latitudes.[53]

Perhaps the most dramatic recent consensus among scientists has been that global warming should cause a rise in the global mean sea level. The major cause would be the thermal expansion of oceans, possibly aggravated by changes in land ice. The sea level has probably already risen 7 to 17 cm during the twentieth century, although it is not possible to attribute this solely to the greenhouse effect. On the basis of these observed changes, it is assumed that the predicted global warming of 1.5 to 5.5°C would lead to a sea-level rise of 20 to 165 cm. The "best guess" for sea level rise by the year 2030 is 20–40 cm; however, the rise could conceivably be as much as 1.5 meters.[54]

In an extremely pessimistic scenario, any rise in temperature of 2–4°C due to an increase in atmospheric carbon dioxide to 600 ppmv or more, may cause the polar ice caps to melt sufficiently to raise the sea level of the major oceans by 5 m or more.[55] However, disintegration of the West Antarctic Ice Sheet is not thought to be imminent and, if it were to happen, would take at least a century. Yet some disintegration of the West Antarctic Ice Sheet has been observed: along a 1,200-km ice front on the Sheet, some 500 cubic km of ice are being deposited each year into the sea in the form of huge icebergs. This could result in a rise in the sea level of 1.5 mm per year, which has in fact been observed by independent studies of global tidal patterns.[56] These recent trends are inconclusive, and further research is required before a reliable assessment of the possibility and timing of this scenario can be made.[57]

## Short-term effects: Agricultural and ecological disruption

The most likely impact of any global warming in the near future will be on world rainfall distribution. As rainfall patterns change, climatic zones will shift and the earth's principal areas of agricultural cultivation and vegetation cover will be displaced.

### *Agriculture*
As shown in Table 6.2, several major agricultural producing regions may be at risk from global warming. These include:

  i) the irrigated semi-arid areas of Northern mid-latitudes, particularly in the US MidWest;
 ii) the lowland areas and island countries of the humid tropics in Asia, the Pacific and Caribbean that are susceptible to excessive precipitation, violent storms and flooding;
iii) the arid and semi-arid tropics of Africa, South Asia and the Mediterranean climate of West Asia and North Africa that are already vulnerable to climate variability;
 iv) rain-fed upland and highland regions, particularly with poor soil conditions; *and*
  v) livestock raising in extreme Northern latitudes.[58]

**Table 6.2: Regional Scenarios for Climate Change**

| Region | Temperature change (as a multiple of global average) Summer | Winter | Rainfall Change |
|---|---|---|---|
| High latitudes (60–90 deg) | 0.5× – 0.7× | 2.0× – 2.4× | Enhanced in winter |
| Mid latitudes (30–60 deg) | 0.8× – 1.0× | 1.2× – 1.4× | Possibly reduced in summer |
| Low latitudes | 0.9× – 0.7× | 0.9× – 0.7× | Enhanced in places with heavy rainfall today |

*Source:* Jill Jaeger, "The development of an awareness of a need to respond to climatic change", Expert Group on Climatic Change and Sea Level Rise (Beijer Institute and Commonwealth Secretariat: London, 19–20 May 1988, Table 1.

Bryson estimated that the 0.1⁰C rise in global mean temperatures between 1957 and 1970 (due to increased atmospheric $CO_2$) should have led to an 86-mm decrease in annual rainfall levels in the Sahel of West Africa. In fact, the actual decrease in the Sahel over this period was 96 mm.[59] Similarly, Glantz and Ausubel have argued that if atmospheric $CO_2$ accumulation increases the frequency, duration and severity of droughts in the Great Plains of the U.S., more rapid depletion of water contained in the Ogallala Aquifer – the underground geological formation of water-bearing porous rocks – would occur. The Aquifer's reserves currently serve eight Western states. Depletion of these reserves could have serious consequences for agricultural production in the Great Plains, one of the world's major food-exporting regions.[60]

Table 6.3 summarizes the alterations in some of the world's major river systems that global warming has caused. All those affected, listed in Table 6.3, form the basis of highly productive irrigated agricultural systems. Changes could occur in the flows or storage capacities of these rivers. There could be less surface and underground flow, or more frequent flooding both of which would be disastrous for irrigated agriculture. In many countries, these systems have been intensively developed in correspondence with the precise seasonal variations of delta flooding and run-off. Changes in seasonal flows would mean severe disruptions in cultivation. Moreover, many river systems do not have adequate water control and management facilities to cope with any variations in flooding

**Table 6.3: Major River Systems Affected by Carbon-Dioxide Induced Climatic Change**

A. Rivers Experiencing Decreases in Flows

| River System | Location |
|---|---|
| Hwang Ho | China |
| Amu Darya | Soviet Union |
| Ayr Darya | Soviet Union |
| Tigris-Euphrates | Turkey, Syria, Iraq |
| Zambezi | Zimbabwe, Zambia |
| Sao Francisco | Brazil |

B. Rivers Experiencing Some Flow and Storage Loss

| River System | Location |
|---|---|
| Congo | Central Africa |
| Rhone | Western Europe |
| Po | Western Europe |
| Danube | Eastern Europe |
| Yangtze | China |
| Rio Grande | United States, Mexico |

C. Rivers Experiencing Increases in Flows

| River System | Location |
|---|---|
| Niger | Africa |
| Chari | Africa |
| Senegal | Africa |
| Volta | Africa |
| Blue Nile | Africa |
| Mekong | Indochina |
| Brahmaputra | South Asia |

*Source:* Roger Revelle, "Carbon dioxide and world climate," *Scientific American*, Vol. 247 (1982), pp. 753–9.

or underground storage. For example, in the lowlands of the humid tropics, the result could be destructive flooding in the vast delta networks of Thailand, Laos, Cambodia, Vietnam, India, China and Bangladesh.

A more detailed analsis of the impact of temperature rises on the river systems of the semi-arid Western and mid-Western states in the US suggests that only modest changes in temperatures are necessary for severe agricultural disruptions to occur. For example, a $2^0$C warming combined with a 10 % decrease in precipitation would cause surface run-off into rivers to decline by between 40 and 76 %. For the Rio Grande, Colorado and Missouri Rivers in particular, the result could mean water requirements exceeding supplies by 20 to 270 %.[61] In the region of the

Colorado River, such a climate change would be particularly severe. Currently in this area, 85 % of the rainfall evaporates and only 15 % (as run-off) feeds the Colorado River. Even this flow has to be backed up by large volumes of reservoir water in order to meet the present agricultural demands of the region.[62] As noted above, however, the region's main reservoir source – the Ogallala Aquifer – cannot be expected to sustain any long-term increase in demand.

With the possible exception of semi-arid irrigated agriculture in the Western and mid-Western US, the overall impact of global warming on temperate agriculture in the mid-latitudes of the northern hemisphere is unclear. For example, many crops (such as rice, wheat, alfalfa, maize, sugar cane and sorghum) suffer productivity losses due to a decrease in rainfall and an increase in evaporation; this problem may be alleviated by the increased photosynthesis and improved water efficiency of plants that can result from raised $CO_2$ levels.[63] At higher northern latitudes, rising temperatures may lead to a longer growing season and so to the possible expansion of rain-fed areas. In the lower latitude zone of the 30 to 60°N band, agriculture might be adversely affected because of the increased evapo-transpiration.[64]

It is clear that farmers in the mid-latitudes of the northern hemisphere will have to respond to any greenhouse effect by modifying seed varieties and cultivation methods, changing crops, and moving agricultural operations away from the worst affected areas. As Oram has pointed out, this in itself may cause significant declines in productivity: first, because it is by no means certain that a rise in temperature would enable large new areas of land at higher latitudes to be brought into cultivation – land at higher latitudes is at the margin of cultivation and often of very low fertility, with low pH and anaerobic conditions due to low drainage; and secondly, as modern agriculture has become more sophisticated, there has been a trend away from trying to breed for wide adaptability toward tailoring varieties to favourable agro-climatic conditions.[65]

Similarly, a study by the US National Academy of Sciences has concluded that, although the direct impact of $CO_2$ enrichment in the US (to 400 ppmv by the year 2000) may be to increase yields of well-tended crops by 5 %, the accompanying 1°C rise in temperature and 5–10 % decrease in precipitation may actually produce a negative net effect on agricultural production.[66] Other crop impact analyses also show that warmer average temperatures are detrimental to both wheat and maize yields in the mid-latitude regions of North America and Western Europe. Given current technology and crop varieties, a sudden warming of 2°C with no change in precipitation might reduce average yields by 3 to 17 %.[67]

The sensitivity of the marginal agricultural lands in the developing world to climatic change is of the greatest concern. How a global warming might interact with the increasing desertification of both rain-fed croplands and rangelands is particularly uncertain in the arid and semi-arid tropics. At present, 1,300 million hectares (ha) of rangelands (35 % of their dryland total) and 170 million ha of rain-fed croplands (30 % of their dryland total) are severely or very severely desertified. That is, they have lost more than 25 % of their productivity and require extensive reclamation. The areas most vulnerable are the semi-arid and arid humid tropics – the regions at great risk from the greenhouse effect. By the year 2000, desertification is expected to have accelerated greatly in the rangelands of Andean South America, in Africa south of the Sudano–Sahel region, and, to a lesser extent, in the Sudano–Sahel region and parts of South Asia. For rain-fed croplands, desertification is accelerating in tropical Africa, South Asia and South America.[68]

Any worldwide impacts on agriculture and human welfare from a global warming will undoubtedly be unevenly spread. As Oram has pointed out, in analysing these impacts, "the first step would be to look at global supply and demand for food with emphasis on cereals for food and feed, and on the major consuming and exporting countries." The two key groups to look at would be the major Northern food-exporting countries and the low-income, food-deficit developing countries. Clearly, the ability to adapt agriculture to changing climatic and environmental conditions will also be distributed unevenly between these two groups. "In a tight grain situation prices would rise and richer countries would have the first call; little might be left for concessional sales or aid. Internationally, the major food-exporting countries would probably benefit substantially; and importers with weak bargaining power, and the poor in those countries, especially the landless labourers, would be the chief sufferers."[69]

Although the wealthier nations of the northern hemisphere could face drastic changes in areas of arable land, the distribution of water resources and the type of products cultivated, these countries tend to have a surplus of land available for production as well as accumulated surplus stocks of some produce, highly developed agricultural R & D infrastructure and techniques, efficient marketing, credit and information systems and extensive water management and control systems. It is more likely, therefore, that Northern nations will be able to meet most of their own agricultural and food needs despite any adverse climatic and environmental changes. It is also likely, however, that the need for these countries to adjust their agricultural production to such changes may involve less production for export and thus fewer global supplies of many essential agricultural products. In addition, any adjustments to major changes in climate, precipitation and temperature will require extensive modifications in existing patterns of cultivation and water management. For Northern countries, this may mean diverting resources from other areas of economic activity and a corresponding rise in the costs of agricultural production.

The most serious repercussions, however, may be on the export and distribution of world food and feed supplies, particularly cereals. Cereals are the dominant crop in the global agricultural system, and wheat is the major surplus food commodity both in world trade and aid. As shown in Table 6.4, the majority of global cereals (including wheat) are produced in the temperate northern hemisphere. Given the surplus production in some of these countries (e.g., the US, Canada and Western Europe), it is not surprising that wheat has become a major feed crop in industrialized countries, and the main fallback for much of the world in terms of reserve stocks and contingency aid. Wheat and barley are also extremely important staple crops in the developing countries of North Africa and the Middle East, as well as in Pakistan, Northern India and China.

By contrast, in the semi-arid tropics – the region of high climatic risk – maize, sorghum, millet, pulses and groundnuts are the major staples. However, countries of this region are also heavily dependent on cereal (mainly wheat) imports and food aid.[70] Although many countries of the lowland humid tropics – especially in Asia – are major producers of rice and other crops, some of them may cease to be self-sufficient if their main food crops (e.g. rice, cassava, sweet potatoes and yams) are adversely affected by a greater intensity of rainfall, tropical storms and flooding. This suggests that during periods of global climatic instability, the failure or unwillingness of the food-exporting northern hemisphere producers to supply, at reasonable prices, the rest of the world with cereal imports or aid may have important implications for global food security.

The food-security needs of the very poor in all developing regions, and the food-deficit low income countries in particular, are vulnerable to the agricultural shocks and stresses posed by climatic instability. Between 1980 and 2000, increased total food demand is projected to exceed the growth of food output in all developing regions except Asia. This is despite increases in per capita food production in Latin America, North Africa and the Middle East. Even though Latin America is expected to have the highest food production per capita growth rate, demand is projected to increase even more rapidly. With its fast population growth, Sub-Saharan Africa's food consumption is estimated to grow by 3.6 % a year, substantially outpacing the projected growth in food output. Per capita food production in the region is expected to continue to decline.[71]

Even in the absence of disruptions to agriculture from climatic change, many developing regions will continue to be dependent on food imports, and in some instances external assistance, in order to meet domestic consumption needs. The lack of food security – defined as the access by all people at all times to enough food for an active, healthy life – may therefore increasingly arise from a lack of purchasing power on the part of nations and households rather than from inadequate food supplies.[72] The disturbing facts are that food security is already worsening in many developing countries, despite higher per capita food production; despite record levels of world food production and excess supplies, about 730

**Table 6.4: Share in Principal Crops and Livestock of Major Producers in Affected Regions**

| | Cereals | Soya Beans | Maize | Wheat | Barley | Oats | Rice | Potatoes | Coffee | Cocoa | Livestock |
|---|---|---|---|---|---|---|---|---|---|---|---|
| **I. 30–50°N** | | | | | | | | | | | |
| Canada | 3.0 | 0.7 | 1.4 | 5.3 | 8.4 | 8.1 | – | 1.0 | – | – | 0.7 |
| United States | 20.1 | 62.8 | 46.1 | 16.6 | 6.6 | 16.8 | 2.0 | 5.9 | – | – | 6.2 |
| Europe | 14.7 | 0.6 | 11.9 | 20.1 | 41.8 | 32.6 | 0.4 | 43.3 | – | – | 14.0 |
| Soviet Union | 10.1 | 0.6 | 1.8 | 19.2 | 27.1 | 34.4 | 0.6 | 28.0 | – | – | 10.4 |
| China | 17.2 | 9.1 | 13.6 | 12.4 | 2.1 | 1.4 | 35.4 | 5.8 | 0.2 | – | 15.2 |
| | 65.1 | 73.8 | 74.8 | 73.8 | 86.0 | 93.0 | 38.4 | 84.0 | 0.2 | – | 36.2 |
| **II. 0–20°S** | | | | | | | | | | | |
| Brazil | 1.9 | 17.0 | 4.7 | 0.5 | – | 0.2 | 2.0 | 0.7 | 32.1 | 20.7 | 4.8 |
| Indonesia | 2.2 | 0.7 | 0.9 | – | – | – | 8.0 | 0.1 | 4.5 | 0.6 | 0.4 |
| | 4.1 | 17.7 | 5.6 | 0.5 | – | 0.2 | 10.0 | 0.8 | 36.6 | 21.3 | 5.2 |
| TOTAL | 69.2 | 91.5 | 75.4 | 74.3 | 86.0 | 93.2 | 48.4 | 84.8 | 36.8 | 21.3 | 41.4 |

*Source:* Edward B. Barbier, "Economic and environmental aspects of rising carbon dioxide levels", paper presented at the Input–Output Research Association Conference, The Environment and Input–Output Analysis (Pembroke College: University of Cambridge, 29 June 1985), Table 2.

million people in developing countries do not obtain enough energy from their diet to allow them to lead an active working life. About two-thirds of the undernourished live in South Asia and a fifth in Sub-Saharan Africa; four-fifths live in countries with very low average incomes.[73]

Although all 65 low-income food-deficit countries identified by the Food and Agricultural Organization of the United Nations (FAO) are potentially vulnerable to climatic instability,[74] those that have failed to increase per capita food production are especially at risk (see Table 6.5). Increasing food production in these countries is essential in order to meet long-term food needs, as their extremely limited ability to purchase food imports is unlikely to improve in the near future. Moreover, data collected up to 1982 suggest that adequate growth in domestic cereal production in low-income food-deficit countries and a healthy growth in export earnings generally go together; both are important determinants of the ability of a country to ensure food security.[75] Yet, most of the countries listed in Table 6.5 have substantial agricultural lands in arid and semi-arid regions or at high altitudes – areas at the greatest risk from a global warming.

The economic impact of any greenhouse effect will most likely be in terms of the rising costs of agricultural displacement and adaption in the face of climatic instability, with potentially grave consequences for the pattern and distribution of global food production and for food security in many developing regions. As a result, sustaining even minimal nutritional standards for millions of people in the Third World will require a generous surplus of world agricultural supplies to be made available through food imports or aid. In recent years, the demand for such a surplus has been steadily rising – during the frequent drought crises it has shot up.[76]

Any decline in production in Northern countries may either perpetuate a global food shortage or raise food prices beyond levels that many low-income importing countries can afford. In either situation, the ability of millions to survive in the Third World would depend on the political will of Northern countries to ration existing global supplies at lower prices and to establish an international system of food security for the world's population. Northern countries would not only have to set aside more economic resources for adjusting their agricultural systems to the changing global climate and environment, but would also have to be willing to expend further resources to support a global food-security system and to expand agricultural investment in developing countries. The alternative is to allow developing countries to bear the brunt of the costs of global warming.

*Forests*
Any impacts that climatic change had on the world's major ecosystems would also affect human welfare. This may be particularly true for the

**Table 6.5: Low Income Food Deficit Countries with Low Food Production Growth[a]**

| | Value added in agriculture (millions of 1980 dollars) | | Cereal imports (thousands of tonnes) | | Food aid in cereals (thousands of tonnes) | | Average index of food production per capita (1979–81 = 100) |
|---|---|---|---|---|---|---|---|
| | 1970 | 1985 | 1974 | 1985 | 1974/75 | 1984/85 | 1983–85 |
| *Africa* | | | | | | | |
| Angola | x | x | 149 | 377 | 0 | 78 | 102 |
| Burundi | 468 | 598 | 7 | 20 | 6 | 17 | 106 |
| Cen.Afri.Rp. | 256 | 333 | 7 | 17 | 1 | 12 | 105 |
| Chad | 416 | x | 37 | 134 | 20 | 163 | 106 |
| Ethiopia | 1,634 | 1,531 | 118 | 986 | 54 | 869 | 97 |
| Guinea | x | 805 | 63 | 140 | 49 | 47 | 102 |
| Kenya | 1,198 | 2,263 | 15 | 365 | 2 | 340 | 99 |
| Lesotho | 88 | x | 49 | 118 | 14 | 72 | 93 |
| Malawi | 258 | 426 | 17 | 23 | x | 5 | 105 |
| Mauritania | 200 | 222 | 115 | 240 | 48 | 135 | 94 |
| Mozambique | x | 477 | 62 | 426 | 34 | 366 | 98 |
| Niger | 1,466 | 1,070 | 155 | 247 | 73 | 218 | 96 |
| Rwanda | 295 | 614 | 3 | 24 | 19 | 36 | 106 |
| Senegal | 603 | 615 | 341 | 510 | 27 | 130 | 105 |
| Somalia | 589 | 911 | 42 | 344 | 111 | 248 | 102 |
| Togo | 238 | 325 | 6 | 79 | 11 | 23 | 103 |
| Zambia | 473 | 659 | 93 | 247 | 5 | 112 | 107 |
| *Near East* | | | | | | | |
| Afghanistan | x | x | 5 | 50 | 10 | 50 | 104 |
| Sudan | 1,754 | 1,511 | 125 | 1,082 | 46 | 812 | 103 |
| Yemen, PDR | x | x | 149 | 357 | x | 25 | 100 |
| *Far East* | | | | | | | |
| Philippines | 5,115 | 9,104 | 817 | 1,524 | 89 | 68 | 103 |
| Sri Lanka | 812 | 1,294 | 951 | 1,071 | 271 | 276 | 98 |
| *Latin America* | | | | | | | |
| Bolivia | 380 | 496 | 209 | 459 | 22 | 111 | 101 |
| El Salvador | 740 | 847 | 75 | 224 | 4 | 194 | 100 |
| Haiti | x | x | 83 | 227 | 25 | 101 | 104 |
| Honduras | 477 | 702 | 52 | 99 | 31 | 118 | 104 |

*Notes:* [a] Low-income food-deficit countries as defined by FAO (1985), below.
x = figures not available.

*Sources:* FAO, Committee on Commodity Problems, 55th Session, *International Trade and World Food Security*, Rome, 21–25 October 1985; and *World Bank, World Development Report 1987*, Washington, DC, 1987.

major forest systems which are so crucial in stabilizing regional climates. For example, the boreal forests found at higher northern latitudes across the continents of Eurasia and North America are particularly vulnerable. However, current evidence is inconclusive. Some studies indicate that rising temperatures might cause the boreal forests to be replaced either by cool temperature forest or by steppes, depending on the accompanying changes in precipitation. The generally warmer conditions at these high latitudes could possibly lead to large reductions in the areal extent of boreal forests and a shift toward the North Pole in their boundaries.[77] In contrast, a study based on Icelandic conditions estimates a net increase in the growth of boreal forest systems as the climate warms.[78] Nevertheless, any major change in the boreal forests, whether a net growth or a decline, will most probably affect the overall ecological balance of higher Northern latitudes and lead to important feedback effects between local climatic zones and vegetation cover.

For the mid-latitude temperate forests in the northern hemisphere, a high rate of warming (0.8 to 1°C) per decade will cause major impacts including large-scale forest dieback between 2000 and 2050. The result would be that more and more production forests would need replanting and increased management. The additional costs may not be economically worthwhile for formerly unmanaged forests.[79] Furthermore, there will be impacts on recreational values if important national parks and wildlife habitats are decimated.

There could also be dramatic impacts on the major tropical forests of the world, such as the extensive Indonesian, Amazonian and Central African tropical forest systems. A typical rain forest system such as Amazonia is dependent on only small variations in average annual temperatures (such as 3°C) and high annual rainfall (such as 1,500 to 3,000 mm). Changes in these conditions would destabilize the unique climate and nutrient-cycling systems of tropical forests, and may also affect neighbouring ecosystems and climatic zones. As tropical deforestation is expected to increase over the coming decades, tropical forest systems will become even more vulnerable to any additional climatic stress induced by the greenhouse effect. Thus, not only will tropical deforestation contribute in a major way to this greenhouse effect but tropical forest themselves may fall victim to any resulting global warming.[80]

## Long-term effects: sea level rise

Although the pessimistic scenario of the collapse of the West Antarctic Ice Sheet may not occur for a century or two, if ever, the possibility of a rise in global sea levels has been taken seriously by many scientists. Even a modest sea-level rise could have grave implications, particularly for low-lying, island and coastal nations. This could occur in the following way:

The primary effects on coastal environments result from increased rates of coastal erosion, salt intrusion into surface groundwater systems and coastal ecosystems, and temporary and permanent flooding, including the risks from storm surges. These, in turn, have secondary impacts on agriculture, water resources, commercial and residential property, energy systems, transportation systems, and so on. These effects can then be evaluated in terms of their 'down-stream' tertiary impacts: on human health (e.g., mortality and morbidity), economic loss (e.g., loss of agricultural production), loss of valued environments (e.g., recreational beach) and social disruption (e.g., from storm surge disasters). The evaluation of policies and strategies to reduce the potential adverse effects depends on impact assessments which integrate these first, second and third-order effects.[81]

Almost every country with significant regions near sea level would be affected. For example, even a one-meter rise would require expenditures of between US$ 10 to 100 billion to maintain threatened beaches and coastal areas on the eastern coast of the US. A study of the Delaware Estuary has shown that over the next 40 years, an additional upstream reservoir capacity of 136 million m³ will be required to protect Philadelphia's domestic water supply from salt-water intrusion.[82]

In particular, low-lying, densely populated countries – such as Bangladesh and the Netherlands – will be affected. In the Netherlands, existing dikes and other protection against storm surges would have to be reinforced at a cost of US$ 3.1 to 8.8 billion for a 70- or 200-cm sea-level rise respectively. In contrast, the densely populated and mainly agricultu-ral low-lying Ganges–Brahmaputra–Meghna River Delta in Bangladesh has always been poorly protected from frequent tropical cyclones, storm surges and flooding. If rising sea levels increase the risks of storm surges and intensified land degradation, the consequences could be disastrous; the combination of sea-level rise and subsidence of the river system could flood the Delta region and threaten anywhere between 8 and 24 million people.[83]

A rise of half a meter would also severely affect small oceanic islands, particularly the low-reef islands and atolls. The result could be a substantial reduction in island size, and shifts and reductions in shorelines. Other direct impacts include decreased fresh-water capacity due to salt-water intrusion, greater exposure to salinization, and the increased risk of sea surge and storm damage. This would mean less land available for food production, more extensive food shortages, and a greater risk of malnutrition and other health problems. The eventual consequences for human populations would certainly be the movement of settlements from coastlines, possibly with mass migrations from low to high islands, to urban centres, and to continental countries.[84]

The above evidence suggests that a major sea-level rise over the next century, could entail the most significant change in global economic systems and standards of living since the Industrial Revolution. Any shift of coastal populations to the remaining land mass areas would lead to an intensification of population densities. Increased population pressure would in turn place greater stress on the people–nature balance of these interior regions, and many areas of previously undisturbed ecosystems would be converted to replace lost areas of cultivation and industry. The resulting stress on the biosphere may be unsustainable. Many regions, particularly the most overpopulated ones, could suffer from severe drought, famine and shortages of essential raw materials. The net global impact may be a drastic lowering of standards of living, physical well-being and even substantial loss of life.

On the other hand, if the rise in sea level is a more gradual process that takes over a century to happen, and one that is carefully monitored and accurately forecast, then some of the consequences could be avoided by constructing extensive dikes and water control systems, and by moving populations and economic activities to unaffected areas. Nevertheless, this would still involve major global economic and political co-operation, at significant costs. As always, wealthier nations with better resource endowments – especially fertile land available further inland and/or above sea level – will be tempted to 'look after their own' rather than to assist less fortunate regions.For all nations, careful monitoring of the sea-level rise – particularly the process of ice-cap disintegration – would at least help the necessary planning effort and reduce some of the economic costs and social burdens of any future catastrophes.

### Appropriate policy responses

In considering appropriate policy responses to global warming, it is necessary to keep in mind two additional aspects of the problem: the unpredictable discontinuity of climatic changes and the way in which they magnify the likelihood of so-called "natural" disasters. For example, commenting on the greenhouse effect, Broecker makes the case that changes in the earth's climate are more likely to be sudden than gradual:

> Earth's climate does not respond to forcing in a smooth and gradual way. Rather, it responds in sharp jumps which involve large-scale reorganization of Earth's system. If this reading of the natural record is correct, then we must consider the possibility that the main responses of the system to our provocation of the atmosphere will come in jumps whose timing and magnitude are unpredictable. Coping with this type of change is clearly a far more serious matter than coping with a gradual warming.[85]

Similarly, "in terms of environmental and socio-economic impacts, the slow changes in mean climate or sea level may often be manifested as large changes in the risks of extreme events." For example, "threats from future sea level rise and salt water intrusion are linked to extreme drought occurrence, since existing water resource supply systems are, based on past experience, already adjusted to only comparatively moderate fluctuations in precipitation and resultant salt intrusion."[86] Both these aspects of climatic change need to be carefully considered in the design of policy measures to counter the greenhouse effect.

Figure 6.2 shows the likely range of policy responses to global warming and their appropriate stage of intervention in the greenhouse effect "causal chain". Note that the essential trade-off is between doing nothing now – which obviously involves smaller current costs but obviously may incur greater future costs in terms of reducing vulnerability and modifying effects – and investing heavily in the control and reduction of fossil fuel emissions, or in the more sustainable management of tropical forests, in order to avoid anticipated future costs. This trade-off is also illustrated in Figure 6.3, which indicates that a concerted effort to limit the greenhouse effect in advance through reducing emissions for example, would involve higher relative costs in the present but would avoid the costs incurred by forced adaption and residual impacts in the future. However, a concerted effort to reduce emissions would at least lower the costs of an anticipatory action, such as the building of dikes, water storage, irrigation and so forth.

We are only beginning to understand the nature of the policy options available to us in the face of a global warming; a full assessment of the costs and benefits of each option is not yet possible. Nevertheless, several points crucial to this analysis are worth highlighting:

i) There is clearly a *waiting cost for doing nothing*; the best guess is that we are already committed to some global warming in the near future (e.g., 1.5 to 4.5°C). The longer we do nothing, the higher will be the future costs of forced adaption and residual effects (see Figure 6.3). The crucial questions are how large is this waiting cost and how fast is it growing over time?

ii) As Figure 6.3 shows, there is also *a high cost attached to the surprise* of an extreme event suddenly occurring. Both the unpredictability surrounding the impacts of the greenhouse effect and the tendency of these impacts to increase the risk of extreme events suggests that we should be careful not to underestimate the probability of a surprise occurring or to make inflexible assumptions concerning the timing of these events.

iii) As a result, *conventional discounting assumptions may need to be modified* in analysing the policy responses to the greenhouse effect. For example, using a positive discount rate in project or policy analysis virtually eliminates the net present value of effects occurring 30 or more years in the future. The policy analysis must

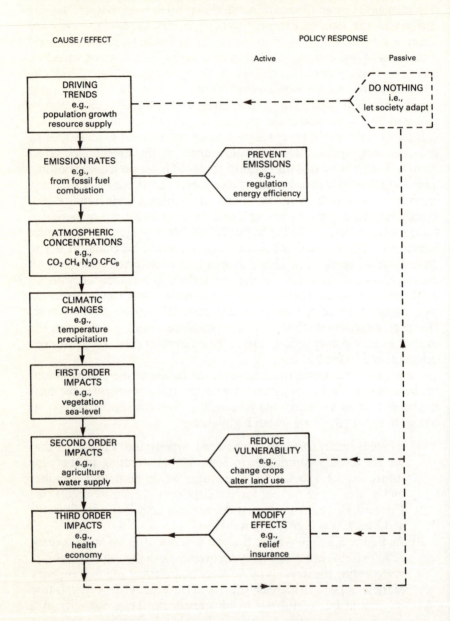

**Figure 6.2: Schematic Diagram of the Greenhouse Effect, Impacts and Policy Responses**

*Source:* R.A. Warrick, P.D. Jones and J.E. Russell, "The greenhouse effect, climatic change and sea level: An overview", Expert Group on Climatic Change and Sea Level Rise (Commonwealth Secretariat: London, 19–20 May 1988), Figure 1.

**Figure 6.3: Relative Costs of Four Different Types of Effort Undertaken in Three Different Strategies for Responding to Climate Change**

| | LIMITATION | ANTICIPATORY ADAPTATION | FORCED ADAPTATION | RESIDUAL |
|---|---|---|---|---|
| | (reduce emissions) | (primarily adjust to effects) | | (absorbed costs) |
| Business as Usual | w | xx | yyyyy | zzzzz |
| Moderate Efforts | ww | xxxx | yyy | ? |
| Concerted Efforts | wwwww | xx | y | z |
| Surprise | | | yyyyyyy | zzzzzzzz |
| Comments | long lead time | varying lead time | no lead time | |

*Notes:* The relative costs are indicated by w, x, y, z. In addition, the relative costs of a surprise occurrence are shown.

Units of Costs: different types of costs (symbolized by the use of w, x, y, and z) are used to emphasize that the costs of limitation and of anticipatory adaptation can be monetized. Forced adaptation, however, would involve both monetized costs (e.g., costs of rebuilding a flooded village) and unmonetized costs (e.g., loss of human life, environmental damage). Residual costs will be almost entirely unmonetized.

*Source:* Jill Jaeger, "The development of an awareness of a need to respond to climatic change", Expert Group on Climatic Change and Sea Level Rise (Beijer Institute and Commonwealth Secretariat: London, 19–20 May 1988), Figure 2.

not always be biased by such a standard result and automatically reject options that involve future costs and benefits. Rather, in addition to using sensitivity analysis with different discount rate assumptions, there should a modification of the benefits and costs under various contingencies concerning risk, as well as a full assessment of the costs of maintaining the sustainability of economic activities and essential natural resources.[87]

iv) The analyst of policy options will need to be aware of both *monetized and unmonetized costs*, and not to be automatically biased to consider the former alone. For example, in Figure 6.3, the costs of limitation and anticipatory adaption can be monetized. Forced adaptation, however, would involve both monetized costs (e.g., the cost of rebuilding a flooded village) and costs that are more difficult to monetize (e.g., environmental damage, human mortality and detrimental effects on health). Residual costs will also be extremely difficult to monetize. A fair assessment of the trade-offs among policy options will therefore require a thorough analysis of both monetized costs and those that are less easily monetized.

The purpose of such an analysis should be to determine whether it is worth investing today in a number of important anticipatory, adaptive and preventive measures for controlling a global warming and limiting the impacts of its effects.

Important *adaptive measures* would include:

i) the development of a global food-security system while Northern countries are still able to generate an agricultural surplus at relatively low costs;

ii) the provision of additional financial assistance to developing countries, especially those in semi-arid and flood-prone regions, to help them establish a self-supporting agricultural infrastructure, appropriate techniques and improved water management and control;

iii) the allocation of development funds in Third World countries to expanding food production and sustainable agricultural development;

iv) a greater international effort to halt the trend of accelerating global desertification; *and*

v) a commitment to humane methods of curbing population growth where it inhibits development.

To some extent, these adaptive measures would lessen the more severe impacts of the economic and environmental disruptions of human welfare which would accompany any global greenhouse effect. They would also involve economic costs that would necessitate the diversion of resources from other economic activities. On the other hand, some of these options (such as the commitment to sustainable agricultural development in the Third World) have long been advocated in their own right; the greenhouse effect just adds force to the arguments in their favour.

The total economic costs of all these options are just one estimate of the consequences that climatic instability and change would mean for human welfare. The alternative to paying these costs may be to face the full brunt of these consequences.

*Preventive measures* would essentially involve:

i) reducing fossil-fuel burning, particularly through the development of non-fossil fuel energy-source, through improvements in the efficiency of extracting useful energy from fossil fuels, and in pollution control;

ii) reducing the emissions of trace gases from other anthropogenic sources;

iii) developing technological processes to "scrub", recover and recycle the carbon and other trace residuals emitted after fossil fuels are burned.

iv) halting unnecessary tropical deforestation through alternative development strategies and incentives; *and*

v) increasing the rate of replanting in deforested areas, encouraging afforestation and improving forest management.

To make any major impact on reducing carbon and trace-gas emissions as soon as possible would again mean rapidly instigating these measures by diverting resources from economic activity, with possibly some sacrifice in short-term economic growth. This may not necessarily be the case, however, for measures that improve the efficiency of fossil-fuel consumption and thus simultaneously allow overall savings in energy costs.

The effective implementation of these preventive measures will eventually require their acceptance by developing countries, whose consumption of fossil fuels is continually increasing. However, these countries cannot be expected to invest in such measures without assistance from more advanced industrialized nations, either in the form of specific investment flows or by making the appropriate emission-reduction and non-fossil fuel technology available. With the possible exception of investments to improve energy efficiency that directly influence costs, one cannot expect developing countries to go it alone in implementing such preventive measures. Indeed, without a substantial commitment to adopting such measures in their own countries, advanced industrialized nations have little moral authority in persuading the developing and newly industrializing countries to adopt them. On the positive side, these same preventive investments are being linked to controlling other global and transnational problems (such as acid rain and the impacts of CFCs on the ozone layer) which are influencing public opinion and policymakers in advanced industrialized countries.

Such problems are vital and plagued with uncertainties over the extent of climatic change and rises in sea level, and over the sustainability of our current pattern of global economic activity. This means that there is usually a rudimentary call for further research. In the case of the greenhouse effect, the need for research is absolute and, fortunately, research in this field is growing. The next and most urgent step, however, is more rigorous analysis of the policy options currently available. This, in turn, requires the continuation of three major thrusts of international co-operation in future research. The first is the monitoring of climatic changes, ocean and atmospheric circulations, biogeochemical and other ecological processes, and changes in the sea level and ice caps. The second is research into and the development of warning systems for predicting sudden disasters from climatic and sea-level changes. The third is the analysis of the costs and benefits of both the impacts of global warming and the adaptive and preventive measures necessary to ameliorate them.

## SUMMARY AND CONCLUSION

Both deforestation in Amazonia and the global greenhouse effect are generating the type of short- and long-term scarcity impacts depicted by the alternative view of natural-resource scarcity. In Amazonia, the loss of environmental quality due to forest alteration – which is severe in some areas – has already led to a deterioration in many of the environmental functions essential to economic activity and human welfare. Eventually, the disruption of the crucial hydrological, nutrient and energy cycles that link the integrated Amazonian ecosystem may destabilize the climate in this and neighbouring regions. In contrast, the greenhouse effect will alter climate on a global scale. In the near future, climatic instability and ecological stress could significantly affect world agricultural production and distribution, as well as disrupt major terrestrial ecosystems. In the long run, sea levels might rise – with devastating consequences for island countries and low-lying regions.

This chapter has also shown how these scarcity effects might be ameliorated by appropriate policy responses. For example, behind Amazonian deforestation is a whole economic strategy that is biased towards large landholdings and commercial developments at the expense of small-scale ownership and sustainable forest management. This strategy and attitude towards forest exploitation needs to be reversed if the resulting short- and long-term scarcity effects are to be avoided. Similarly, to avert the climatic disturbances associated with a global warming, a range of preventive and adaptive policy measures may need to be implemented. The benefits and costs of the various policy options, as well as their trade-offs with the costs of doing nothing, must be analysed further.

In short, economic analysis has quite a lot to say about the type of scarcity effects depicted by the alternative view – once it is recognized that such effects are real phenomena and truly constitute an economic problem. Amazonian deforestation and the global greenhouse effect are just two examples of the increasing number of environmental degradation problems that economics will need to come to grips with in the near future. As demonstrated in this chapter, the alternative view of natural-resource scarcity can provide the proper economic framework for analysing such problems and their impacts. The next step is to build on the insights afforded by this view in order to establish the appropriate policy responses and strategies.

## NOTES

1. Norman Myers, *Conservation of Tropical Moist Forests* (National Academy of Sciences: Washington, DC, 1980), defines tropical forests as "forests that occur in

areas that have a mean annual temperature of at least 75 degrees Fahrenheit and are essentially frost-free – in areas receiving 2,000 mm or more of rainfall per year and not less than 100 mm of rainfall in any one month for two out of three years. They are mainly, if not entirely, evergreen." Norman Myers, *The Primary Source: Tropical Rain Forests and Our Future* (W.W. Norton: New York, 1984), notes that all tropical forests are commonly called "rain forests". However, he suggests that true rain forests are only those tropical forests that receive at least 4,000 mm of rain annually and at least 200 mm in 10 months of the year. The more appropriate term for most tropical forests is "tropical moist forest".

2. See David W. Pearce and Norman Myers, "Economic values and the environment of Amazonia" in David Goodman and Anthony Hall (eds), *The Future of Amazonia: Destruction or Sustainable Development*? (Macmillan: London), forthcoming; Enos Salati and P.B. Vose, "Amazon basin: A system in equilibrium", *Science*, Vol. 225 (1984), pp. 129–38; and Daniel Vidart, "Amazon roulette: Destruction or development" in IDRC *Reports*, Vol. 10 (1981), pp. 10–11. The "Legal Amazon" region of Brazil includes the country's traditional "Northern Region" plus Mato Grasso and parts of Goias and Martanhao States. It comprises an area of around 5 million km², or around 57 % of the country. In 1980, the tropical forest zone was almost 3.7 million km², or about 67 % of the Legal Amazon. Moist forest proper covered almost 2.9 million km², or about 57%. There are another 1.3 million km² of tropical forests located in Amazonian regions outside of Brazil. Venezuela has 0.31 million km², Colombia 0.27 million km², Ecuador 85,000 km² and Peru 0.6 million km². This makes a total Amazonian forest area of about 4.2 million km². See Pearce and Myers, op. cit.

3. Myers, *The Primary Source*. op. cit., p. 280.

4. Salati and Vose, op. cit., p. 129.

5. Catherine Caufield, *Tropical Moist Forests: The Resource, the People, the Threat* (Earthscan: London, 1982); and Darrell Addison Posey, "Indigenous management of tropical forest ecosystems: The case of the Kayapo Indians of the Brazilian Amazon", *Agroforestry Systems*, Vol. 3 (1985), pp. 139–58.

6. Caufield, op. cit.; Philip M. Fearnside, "Agricultural plans for Brazil's Grande Carajas Programme: Lost opportunity for sustainable local development?", *World Development*, Vol. 14 (1986), pp. 385–409; Anthony Hall, "Agrarian crisis in Brazilian Amazonia: The Grande Carajas Programme", *Journal of Development Studies*, Vol. 24 (1987), pp. 522–51; and C. Padoch, J. Chota Inuma, W. De Jong and J. Unruh, "Amazonian agroforestry; A market-oriented system in Peru", *Agroforestry Systems*, Vol. 3 (1985), pp. 47–56.

7. Christopher J. Barrow, "Development of the Brazilian Amazon", *Mazingira*, Vol. 5 (1981), pp. 36–471; Hall, op. cit., and Pearce and Myers, op. cit.

8. *Deforestation and Development*, a newsletter for environmental and development organizations (European Economic Bureau: Brussels, 1982); Norman Myers, "The present and future prospects of tropical moist forests", *Environmental Conservation*, Vol. 7 (1980), pp. 101–14.

9. For example, although attempts have been made to develop commercial brazil-nut plantations, many pilot projects have failed because the trees are pollinated by one species of bee that, in turn, requires other tree species for feeding when the nut trees are not flowering. Moreover, as the trees depend for germination on a particular species of rodent that chews and softens the seed coat of the nut, either brazil-nut reserves need to be large enough to support a breeding population of this rodent or the seed coat has to be softened artificially. See Caufield, op. cit.

10. Myers, "The present and future prospects", op. cit.; Pearce and Myers, op. cit.; and *Deforestation and Development*, op. cit.

11. John O. Browder, *Subsidies, Deforestation, and the Forest Sector in the Brazilian Amazon* (A Report to the World Resources Institute: Washington, DC, December,

1985); and Philip M. Fearnside, "Spatial concentration of deforestation in the Brazilian Amazon", *Ambio*, Vol. 15 (1986), pp. 74–81. See note 2 for the definition of Brazil's "Legal Amazon" region.

12. Pearce and Myers, op. cit. and Salati and Vose, op. cit. Pearce and Myers, op. cit., estimate the amount of deforestation in Non-Brazilian Amazonia to be: 19,000 km² (7 %) of Colombian Amazonia; almost 73,000 km² (12 %) of Peruvian Amazonia; 7,000 km² (8 %) of Ecuadorian Amazonia and 14,000 km² (4 %) of Venezuelan Amazonia. The authors note that the comparatively low rate of deforestation in Venezuela is most likely due to the country's oil revenues, which reduce the incentive to maximize revenues from forest exploitation.

13. Fearnside, "Spatial concentration", op. cit.

14. See Food and Agricultural Organization (FAO), *Tropical Forest Resources Assessment Project* (FAO/UNEP: Rome, 1982); Fearnside, "Spatial concentration", op. cit.; and Myers (1980a, 1980b and 1984). The extent and rate of deforestation and degradation in these nuclei of intense activity can be dramatically illustrated by the case of Rondonia in Brazil (see Pearce and Myers, op. cit.). It is a vast State of 244,000 km², and in 1975 only 1,200 km² of forests had been cleared. From 1975 to 1986, however, colonial settlement and other economic activities had increased the population by almost ten-fold from 111,000 to over one million. Thus, by 1987 a total of at least 147,000 km² of forest had been either degraded or deforested – roughly 60 % of the State. If this exponential rate of destruction continues, the entire forest of Rondonia would disappear by the year 2000.

15. Browder, op. cit., p. 21; Caufield, op. cit.; FAO, op. cit.; and Myers, op. cit.

16. Robert Repetto, *The Forests for the Trees? Government Policies and the Misuse of Forest Resources* (World Resources Institute: Washington DC, 1988), pp. 74–5.

17. Pearce and Myers, op. cit.

18. Vidart, op. cit.

19. Repetto, op. cit., p. 74. For example, wood products account for more than a quarter of industrial output in four of the region's six states, exceeding 60 % in Rondonia and Roraima, but the *entire* Brazilian wood industry, of which the Amazonian contribution is relatively small, accounted for only 12.9 % of industrial output and 4.9 % of foreign-exchange earnings in 1980.

20. G.J. Dowling, "Growing goodwill in Brazil", *Timber Trades Journal Hardwood Supplement*, August 1981, pp. 27–9.

21. Pearce and Myers, op. cit.

22. For example, Harald Sioli, "The effects of deforestation in Amazonia", *The Geographical Journal*, Vol. 151 (1985), pp. 197–203, argues that when a certain percentage of Amazonian forests has been destroyed, the environmental threshold effects "will probably have a disastrous effect on the survival of spared forest areas which are intended as 'nature reserves' or the like."

23. For example, according to Caufield, op. cit., although Brazil's Indian population was an estimated 6–9 million in 1500, it had dropped to one million by 1900, and to under 200,000 by the early 1980s. Of the 230 tribes living in Brazil in 1900, only 143 survive.

24. See Vidart, op. cit. E.H. Butler and C.J. Schofield, "Economic assault on *chagas* disease", *New Scientist*, 29 October 1981, pp. 321–4, have also established a link between the conversion of forest land to pasture and the spread of *chagas* disease, which has already affected 10 million South Americans.

25. For example, Sioli, op. cit., reports that the carrying capacity of converted pastures near the Belem–Brasilia highways decreased from 0.9 to 1 head of cattle on young pastures to only 0.3 head after some six years. Because of the declining phosphorous in soil combined with compaction and weed invasion, cattle pasture is not sustainable under the low-input system that is generally used among ranchers in Amazonia. By 1981, over 50 % of the pastures established in the Paragominas area were degraded, and the observed trend is for ranches to become uneconomic after 5 to 8 years under

standard low-input conditions, and after 12 to 14 years with adequate management. See Fearnside, "Agricultural plans", op. cit. The same problem of nutrient loss faces cultivation on converted forest lands, especially as many colonists are ignorant of traditional tropical cultivation skills, do not have sufficient land to practice shifting cultivation sustainably and often cannot afford appropriate fertilizers or crops. However, Fearnside, op. cit., notes that the poor economics of pasture from converted Amazonian forest land is overridden by the use of cattle pasture as a rapid and cheap means of securing claim to the land for speculative purposes in the advance of anticipated development and farmer settlement. As will be discussed below, the economics of cattle ranching are also distorted by fiscal incentives through numerous subsidies.

26. For example, there is evidence that the annual floods experienced in Amazonia since 1970, especially the high peak flows of 1981 and 1982, and the commonly reported incidence of river flooding, are connected with the increased deforestation of upland areas. See Salati and Vose, op cit.

27. G.L. Potter *et al.*, "Possible climatic impact of tropical deforestation", *Nature*, Vol. 258 (1975), pp. 697-8; G.L. Potter *et al.*, "Albedo change by man", *Nature*, Vol. 291 (1981), p. 291; Salati and Vose, op. cit.; and Siolo, op. cit.

28. Salati and Vose, op. cit.

29. For example, in the region of Manaus, the present dry period is at the maximum that the local ecosystem can tolerate. Any lengthening of this dry season or further reductions in rainfall at other times would induce irreversible ecological changes. See Salati and Vose, op. cit.

30. *Deforestation and Development*, op. cit., and Sioli, op. cit.

31. Salati and Vose, op. cit.

32. R.E. Newell, "The Amazon Forest and atmospheric general circulation" in W.H. Matthews *et al.* (eds), *Man's Impact on the Climate* (MIT Press: Cambridge, Massachusetts, 1971).

33. Sioli, op. cit., and American Geophysical Union, *Journal of Geophysical Research*, Vol. 93 (1988), pp. 1389-95.

34. Anthony L. Hall, "More of the same in Brazilian Amazonia: A comment on Fearnside", *World Development*, Vol. 14 (1986), pp. 411-14.

35. Fearnside, "Agricultural plans", op. cit. See also Hall, op. cit.

36. Browder, op. cit., p. 6.

37. Ibid.

38. Ibid., pp. 21-3 and 29. Browder (note 7) acknowledges that other estimates of the average size of SUDAM livestock projects range from a low of 18,126 ha (by SUDAM itself) to 28,860 ha. On the other hand, for the traditional North region and Mato Grasso, the average size of cattle ranches is 872 ha.

39. Hans P. Binswanger, "Fiscal and legal incentives with environmental effects on the Brazilian Amazon", Discussion Paper (World Bank: Washington, DC, May 1987), p. 14.

40. Repetto, op. cit., pp. 79-80. It is also noted that only 20 % of SUDAM-financed livestock projects market their timber, compared to 47 % of non-subsidized ranches. For all projects, this equates to a potential loss of nearly 50,000,000 m³ of roundwood, or an opportunity cost of US$ 100-250 million. This is equivalent to one eighth to one third of all SUDAM tax credits distributed to Amazonian livestock projects from 1966 to 1983.

41. Browder, op. cit., pp. 53-62.

42. Ibid., pp. 16-20. Binswanger (p. 18) also notes that "small scale squatters are frequently accused of contributing in a major way to the deforestation. While this may be of local importance in several regions, it is probably less of a problem than the ranchers ... for the entire legal Amazon area the bulk of deforestation is accounted for by large private and corporate ranches." The exception would be in Rondonia, which

is the region for the major colonization programmes.

43. Ibid., p. 8.
44. Ibid., pp. 6–7.
45. Sioli, op. cit. See also, Salati and Vose, op. cit.
46. An earlier version of this section appeared as Edward B. Barbier, "Economic and environmental aspects of rising carbon dioxide levels", paper presented at the Input–Output Research Association Conference, The Greenhouse Effect, the Environment and Input–Output Analysis (Pembroke College; University of Cambridge, 29 June 1985).
47. In 1980, the developing countries accounted for only about 13 % of global carbon emissions, whereas the industrialized market economies of North America, Western Europe and Asia accounted for about 57 %. At current annual growth rates of 0.5 % for industrialized countries and 6.2 % for developing countries, the developing world would become the major source of $CO_2$ emissions by the year 2007. Thus the policies and strategies for development in the Third World, particularly the expansion of energy-use for economic development, may be the most significant determinant of future global carbon emissions. See J. Darmstadter, "Energy patterns – In retrospect and prospect" in W.C. Clark and R.E. Munn (eds), *Sustainable Development of the Biosphere* (Cambridge University Press: Cambridge, 1986) and R.A. Warrick, P.D. Jones and J.E. Russell, "The greenhouse effect, climatic change and sea level: An overview", Expert Group on Climatic Change and Sea Level Rise, (Commonwealth Secretariat: London, 19–20 May 1988).
48. On the different sources of carbon emission see B. Bolin, B. Doos, J. Jaeger and R.A. Warrick (eds), *The Greenhouse Effect, Climatic Change and Ecosystems*, SCOPE 29 (John Wiley: New York, 1986); R.P. Detwiler and Charles A.S. Hall, "Tropical forests and the global carbon cycle", *Science*, Vol. 239, 1 January 1988, pp. 42–7; R.M. Rotty, "Data for global $CO_2$ production from fossil fuels and cement" in B. Bolin (ed.), *Carbon Cycling Modelling*, SCOPE 16 (John Wiley: New York, 1981); United States National Academy of Sciences (USNAS), *Changing Climate: Report of the Carbon Dioxide Assessment Committee* (National Academy Press: Washington, DC, 1983); World Climate programme, "Report of the International Conference on the Assessment of the Role of Carbon Dioxide and of Other Greenhouse Gases in Climate Variations and Associated Impacts" (World Meterological Organization: Villach, Austria, 9–15 October 1985). The biggest controversy appears to be over the contribution that land clearing, particulary tropical deforestation, makes to total carbon emissions. Initial estimates placed it at about 1–2 gigatonnes, and from all terrestrial ecosystem disturbances anywhere from 1.5 to 5 gigatonnes. See, for example, A.T. Wilson, "Pioneer agricultural explosion and $CO_2$ levels in the atmosphere", *Nature*, Vol. 273 (1978), pp. 40–1; C.S. Wong, "Atmospheric impact of carbon dioxide from burning wood", *Science*, Vol, 200 (1978), pp. 197–9; and George M. Woodwell *et al.*, "Global deforestation: Contribution to atmospheric carbon dioxide", *Science*, Vol. 222 (1983), pp. 1081–6. More recent modelling (e.g., Detwiler and Hall, op. cit.) has led to a downward revision in these estimates. Nevertheless, some analysts have suggested that the annual rate of carbon release from deforestation may actually reach 7–9 gigatonnes before tapering off dramatically as the world's major forests begin disappearing completely during the middle of the next century (e.g., Woodwell *et al.*, op. cit.).
49. Bolin *et al.*, op. cit.; Robert E. Dickinson and Ralph J. Cicerone, "Future global warming from atmospheric trace gases", *Nature*, Vol. 319 (1986), pp. 109–15; Michael MacCracken and Frederick M. Luther, *Projecting the Climatic Effects of Increasing Carbon Dioxide* (United States Department of Energy: Washington, DC, December 1985); V. Ramanathan, R.J. Cicerone, H.B. Singh and J.T. Kiehl, "Trace gas trends and their potential role in climate change", *Journal of Geophysical Research*, Vol. 90 (1985), pp. 5547–66; and World Climate Program, op. cit. Warwick *et al.*, op.

cit., cite four reasons for the growing importance to the greenhouse effect of CFCs: (1) molecule for molecule, some are as much as ten thousand times more effective than $CO_2$ in terms of their radiative effects; (2) most are "long-lived" in the atmosphere; (3) they destroy stratospheric ozone, which in turn may enhance the greenhouse effect; and (4) the annual growth rates in atmospheric concentrations of CFCs are high.

50. Warrick, *et. al.*, op. cit. Some observers have expressed important reservations over assuming that such predictions of global warming are inevitable. For example, some time ago, Bryson pointed out that the supposed effect of increasing carbon dioxide levels on the earth's surface temperatures may be cancelled out in time by other factors tending to lower temperatures, such as the increased turbidity of the atmosphere from volcanic dust, man's disturbance of the soil and particulate waste, and the long-term climatic change from an interglacial to a glacial age. See Reid A. Bryson, "A perspective on climatic change", *Science*, Vol. 184 (1974), pp. 753–9. More recently, Maddox has cautioned that "although it has been known for nearly three decades that the quantity of carbon dioxide lodging in the atmosphere is only half of that discharged into it, whether the missing half finishes up in the biosphere or in the oceans is unknown – but is critical for the long-term prognosis. The link between an accumulation of excess heat and the surface temperature is similarly, but seriously, complicated by uncertainty about the role of the oceans as heat reservoirs." See John Maddox, "Jumping the greenhouse gun", *Nature*, Vol. 334 (1988), p. 9.

51. S. Manabe and R.J. Stouffer, "Sensitivity of a global climate model to an increase of $CO_2$ concentration in the atmosphere", *Journal of Geophysical Research*, Vol. 85 (1980), pp. 5529–5554; S. Manabe and R.T. Wetherald, "On the distribution of climatic change resulting from an increase in $CO_2$ content in the atmosphere", *Journal of Atmospheric Sciences*, Vol. 37 (1980), pp. 99–118.

52. T.M.L. Wigley, P.D. Jones and P.M. Kelly, "Scenario for a warm, high-$CO_2$ world", *Nature*, Vol. 283 (1980), pp. 17–21.

53. Jill Jaeger, "The development of an awareness of a need to respond to climatic change", Expert Group on Climatic Change and Sea Level Rise (Commonwealth Secretariat and Beijer Institute: London, 19–20 May 1988).

54. See Bolin *et al.*, op. cit.; Jaeger, op. cit.; James Lewis, "The implications of sea level rise for island and low-lying countries", Expert Group on Climatic Change and Sea Level Rise (Commonwealth Secretariat: London, 19–20 May 1988); Warrick, *et al.*, op. cit.; T.M.L. Wigley and S.C.B. Raper, "Thermal expansion of sea water associated with global warming", *Nature*, Vol. 330 (1987), pp. 127–31; and World Climate Programme, op. cit.

55. J.H. Mercer, "West Antarctic Ice Sheet and $CO_2$ greenhouse effect: A threat of disaster", *Nature*, Vol. 271 (1978), pp. 321–5; Roger Revelle, "Carbon dioxide and world climate", *Scientific American*, Vol. 247 (1982), pp. 753–9; USNAS, op. cit., and Woodwell *et al.*, op. cit.

56. See Bolin *et al.*, op. cit.; Revelle, op. cit.; World Climate Programme, op. cit.

57. For example, the USNAS, op. cit., study concluded that any polar ice-cap melting would, at most, increase the rate of sea-level rise to anywhere from 15 to 70 cm per century, a process that would take several centuries before a 5- to 6-m total rise would occur. In contrast, theoretical models developed at Ohio State University have indicated that the disintegration of the West Antarctic Ice Sheet could conceivably accelerate to a sea-level rise of 3 cm per year, or 3 m in one century. See Revelle, op. cit.

58. The last four are especially singled out by P.A. Oram, "Sensitivity of agricultural production to climatic change", *Climatic Change*, Vol. 7 (1985), pp. 129–52.

59. Bryson, op. cit.

60. Michael H. Glantz and Jesse H. Ausubel, "The Ogallala aquifer and carbon dioxide: Comparison and convergence", *Environmental Conservation*, Vol. 11 (1984), pp.

123–31. The eight Western states are Colorado, Kansas, Nebraska, New Mexico, Oklahoma, South Dakota, Texas and Wyoming.

61. USNAS, op. cit.

62. Revelle, op. cit.

63. Bolin *et al.*, op. cit.; Oram, op. cit.; N.J. Rosenberg, "The increasing $CO_2$ concentration in the atmosphere and its implications on agricultural productivity – II. Effects through $CO_2$-induced climatic change", *Climatic Change*, Vol. 4 (1982), pp. 239–54; USNAS, op. cit. and World Climate Programme, op. cit. For example, the World Climate Programme, op. cit., p. 21 notes that: "It is estimated from laboratory experiments on individual plants that, in the absence of climatic change, a doubling of the $CO_2$ concentration would cause a 0–10 % increase in growth and yield of $C_4$ crops (e.g. maize, sorghum, sugar cane) and a 10 to 50 % increase for $C_3$ crops (e.g. wheat, soya bean, rice), depending on the specific crop and growing conditions." The USNAS study, op. cit., however, has pointed out that positive feedback effects between higher atmospheric $CO_2$ levels and rain-fed crop productivity have so far been analysed only under the controlled conditions of greenhouses and growth chambers. In natural environments, such feedback effects would not only affect crops but also weeds, pests and their inter-relationships.

64. Jaeger, op. cit.; Oram, op. cit.; Rosenberg, op. cit.; USNAS, op. cit.

65. Oram, op. cit.

66. USNAS, op. cit.

67. Bolin, *et al.*, op. cit.; World Climate Programme, op. cit.

68. Jack A. Mabbutt, "A new global assessment of the status and trends of desertification", *Environmental Conservation*, Vol. 11 (1984), pp. 103–13.

69. Oram, op. cit.

70. See also the discussion in Oram, op. cit.

71. Leonardo A. Paulino, *Food in the Third World: Past trends and projections to 2000*, Research Report 52 (International Food Policy Research Institute: Washington, DC, 1986), pp. 38–9.

72. World Bank, *Poverty and Hunger* (World Bank: Washington, DC, 1986). The report distinguishes between "chronic" and "transitory" food insecurity. Chronic food insecurity is a continuously inadequate diet caused by the inability to acquire food. It affects households that persistently lack the ability either to buy enough food or to produce their own. Transitory food insecurity is a temporary decline in a household's access to enough food. It results from instability of food prices, food production, or household incomes – and in its worse form produces famine.

73. Ibid.

74. See, for example, FAO, Committee on Commodity Problems, 55th Session, *International Trade and World Food Security*, Rome, 21–25 October 1985.

75. Ibid.

76. In Africa, the increasing dependency on food imports and aid has been evident. From 1974 and 1982, between the major drought years, the average annual growth rate in cereal imports was 9.5 % and in food aid, 16.6 %. During the most recent major drought crisis of 1983–84, it was estimated that the 24 affected countries had to import an additional 5.3 million tonnes of cereals, of which 3.4 million was emergency aid. See *UN Chronicle*, "Perspectives: Crisis in Africa", Vol. 21 (1984), pp. i–xxviii.

77. Bolin *et al.*, op. cit.; W.R. Emanuel *et al.*, "Climatic change and the broad-scale distribution of terrestrial ecosystem complexes", *Climatic Change*, Vol. 7 (1985), pp. 45–54; and World Climate Programme, op. cit.

78. P. Kauppi and M. Posch, "Sensitivity of boreal forests to possible climatic warming", *Climatic Change*, Vol. 7 (1985), pp. 45–54.

79. Jaeger, op. cit.

80. See, for example, pp. 128–9; and Woodwell *et al.*, op. cit.

81. Warrick *et al.*, op. cit. The authors go on to note: "Clearly, any future projections for

specific localities must consider the combination of global, regional and local effects on sea level.... In south-eastern England, for example, the local sea level has been rising at a rate about twice the global average, partly because the land is submerging. In Scandinavia, sea level has been falling, due to isostatic uplift. Most of the Pacific islands have shown little change. Local influences can have a marked effect, such as on the Mississippi Delta which is experiencing a sea level rise of about one meter per century due to subsidence related to decreased sedimentation as a result of human interference in the flow of the Mississippi River."

82. Jaeger, op. cit., and Warrick *et al.*, op. cit. In the extreme case of a rise of five to six m in sea levels, the United States would lose most of its southern coastal lowlands, including half of the state of Florida. See Revelle, op. cit.

83. Jaeger, op. cit.; Warrick *et al.*, op. cit.

84. Lewis, op. cit.

85. Wallace S. Broecker, "Unpleasant surprises in the greenhouse?", *Nature*, Vol. 328 (1987), pp. 123–6.

86. Warrick *et al.*, op. cit., p. 30.

87. Thus "modifying conventional discounting assumptions" does not strictly mean simply universally adopting a lower or zero discount rate; rather, adjusting the cost and benefit values to allow the actual costs of risk, irreversibility and lost future values may be more appropriate. See, for example, Anil Markandya and David Pearce in *Environmental Considerations and the Choice of Discount Rate in Developing Countries*, Environment Department Working Paper No. 3 (World Bank: Washington, DC, May 1988).

# 7
# Upper Watershed Degradation in Java[1]

On the densely populated island of Java in Indonesia, the area of severely eroded upland is increasing at the rate of 1–2 % per annum and now covers a total of over 2 million hectares (ha), approximately one third of Java's cultivated uplands. The population of the uplands is roughly 12 million. Population densities in these areas average 600–700 people per km[2], and holdings averaging 0.4 ha or less. In some areas, up to 20–25 % of the population are landless. Yields for upland rice and corn average 0.9 to 2.5 tonnes per hectare. The general pattern is one of poor, predominantly subsistence households struggling to feed themselves and to meet other basic needs by using inappropriate cropping patterns that result in high levels of soil erosion on their rainfed lands. Significant erosion is also caused by absentee and better-off farm owners who cultivate highly profitable but erosive crops such as vegetables. An additional cause is the failure to police state-owned tree plantations properly, particularly in preventing illegal fuelwood collection and agricultural conversion.[2]

Although natural-erosion rates on Java (resulting from the interaction of climate, bed-rock geology, soils and vegetation) are among the highest in the world, human-induced erosion through inappropriate land use (particularly the continual cultivation and expansion of annual cropping systems on erodable soils) is clearly significant. A recent World Bank report suggested that upper watershed degradation has led to concern over three dominant cycles of interaction:

i) the on-site effects of land-use patterns and practices in upper watersheds on the natural-resource base and on the livelihoods of upland people;
ii) the off-site effects of upland activities on the environment downstream and the agricultural, industrial and urban livelihoods of lowland people; *and*
iii) the impact of policies, programmes and projects, both government of Indonesia (GOI) and foreign-donor funded, and of private investment on these on and off-site effects.

The on and off-site effects of upper watershed degradation on Java are very good examples of the type of natural-resource scarcity problems that concern the alternative view. Instead of focussing on these effects, this chapter will concentrate on the third concern – the role of economic policies, incentives and investment strategies in controlling upland erosion on Java. The chapter will examine two aspects of this role in particular: the incentives for upland farmers to adopt soil-conservation packages as a means of combatting erosion and improving long-term land productivity and agricultural growth, and the design of appropriate policies and incentives to facilitate the control of soil erosion on upland farms.

## ON- AND OFF-SITE EFFECTS

Usually, the on-site effects of soil erosion on farm productivity are distinguished from the off-site impacts of downstream environmental degradation. Both need to be studied and evaluated in any complete economic analysis of erosion control.[3]

The on-site impacts consist of a decline in the yields of agro-ecosystems arising from mass wasting, soil and nutrient losses and changes in the water-holding capacity of the soil. The use of the term "on-site" to describe these effects seems conceptually appropriate, as they are the user costs that farmers must eventually face for their choice of land-use patterns. By improved land management and the application of farm and soil-conservation techniques, farmers may be able to reduce on-site effects. but will generally only do so if the benefits appear to exceed the costs. In addition, however, the erodability of the land and thus the effectiveness and appropriate choice of land-management and conservation techniques will depend a great deal on the soil's characteristics, its interactions with the climate, slope and topsoil depth. On Java, the recent volcanic soils are generally less erodable than the more shallow, poorly drained sedimentary (limestone) soils.[4]

Soil erosion in the uplands of Java is thought to be the main determinant of downstream environmental degradation that results from off-site siltation, water flow irregularities and agro-chemical run-off. Again, the term "off-site", or "downstream", is appropriate as the costs of these impacts are external to the upland farm; that is they are not borne by the farmers whose upland agro-ecosystems are causing the problems. As erosion from cultivation often takes the form of sheet, rill or gully erosion, the off-site effects may be pervasive. They generally include:

i) increased sedimentation in reservoirs, rivers, channels, irrigation canals and other waterways;

ii) the increased irregularity of river flow, resulting in greater flooding after rains and reduced flow during dry periods;

iii) the loss of infrastructure, human lives, livestock and crops as a result of flooding;

iv) shortage of domestic, industrial and irrigation water supply as a result of reduced water flow in the dry season;

v) general pollution and eutrophication of water in reservoirs and rivers with resulting damage to water supply systems and inland fisheries; *and*

vi) progressive obstruction of navigation in rivers, channels and estuaries.[5]

To the extent that farmland erosion is a major factor, the on- and off-site impacts of upper watershed degradation on Java are one illustration of the effects, suggested by the alternative view, of natural-resource scarcity. In this case, improper land management in the uplands not only leads to deteriorating soil quality and formation in the upper watershed but also degrades important environment functions downstream. The result is, on the one hand, less sustainable agriculture and lower yields in the uplands and, on the other, a decline in environmental quality in the lower watershed with adverse consequences for various economic activities and welfare.

As upper watershed degradation continues, agro-ecosystems in some upland areas will eventually become destabilized and finally unsustainable. This may cause the widespread collapse of agricultural livelihoods. At the same time, the frequency of flooding, drought and other off-site effects may severely disrupt economic activity and populations downstream. In general, the cumulative costs of upper watershed degradation may be very high.

A recent study estimated that the on-site crop productivity losses from human-induced soil erosion on upland farms on Java were US$ 324 million annually, compared to the additional off-site sedimentation costs of US$ 25 to 91 million.[6] However, the authors stress the difficulty in estimating the off-site impacts accurately – particularly in separating sedimentation arising from "natural" geological and non-farm erosion from erosion caused by upland farming. The study estimated the off-site costs of damage to irrigation systems, sedimentation of reservoirs and harbour dredging; insufficient information was available to assess other off-site effects. Nevertheless, as a rough order of magnitude, these estimates suggest that the downstream costs of upper watershed degradation on Java are currently relatively less important than the costs of on-site productivity.

Whatever the exact costs of soil erosion, it is clear that to reduce them and to encourage sustainable agricultural development in the Javan uplands, a major change in economic strategy is required. There are three parts to such a strategy:

i) Directing increased investments in upland watershed projects to reduce soil erosion and raise agricultural productivity through developing and improving farming systems for specific agro-ecological zones and the physical infrastructure serving these zones.

ii) Improving the incentives for the adoption of soil conservation packages, improved farming systems and better land-management techniques through essential economic policy reforms.

iii) Designing the necessary institutional framework and planning capacity for implementing the desired policy and investment strategies.

The rest of this chapter will focus on the first two parts of this strategy.

## INCENTIVES FOR SOIL CONSERVATION

The effectiveness of economic policies and investment strategies in combatting upper watershed degradation and sustaining agricultural development depends crucially on the incentives for upland farming households. It is therefore necessary to understand the key economic factors which influence the decisions of upland farmers about the best way to manage their land and, in particular, about whether or not they see upland watershed management projects as beneficial and so adopt the available soil-conservation practices and technologies demonstrated on model farms.[7] The development of farming systems appropriate to upland conditions and capable of improving soil and water conservation will not succeed unless economic incentives are sufficient to encourage farmers to change their existing systems and land-use patterns. This section examines the technical packages advocated for upland soil conservation on Java and the various economic incentives given for their adoption.

The predominant technical approach for combatting upper watershed degradation on privately owned land has evolved from the FAO-funded Solo Watershed project (1972–78). In upper watershed areas of up to 50% slopes, the basic approach involves subsidizing bench-terrace construction through cash wages and/or free agricultural inputs, either directly or on credit. After the terraces are built, food crops are planted on the horizontal surface and grasses on the riser and lip to support livestock and help control erosion. Farmers are also encouraged to adopt improved cropping patterns which, together with the introduction of new varieties, increased inputs (e.g., fertilizer and pesticides) and better technical information, are intended to improve the net returns from cultivation. For example, in the Citanduy II project in West Java, farmers were advised not to monocrop corn and cassava but to switch to growing higher valued crops. As a result, increased returns from terracing have been largely associated with changing crop patterns: cassava production fell from 42.4 to 12.4 % of the average value per plot, while rice production increased from 7.1 to 26.8 % and peanut production rose from 3.4 to 17.8 %.[8]

Dependence on a single technical package to reduce soil erosion and improve the livelihoods of upland farmers throughout all the watersheds of Java is unrealistic. There is a growing recognition that approaches have to be more varied, given the great variability in topographic, soil, agro-ecological and even socio-economic conditions across these watersheds. For example, a study of bench terracing and related farming practices in the Citanduy basin revealed that model farms based on recent and pliocene volcanic soils have the lowest relative erodability index and the highest net returns, whereas those located on the sedimentary derived (limestone) soils have low returns, and in some cases, actual losses. This is due not only to the generally lower fertility of the limestone soils but also to the greater amount of labour involved in building and maintaining terraces, the higher rate of topsoil lost through erosion and, finally, the frequent collapse of terraces built on these soils.[9] During periods of peak rainfall, inappropriately bench-terraced fields can lose just as much if not more soil than adjacent fields cultivated using traditional methods (similar to ridge terracing).[10]

The livestock component of upper watershed projects is also intended to increase household income and nutrition, reduce vulnerability to crop failure and to encourage farmers to maintain a grass cover on their terraces. In general, the intention has been for a project to provide small ruminants (sheep or goats) for participants, who are then expected to give back one or two of the first offspring for distribution to others. In practice, several projects have had difficulty in implementing a livestock credit programme and/or have been unable to make livestock available on site. Consequently, farmers have had no incentive to maintain a forage cover crop.[11] The Kali Konto Project in East Java has had more success in implementing goat and sheep schemes, which are aimed at increasing the income of the poor, landless farmers. Participants are expected to plant fuel and fodder trees in their homeyards and/or on forest land, which they could also use for their own needs. Some farmers prefer goats to sheep, because the manure is used in onion production, and also because of their quicker reproduction rate and higher sales prices. Others have chosen sheep because they require less maintenance, can be fed with low quality fodder and are considered to be more resistant to disease.[12]

On slopes greater than 50 %, the basic approach has been to persuade farmers to grow tree crops rather than annual crops. These would include cloves, fruits, coffee, cocoa and tea, fuelwood for domestic consumption and sale, fodder trees, and grass under the canopy for livestock. All of these would contribute to a cash income. As the main constraint on developing agroforestry based systems is the long wait before trees mature, the usual strategy (as employed in Citanduy II), has been to intercrop food crops and tree species. It would be better to develop farming systems that incorporate a mix of trees which can be harvested or produce fruit at different times and so spread income flows throughout the year. This would gradually induce the phasing out of annual cropping in the medium and long run.[13] In the Kali Konto Project, a key component in the establishment of perennial crop gardens and agroforestry systems on steep slopes was seen to be the development of village-level nurseries. These are backed up by central forestry and perennial crop nurseries at a (sub)district level which supply planting material required for village land. They also train and encourage farmers in the establishment of nurseries for their own requirements and demonstrate the success of high yielding varieties. In order to increase the production of fuelwood, fruits and fodder in watershed areas, it was considered essential to provide high quality seedlings in adequate quantities, at reasonable prices, and from nurseries close to the farming population.[14]

In spite of some input subsidies, the introduction of many soil conservation techniques to upland farms may require a substantial investment of time and money by farmers. For slopes of 50 % or less, to introduce bench terracing often requires a signicant input of human labour, ranging from about 750 to over 1800 person-days (PD) per ha depending on the slope. This implies construction costs of between US$ 420 and US$ 2,060 per ha (1979 prices). In addition, costs of planting material, tools and the fertilizer needed to build a terrace and establish a crop in the first year average US$ 112 per ha (1979 prices). So the total labour and material costs would range from US$ 560 to US$ 2,075 per ha (1979 prices). These estimates do not include the additional costs to the farmer of periodic maintenance of terraces, waterways and drop structures. For farmers to add an intensive livestock system to terracing, the cost of establishing a grass cover on terraces is approximately US$ 72 per ha for material (1979 prices) and an extra 2–5 PD per ha, if 20 % of each hectare is in terrace risers and lips. A mature female sheep or goat costs about US$ 70.[15]

It is generally assumed that the labour for constructing the terraces is provided by the farmer during the dry season. Assuming a four-month dry season and a holding of 0.5 hectares, a single farmer could provide a maximum of 100 PD each dry season. This is far short of the terracing requirements of approximately 375 (low slope) to over 900 (steep slopes) PD per 0.5 ha holding. Alternatively, during a 100 working-day period, a farmer could only terrace 0.14 ha of low slope and 0.06 ha of steep slope.[16] The total labour requirements for terracing may therefore mean additional cash expenditures on hired labour. Thus from the farmer's point of view, the costs of terracing not only imply forgoing his own income-earning opportunities – either in off-farm employment during the dry season and/or less labour time devoted to crop and farm production – but also additional expenditures on material and possibly livestock costs. This suggests that the adoption of terracing-based technology for soil conservation may be limited to households with the cash available to hire additional labour, to those with more than one adult male member to supply labour and wealthier households that can afford to forgo wage employment during the dry season.

In Gubugklakah, East Java, only the relatively wealthy farmers engaged in profitable commercial apple production (approximately US$ 3–6,000 per year profits, 1986 prices) are able to afford to construct the extremely effective back-sloping tied ridges capable of conserving topsoil and reducing erosion rates to less than 10 tonnes per ha (volcanic middle soils with a slope profile of 4 to 8 degrees).[17] Similarly, a survey of farmers who did not adopt bench-terracing technology in the Citanduy watershed of West Java revealed that 87 % of the respondents cited lack of money as the reason for not constructing terraces.[18] Calculations of the net present value of the gains from terracing in the Citanduy II project suggest that, to the extent that terracing costs are around US$ 500 or less (1984–85 prices), farmers could be expected to adopt terracing without subsidies.[19]

One advantage of a livestock-based system is that owning small ruminants provides an opportunity for the household to use its own, often child, labour which has a low opportunity cost. On the other hand, in order to feed small ruminants by cutting grass along roadways and on other public land, the household must devote one hour/animal/day in the wet season and two hours/animal/day in the dry season. Under these conditions, flock size seldom exceeds four to eight animals per household. By establishing grass intensively on terraces, households are able either to raise a greater number of animals with the same labour input or to raise the same number of animals with perhaps only 20 % of the labour required under the extensive cut- and-carry system.[20] With terraces already established, a farming household can significantly raise productivity from animal husbandry with a relatively small additional investment in terms of labour and material costs.

As noted above, on slopes greater than 45–50 %, the recommended soil conservation strategy is for farmers to take land out of annual food-crop production and adopt an agroforestry-based system to produce tree crops for a cash income. For upland farmers, however, there is an additional waiting cost of three or more years to be borne between the initial year of land preparation and planting, and the eventual maturing and harvesting of the trees. For example, although *Albizia falcata* is considered a relatively fast-growing tree with economic potential for fuelwood, sawn lumber and supplementary dry-season forage, harvesting for fuelwood cannot begin before three years (five years for sawn logs), and it takes five years or more for cumulative returns to exceed the initial preparation and planting costs of around US$ 100/ha (1982 prices). Similarly, the preparation and planting of *Glyricidia* requires 7.5 PD per ha and subsequently 3.5 PD per ha for maintenance, as well as a material cost of around US\$ 45 per ha (1982 prices). Farmers, however, have to wait until the third year before making the first cut, and it is not until the fifth year that harvests reach their full economic potential (around US\$ 300 per ha per year – 1982 prices).[21] This suggests that adopting agroforestry systems may be extremely difficult for poorer farmers who are dependent on extremely small landholdings for food production and who have no alternative cropland or employment opportunities. On the other hand, farmers who are relatively well-off, who have sufficient lower sloped cropland to grow food on and/or who have access to off-farm employment opportunities may be able to afford the "waiting cost" associated with agroforestry investments. Security of land tenure is an additional determinant as to whether upland farmers are willing to bear this "waiting cost".

Given that upland farmers face significant costs in adopting soil conservation measures and changes in farming sytems, they are unlikely to make changes in their land management unless they can see an economic advantage in doing so. In addition, the more productive or profitable the land use, the more farmers will be willing to maintain and invest in better land-management and erosion-control practices. Higher productivity and returns will also mean that farmers can afford to maintain terraces and other conservation structures and to continue with labour-intensive erosion control measures. On the other hand, poorer upland farmers dependent on low-return cropping systems, such as maize or cassava, may be aware that soil erosion is reducing productivity but may not be able to afford to adopt conservation measures. At the other extreme, farmers with very profitable crops that are extremely erosive, such as temperate vegetables on steep upper volcanic slopes, may not consider soil conservation measures if their returns do not appear to be affected by soil erosion losses. Thus the relationship between the erodability and profitability of different framing systems on different soils and slopes is an important determinant of whether upland farmers adopt a soil conservation strategy. As shown in Figure 7.1, this relationship varies widely across Java.

## ECONOMIC POLICIES AND INVESTMENT STRATEGIES

The main factors in determining the willingness of upland farmers to invest in improved land-use management practices are:

i) They are not willing to modify their land-management practices and farming systems unless they see an economic advantage in doing so.

ii) This "economic advantage" is largely determined by increased productivity, and thus net returns from working the land, although other factors may also be significant. For example, the ability to earn greater returns from off-farm employment, the insecurity of land tenure, poor transportation and marketing facilities and inadequate information on available technology, inputs and farming methods.

iii) Where they see a direct economic advantage in doing so, farmers appear responsive to new information provided by research and extension services on optimum input and output mixes to achieve greater productivity.

In general, some scope exists for complementary economic policies and investment strategies that both enhance agricultural development in the uplands by increasing farmers' incomes and productivity, and so reduce the economic pressures to deplete the land and accelerate soil erosion. To introduce them, however, may require a re-orientation of agricultural policies and resources directed towards lowlands rice production in order

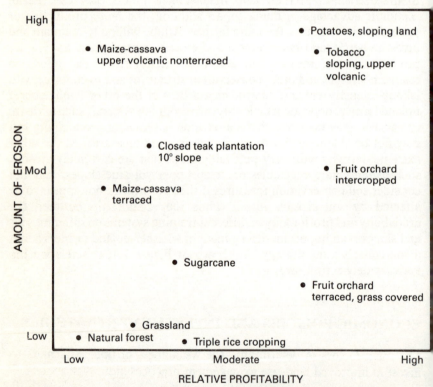

**Figure 7.1: The Relationship Between Relative Profitability and Amount of Erosion of Major Crops, Java Uplands**

*Source:* Brian Carson and Warni Hadi Utomo, "Erosion and sedimentation processes in Java" (KEPAS: Malang, Indonesia, 1986), Fig. 4.

to meet the very specific needs of upland agriculture. It is also clear that for such a reallocation of resources to be successful, it must also be efficient. The input-subsidized and production-oriented targeting approach for each commodity that, as part of the Green Revolution, was successful in achieving rice self-sufficiency in the early 1980s, would be costly to replicate for the uplands of Java.

The highly diversified soil conditions, topography, and agro-ecological zones that comprise the uplands, which are often characterized by non-contiguous smallholdings with mixed cropping patterns, are not ideal for mono-cropping rice, maize, soya beans and other major crops. Consequently, instead of trying to direct cropping patterns and areas to be harvested on a single commodity basis, attempts should be made to control soil erosion effectively, and to boost the productivity of the varied and appropriate mixed cropping, agroforestry and silvo-pastoral systems that would be appropriate under these diverse upland conditions. That is, a more flexible approach to farming systems may also be the most cost effective. To complement this approach, the immediate priorities for investment in the uplands are for research and extension to support the development of appropriate upland-farming systems, and for building up the physical infrastructure of the uplands, such as rural transport, integration of markets, and post-harvest technology and processing.

Given the current climate of slower economic growth, rising external-debt servicing and reduced development expenditures in Indonesia, increasing government investment and subsidy programmes (for irrigation, fertilizers and pesticides, higher yielding varieties (HYVs), management and credit) which currently are predominantly for rice production, are becoming a financial burden. Extending these policies to the uplands would increase this financial burden, which, in any case, may be an inappropriate and costly way of achieving agricultural diversification and upland agricultural development. With Indonesia now producing rice surpluses that have resulted in high storage costs and subsidized exports, there is clearly a case for introducing a phased reduction of these subsidies and reallocating funds towards research, extension and infrastructure for the uplands.[22]

To understand this need for a reorientation in policy requires a brief review of existing agricultural policy and its impact on the uplands.

Agricultural markets in Indonesia are complex, and although government management is pervasive, the degree of intervention varies significantly from market to market for the various crops cultivated. For example, the rice market is tightly regulated, with the government of Indonesia (GOI) procurement agency, BULOG, maintaining floor and ceiling prices through its accumulation and control of inventory stocks and imports. BULOG has been active in the markets for sugar, corn, soya beans and wheat, although mainly in restricting imports. In addition, extremely high effective protection rates exist for fruits, vegetables and dairy products as a stimulus to local production, which for the most part is not traded internationally. In contrast, there has traditionally been little government intervention in the markets for cassava, groundnuts, sweet potatoes and minor legumes (mungbeans, pigeon peas, etc.), which are also predominantly non-tradeables. However, the GOI is currently encouraging the expansion of cassava so as to fulfil its EEC export quota, and increased production of groundnuts to substitute for imports. With declining world prices, the GOI has relaxed its export taxes on tree crops, whose domestic prices are heavily influenced by world markets. The major export crops in Indonesia are rubber, palm oil, coffee, tea, tobacco and pepper.

One indicator of the incentives to domestic production afforded by government intervention is the nominal protection rate (NPR) – the ratio of domestic producer prices to border prices. The NPRs for rice and corn varied considerably between positive and negative levels over the 1972–85 period, whereas over the more recent 1980–85 period, the real protection rate for rice did not change, and for cassava it only increased by 8 %. Despire the varying degrees of GOI market intervention for these crops, the implication is that price distortion in these markets has not been significant. In contrast, the mainly positive NPRs, for soya beans, and particularly for sugar over 1972–85, suggest that import controls have lifted domestic prices well above world levels. The collapse in world commodity prices has significantly eroded the nominal and real incentives to domestic producers of export crops. In the past, effective protective rates for dairy products, and fruits and vegetables have been as high as 221.4 and 208.9 % respectively.[23]

Current GOI pricing policies and general market trends have reinforced the profitability of horticultural crops and, to a lesser extent, of soya beans, livestock products and groundnuts. Rigid import controls, a heavily protected domestic pricing structure and stringent area targeting have all been used to expand smallholder sugar production on Java. In contrast, incentives for increased rice production have come less from producer prices, which have been declining in real terms, but from input subsidies. This in turn may have depressed prices for the less desirable staple substitutes produced mainly on rainfed lands, such as corn and root crops. As these three basic staples are strong substitutes in consumption, especially among the rural poor, the declining price of rice during the 1980s in turn depressed the demand for the two less-preferred substitutes. In recent times, however, the price of cassava has rebounded, doubling in 1985 and again in 1987. This largely reflected the GOI's determination to overcome domestic shortages and to procure sufficient supplies to meet the EEC export quota.[24] Although export crops have suffered from declining world prices, the revaluations of 1983 and September 1986 have somewhat restored Indonesia's relative competitiveness in many export markets.

This agricultural pricing structure has significant implications for the sustainable development of the uplands on Java and the economic incentives for upland farmers to improve their cropping systems and land management. Although there are important regional variations in trends, on the whole over the period 1976 – 86 across Java, the farmer terms of trade for paddy have declined sharply. For secondary food (*palawija*) crops they have risen only marginally, except for more significant increases in Central Java. For commercial crops, the fall in world commodity prices has generally depressed farmer terms of trade whereas for fruits and (especially) vegetables, farmer terms of trade have increased dramatically. With the exception of the recent price rise for cassava, these trends may, in the long run, encourage upland agricultural production to move from less profitable, relatively income-inelastic basic starchy staples to more profitable, income-elastic commodities such as fruits, animal products and tree crops.

As noted above, the increasing profitability of agriculture is an important incentive for upland farmers to invest in soil conservation measures and improved land-management techniques, although increased profitability alone may not be sufficient to induce conservation. Farmers may also be encouraged to adopt agroforestry and livestock-based farming systems that protect steep slopes as fruits, animal products and tree crops become relatively more profitable.

In contrast, the higher farmer terms of trade and therefore profitability of vegetable crops and sugar cane may actually be a disincentive to soil conservation. As the average returns to these highly commercialized and input-intensive crops increase, share tenancy and absentee ownership become more common, which can reduce the incentives for long-term investments in improved land management if tenancy arrangements are insecure and if the objective of absentee owners is short-term profit maximization or land speculation. In addition, the increased profitability of vegetable crops means that farmers are encouraged to cultivate them on steeply sloped volcanic soils, where water run-off, and therefore soil erosion, are greater. Similarly, although the system of controls for sugar has stabilized prices, eliminated imports and increased production, Indonesia has no comparative advantage in this crop. Consumer prices for refined sugar are three times the international price, and sugar production occupies a significant proporion of the scarce irrigated land on Java. The extra costs of expanding domestic sugar cultivation to about 1.8 million tons are estimated to be US$ 125 a tonne, or US$ 225 million per year.[25] Finally, the recent and rapid rise of cassava prices is worrying, as some upland farmers are switching back from more protective farming systems based on livestock rearing, agroforestry and annual multi-cropping, to cassava grown on highly erosive soils.

A key factor contributing to environmental degradation and low productivity on marginal uplands is the failure of farmers to adopt the appropriate farming and cultivating systems for the diverse agro-ecological conditions found here. In order for such diversified small-holder production systems to be viable on marginal lands, improvements in the quality and marketing of smallholder production, particularly of potentially tradeable crops and of import substitutes, are necessary. The ability of farmers to make these improvements and investments, particularly in agroforestry and livestock based systems, will in turn depend on the returns from their marketing efforts.

Although the combined effect of the 1983 and September 1986 devaluations has substantially improved Indonesia's relative competitiveness in a number of important agricultural exports, current evidence suggests that improvements in terms of trade are not directly benefiting upland farmers. The considerable market power of exporter associations, licensed exporters and approved traders and other marketing inter-mediaries means that the farmers, despite the devaluations, are paid little more for their coffee, corn, cassava, spices, pepper and other smallholder commodities.[26] In general, the farmers of the rain-fed drylands which predominate in the uplands of Java, tend to have lower producer margins than those growing crops on the irrigated lowlands. For example, producers receive 80 to 85 % of the retail price for rice, 70 to 75 % of the retail price for soya beans and only 60 to 65 % of the final price for corn, which is predominantly a dryland crop.[27]

Not only have farmers in lowland irrigated areas benefited substantially in the past from disproportionate investments in marketing and transportation, but because in the uplands farmers tend to have holdings that are small- scale and scattered over small and isolated plots, transportation and marketing inefficiencies are increased. In addition, as they have limited labour and capital, very limited market information and more mixed cropping systems yielding smaller volumes of individual crops, upland farmers are less likely to engage in marketing activities and more prone to price discrimination by marketing intermediaries. In the Citanduy River Basin, West Java, only 10–20 % of clove and peanut farmers either dry their crops or transport them to sub-district sellers.[28]

Agricultural input subsidies in Indonesia amounted to around US$ 725 million in 1985. The current effective subsidy for fertilizers to farmers is about 38 % of the farmgate price (a weighted average of the subsidy rates for TSP and urea). For pesticides, the rate is more than 40 %. Irrigation attracts as much as 87 %, and credit is given at an implicit rate of 8 % (based on 1985 average commercial rates and outstanding public credit to agriculture).

The policy of heavily subsidizing agricultural inputs was one of the hallmarks of the Green Revolution rice self-sufficiency strategy of the 1960s and 1970s. Thus, the bulk of these subsidies has benefited the lowland irrigated, mainly rice-producing areas of Java, South Sumatra, South Sulawesi and Bali. As a result of maintaining high input subsidies over the period 1970 to 1984, the area of higher yielding varieties (HYVs) has expanded from 0.8 to 6.8 million ha. On Java, the average area planted with HYVs has reached 94 %; the irrigated area has increased from 3.7 to 4.9 million ha; the distribution of subsidized fertilizers from 0.2 to 4.1 million tons; and the distribution of subsidized pesticides from 1,080 to 14,210 tons.[29]

With the current emphasis on agricultural diversification, these subsidies are increasingly being used to stimulate production of non-rice crops – notably sugar, cassava, maize, palm oil and soya beans. Assuming no change in policy, the total costs of these input subsidies is anticipated to increase as they are gradually extended to agricultural cultivation on marginal lands, including upland areas. For example, rainfed crops on Java (with the exception of high-value vegetables, fruits and estate crops) still tend to use relatively lower subsidized inputs than irrigated rice and sugar. On the other hand, rainfed (dryland) crops appear to use relatively more organic fertilizers.[30] Although the yields and net returns of intensive irrigated rice on Java are substantially higher than those for dryland crops, this does not necessarily imply greater efficiency in the use of inputs. For instance, with the exception of fertilizer use on maize, non-intensive irrigated paddy and the predominantly rainfed staple crops appear to have lower per unit costs of pesticide and fertilizer use than does intensive wetland paddy. This would suggest that subsidies are encouraging the over-use of these inputs in intensive wetland rice cropping. Moreover, per unit irrigation costs for wetland rice are strikingly low, given that irrigation accounts for 91 % of the water use on Java. Finally, the greater availability of HYVs for irrigated rice may account for the much higher use of purchased seeds in intensive irrigated rice cultivation compared to other crop production.[31]

Over-use of fertilizers as a result of the subsidy is a substantial problem, particularly in lowland irrigated areas. With the consumption of fertilizer increasing on average by 12.3 % per annum over 1980–85, the current rate of fertilizer consumption – 75 kg per ha of arable land – is much higher than in other Asian countries (e.g., 32 kg in the Philippines and 24 kg in Thailand). In some areas of Indonesia, applications of urea can reach 200–250 kg per ha. Given that fertilizer comprises less than 10 % of the production cost of rice and that the largest production response is achieved at relatively low levels of application, the current high rice-fertilizer price ratio of 1.5–2 will continue to encourage inappropriate application and waste, with little increase in the output of rice.[32] Moreover, providing subsidized fertilizers to cultivators of marginal lands may be counter-productive. These farmers will apply relatively cheap fertilizers so as to increase their yields rather than consider more expensive but environmentally sound methods such as green manuring, mulching and composting to maintain soil fertility. Thus fertilizer subsidies are a disincentive, at least in the short run. They discourage farmers from facing the full economic costs of declining soil fertility, particularly from soil erosion, and from responding with sound land-conservation measures. For example in Ngadas, East Java, farmers are presently using over 1,000 kg of subsidized chemical fertilizers per hectare to produce two 10-tonne potato crops. These yields are less than one half of what could be attained with improved soil-management techniques and green manuring. Recently, as farmers have come to realize that increased fertilizer use was not offsetting yield reductions, they have returned to using organic fertilizers.[33]

The GOI has recently banned the use of 57 pesticides and is planning an integrated pest-management programme with the World Bank and the FAO. However, the current subsidy levels will probably continue to encourage inappropriate and excessive use of pesticides. In fact, the ban was a belated response to the latest plague of rice brown planthopper. This was associated with the misapplication of pesticides which have wiped out natural pest predators, parasites and pathogens. A major concern is that the pesticide subsidies will discourage traditional methods of eradicating pests, and make integrated and biological pest control relatively less attractive to farmers. Subsidized pesticides encourage farmers to treat fields preventively even before an economically damaging insect population is present, causing natural enemies to be killed and freeing pests (e.g., brown planthopper) from natural control. Even rice varieties normally resistant to the brown planthopper, such as IR–36, have been known to be "hopper-burned" (severely damaged by brown planthopper feeding) when treated too often with insecticides.

In Northern Sumatra, the population density of brown planthopper (between 0.5 and 40 per plant) rose directly as the number of reported insecticide applications. In five areas experiencing hopper-burn, farmers were treating fields six to twenty times in four to eight weeks without any success.[34] Although fiscal outlays for pesticide subsidies have been reduced, preliminary indications suggest that the costs of these subsidies are being shifted from the official budget to the operations of parastatal producers, who are financing it through additional borrowing.

The high level of subsidy for irrigation – US$ 401 million spread over approximately 4 million ha – is also causing problems of over-use. Total spending on operation and maintenance (O & M) has been reduced by budget cuts, and the supply network has been jeopardized by the failure to recover any significant amount of the costs of irrigation. Failure to maintain the irrigation network will, in the long run, translate into losses of agricultural productivity, which will be exacerbated by any water scarcity problems caused by over-use. As municipal and industrial uses continue to expand, the allocation of scarce water supplies will become a pressing problem in the near future.

Despite implicit credit subsidies, public liquidity credit is estimated to meet only 15 % of the demand for credit by farmers; the other 85 % is obtained informally at an interest rate of around 60 %. Small farmers, particularly those outside the lowland irrigated areas, are especially dependent on such high cost, informal sources of funds. Moreover, although sugar production accounts for only 3.3 % of the value of total crop production in Indonesia, in 1985 over 50 % of subsidized liquidity credit went to sugar growers.[35]

These distortions in the credit market and the general lack of multi-purpose credit at affordable rates with medium- and long-term payback periods, are seen to be major constraints on the sustainable development of agricultural lands. They limit particularly the adoption of improved soil-conservation and land-management techniques on marginal lands. For example, investments in bench terracing require a medium-term loan for at least two years and short-term loans for succeeding years. Agroforestry requires long-term loans for at least seven years. Different rates and terms are required for various private smallholder investments in marketing, transport facilities, post-harvesting technologies and quality improvements.[36]

As the producer prices for the major food crops (rice, corn, and until recently, cassava) in Indonesia have generally followed the underlying trend in world market prices, there seems little need to change pricing policies for these crops. Improvements in quality and yield in upland soya bean production and of other higher valued upland crops may, in the long run, be a more effective way of increasing farmer incomes than the current practice of maintaining domestic prices well in excess of world levels. On the other hand, high effective protection rates for vegetables and sugar production are counterproductive in terms of promoting improved soil-conservation practices in upland areas, and may benefit the richer rather than poorer upland farmers.

To encourage the spread of agroforestry and livestock-based forage systems, particularly in the uplands of Java, may mean a continuation of some restrictive import controls for perennial fruits and animal husbandry products. However, in the long run, Indonesia will need to develop export markets for certain products, such as tropical fruits. This will require a gradual dismantling of policies to protect domestic production. In general, for all export crops vital to sustainable upland development (e.g., coffee, cloves, tea, cocoa, etc.), not only must international competitiveness be maintained by an effective exchange-rate policy, but monopolistic trading practices must be removed to allow the benefits of improved terms of trade to reach upland smallholders.

Current agricultural policies – particularly input subsidies and invest-ment strategies for research, extension and infrastructure – are still largely biased towards lowland irrigated agriculture, especially rice cultivation. Not only does this imply an under-investment in other agricultural areas that are currently absorbing labour and could potentially yield higher growth and incomes, but it also artificially overvalues the contribution to agricultural development of the lowlands, compared with the contribution of these other areas. The high-input subsidies also encourage wastefulness which is the direct cause of some environmental problems. They also act as disincentives to the proper management of land and water resources. Moreover, as Indonesia now produces rice surpluses that result in additional high costs for storage and subsidized exports, there is clearly a case for introducing a phased reduction of these subsidies and reallocating funds towards more urgent agricultural investments, such as sustainable agricultural development in upland areas.

Reducing or eliminating input subsidies and reallocating research and extension funds could, in the short term, release US$ 275 million annually for investment in more sustainable agriculture.[37] Assuming a gradual phase-out of the fertilizer subsidy and a fourfold increase in both research and extension budgets, this could increase to as much as US$ 525 million per year. Thus, the following investement programme would be feasible:

| | | |
|---|---|---|
| i) $ 35–40 million | – | Integrated pest management (IPM) for brown planthopper control, gradually to be extended to IPM for other pests. |
| ii) $ 40–45 million | – | Increasing the availability of general rural credit, particularly to marginal farmers, at affordable rates and with multiple terms. |
| iii) $ 60–240 million | – | Research and extension to develop and support new farming systems and land-management techniques appropriate to the marginal (mainly dryland and swampland) sedentary agriculture in the Outer Islands and the uplands of Java, as well as shifting cultivation. This would include the development and dissemination of new varieties appropriate to diverse agro-ecological conditions, research into pest and disease outbreaks, and improvements in smallholder estate crop systems. |
| iv) $ 140–200 million | – | Investment in: a) further improvements in farming systems for specific agroecological zones; and b) improvements in the physical infrastructure serving these zones, including rural transport, integration of markets, credit facilities, post-harvest technology and processing, and produce quality. |

Such an agricultural strategy does not necessarily mean sacrificing the overall government objectives of food self-sufficiency and agricultural diversification. On the contrary, it may be crucial to the achievement of these objectives. Indonesia rice production, which accounts for about 70% of the total food-crop area harvested, already occupies the most fertile lowland areas on the islands of Java, Bali, Southern Sulawesi and Southern Sumatra. The limits on expanding irrigated rice production and increasing yields on these fertile lowlands suggest that agricultural resources there are already being exploited at or near their full potential in production levels.

In contrast, the low yields in the upland areas of Java stem from cropping systems, land-management techniques, input packages and, above all, research and extension advice inappropriate for the more diversified and fragile agro-ecological conditions found on these lands. Nevertheless, dryland – mainly upland – food production accounts for nearly two-thirds or more of maize, cassava, sweet potato and peanut production, and around 40 % of soya bean production on Java (see Table 7.1). The total dryland area planted with paddy and secondary crops on Java amounts to about one-fifth of the total harvested food production area in Indonesia. Food production on the marginal drylands of Java alone may contribute over 3 % of GDP and about 15 % of agricultural GDP. Moreover, Table 7.2 indicates that yields in food production could be substantially increased, particularly on dryland areas, by overcoming inappropriate land-management, cropping-system, and research and extension techniques, as well as other constraints. This suggests that the potential food production on Java's drylands could be almost 25% greater

**Table 7.1: Area Planted of Paddy and Secondary Crops, Java 1985**

|  | Wetland (ha) | Dryland (ha) | Total (ha) | Total Indonesia (ha)[a] |
|---|---|---|---|---|
|  | '000 units | | | |
| Paddy | 4756.5 | 329.7 | 5086.2 | 9902.3 |
| Maize | 541.9 | 1403.6 | 1945.5 | 2439.9 |
| Cassava | 25.6 | 766.9 | 792.5 | 1291.8 |
| Sweet Potatoes | 40.4 | 58.8 | 99.2 | 256.1 |
| Peanuts | 123.8 | 245.7 | 369.5 | 510.1 |
| Soya beans | 378.6 | 238.9 | 617.5 | 896.2 |
| TOTAL | 5866.8 | 3043.6 | 8910.4 | 15296.4 |

a = Area harvested

*Sources:* BPS, *Production of Cereals in Java*, 1985, and *Cost Structures of Farms* Paddy and Palawija, 1985, Jakarta

### Table 7.2:  Indonesia – Main Constraints on Production and Potential

| Commodity<br><br>(1) | Provinces with Major<br>Smallholder Activities in<br>Order of Importance<br>(2) | Main Constraints to Increasing<br>Smallholder Production<br><br>(3) |
|---|---|---|
| Paddy (rice)<br>(dry gabah) | W Java, E Java, C Java, S Sulawesi, N Sumatra, S Sumatra, W Kalimantan, S Kalimantan, W Sumatra, Aceh, Lampung, NTB, Bali, Riau, Jambi, NTT[a] | Pests (chiefly brown planthopper and rats); diseases; limited periods of water supply or flooding; lack of upland blast-resistant varieties |
| Corn<br>(dry seed) | E Java, C Java, S Sulawesi, NTT, N Sulawesi, W Java, N Sumatra, Bali, SE Sulawesi, Yogyakarta, C Sulawesi, Lampung, NTB | Downy mildew and insufficient good seed of mildew-resistant variety; yield closely linked to rainfall; risk factors and unreliable marketing discourage farmers from using cash inputs |
| Cassava<br>(fresh root) | E Java, C Java, W Java, Yogyakarta, Lampung, NTT, S Sulawesi | Poorly developed marketing system and low farmgate price; inadequate supply of improved planting material; crop management poor due to lack of incentives and knowledge |
| Groundnut<br>(shelled) | E Java, C Java, W Java, Yogyakarta, S Sulawesi, N Sumatra, NTB | Marketing system and price fluctuation; inadequate supply of good seed of improved planting material; crop management poor due to lack of incentives and knowledge |
| Soya bean<br>(dry seed) | E Java, C Java, NTB, Lampung, W Java, Yogyakarta, N Sumatra, Mali | Pod-boring insects uncontrolled; intermediate fruiting pattern, cercospora rust disease; rather poor quality due to lack of effective pest control and low standard of management |
| Sweet potato<br>(fresh root) | E Java, W Java, C Java, Irian Java, N Sumatra, NTT, Bali, NTB, Maluku | Lack of effective marketing system and adequate improved planting material; limited use of case inputs due to lack of market and price level |

a = NTT (Nusa Tenggara Timur) and NTB (Nusa Tenggara Batat)
*Source:* World Bank, Indonesia "Agricultural policy: Issues and options", Technical Annex, Table 2 (World Bank: Washington DC, 17 July 1987).

than current output (see Table 7.3). On highly erodable soils (e.g., limestone clays) and on slopes greater than 50 %, switching from annual food cropping altogether to perennial tree crops and livestock-based systems would significantly increase the economic potential of severely degraded uplands.

## for Increasing the Yields of Major Food Crops

| Key Points for Emphasis in Extension (4) | Present Average Smallholder Yield (5) | Agronimically Feasible Average Yield (6) | Expected Yield with Improved Extension (7) |
|---|---|---|---|
| Selection of varieties resistant in local pests/ diseases; improved nursery management; timing, rate and method of application of fertilisers and pesticides; correct time of transplanting; pest surveillance; communal rat control; water management including drainage in maturity period | Java: 4.5 ton/ha Other islands: 3.0 ton/ha | Java: 6.0 ton/ha Other islands: 4.5 ton/ha | Java: 5.0 ton/ha Other islands: 3.5 ton/ha |
| Introduce short duration HYV in E Java and in other provinces mildew-resistant HYV; correct time of planting and pest control; rate, time, method of application of fertiliser; improved processing and storage | Java: 1.7 ton/ha Other islands: 1.6 ton/ha | Java: 2.75 ton/ ha Other islands: 2.3 ton/ha | Java: 2.1 ton/ha Other islands 1.9 ton/ha |
| Selection of high-yielding, bacterial blight-resistant varieties; improved processing to achieve better quality and price; promote use of fertiliser; better plant spacing; erosion control measures | Java: 9.9 ton/ha Other islands: 9.8 ton/ha | Java: 20 ton/ha | Java: 12.3 ton/ ha Other islands: 12.2 ton/ha |
| Introduce improved HYVs; use of good seed rate; improved time, method of applying fertiliser; improved pest and disease control and post-harvest handling; improve sowing timing and land preparation; liming where necessary | 0.94 ton/ha | 1.5 ton/ha | 1.25 ton/ha |
| Introduce improved varieties; improved seed and preparation/planting techniques, pest control, and post-harvest handling; rhizobium inoculation; basal phosphatic and initial nitrogen fertiliser applications | 0.90 ton/ha | 1.50 ton/ha | 1.1 ton/ha |
| Introduce improved planting materials; improved rate, time and method of applying fertiliser and post-harvest handling | 7.8 ton/ha | 20 ton/ha | 10 ton/ha |

## *SUMMARY AND CONCLUSION*

The on- and off-site impacts of upper watershed degradation on Java illustrates the relative and potential absolute natural-resource scarcity effects suggested by the alternative view. As this chapter has emphasized,

**Table 7.3: Actual and Potential Production of Major Food Crops, Java 1985**

|  | Dryland Area ('000 ha) | Actual Yield (tonnes/ha) | Potential Yield (tonnes/ha) | Actual Production ('000 tonnes) | Potential Production ('000 tonnes) |
|---|---|---|---|---|---|
| Paddy | 329.7 | 1.75[a] | 1.94[b] | 576.975 | 639.618 |
| Maize | 1,403.6 | 1.7 | 2.1 | 2,386.12 | 2,947.56 |
| Cassava | 766.9 | 9.9 | 12.3 | 7,592.31 | 9,432.87 |
| Sweet Potatoes | 58.8 | 7.8 | 10 | 458.64 | 588 |
| Peanuts | 245.7 | 0.95 | 1.25 | 233.415 | 307.125 |
| Soybeans | 238.9 | 0.9 | 1.1 | 215.01 | 262.79 |
| Total | 3,043.6 | – | – | 11,462.47 | 14,177.96 |

[a] From Frederick C. Roche, "Sustainable farm development in Java's critical lands: Is a green revolution really necessary?" (Division of Nutritional Sciences, Cornell University, 1987), Table 12, p. 46.

[b] Assumes a 11 % increase, as suggested by Table 7.2

*Sources:* Tables 7.1 and 7.2 except where indicated.

it is necessary to understand the economic incentives determining farmers' decisions over choice of crops, farming systems and land-use patterns in order to design an appropriate investment and policy strategy to overcome these impacts. A major reason for the failure of the current strategy is its disincentives for upland farmers to invest in improvements in their land management and in agricultural systems, and soil and water conservation techniques that control erosion. Moreover, isolated soil and water conservation projects are not sufficient to deal with the problem of upper watershed degradation. What is required are complementary policy reforms as part of a positive strategy for sustainable agricultural development in the uplands.

Thus, the key to sustainable agricultural development in the uplands of Java is appropriate marketing, post-harvest technology and processing, rural credit, research and extension, seeds for high-yielding varieties (HYVs), transport, and other infrastructure and institutional investments. Therefore, what is really needed is a commitment to integrated rural development combining economic incentives through appropriate pricing policies, physical infrastructure and institutional investments.

The additional value of investments in physical infrastructure in rural areas is their capacity, directly and indirectly, to generate off-farm employment. For example, in the lowlands of Java, the rural infrastructure built to accompany the rice-based development strategy allowed for additional employment in trade, transport, private construction and services that especially benefited the landless and those with marginal holdings. Greater investment in infrastructure in the uplands of Java would also have important income-generating and employment multiplier effects. So, too, would the establishment of more processing and transportation in rural areas. This would allow local produce to be stored, moved to nearby or distant markets, sorted, graded and packed for domestic and export markets, and processed into both food and industrial products.[38]

Although there is some evidence that the availability of off-farm income may lessen farmers' attachment to the land and hence their willingness to invest in improved land management, the effective co-ordination of physical infrastructure investment with agricultural and rural development should expand overall incomes and employment opportunities sufficiently to ensure that the majority of households would use these additional resources to invest in and improve their land.


## NOTES

1. This chapter is based on the work the author has done for USAID and the World Bank. Some of it appears in a World Bank report, *Indonesia – Java Watersheds: Java Uplands and Watershed Management* (World Bank: Washington, DC, November 1987). The report was prepared by Peter Arens, Edward B. Barbier, Gordon R. Conway, Dirk Leeuwrik, David S. McCauley and William B. Magrath. See also Edward B. Barbier, "Natural resources policy and economic framework", Annex 1, in James Tarrant *et al.* (eds), *Natural Resources and Environmental Management in Indonesia* (USAID: Jakarta, Indonesia, October 1987); and Edward B. Barbier, "The economics of farm-level adoption of soil conservation measures in the uplands of Java", Environment Department Working Paper No. 11 (World Bank: Washington, DC, October 1988). However, the views expressed in this chapter are those of the author, and do not reflect the policy nor the views of the World Bank or USAID.

2. See World Bank, *Indonesia – Java Watersheds*, op. cit., and Barbier, "Natural resources policy", op. cit.

3. A number of recent studies have developed techniques for this sort of analysis. See, for example, K. William Easter, John A. Dixon and Maynard Hufscmidt (eds), *Watershed Resources Management: An Integrated Framework with Studies from Asia and the Pacific* (Westview Press: Boulder, Colorado, 1986); H.M. Gregerson, K.N. Brooks, John A. Dixon and Lawrence S. Hamilton, *Guidelines for Economic Appraisal of Watershed Management Projects* (FAO: Rome, March 1986); and Alberto Veloz, Douglas Southgate, F. Hitzhusen and Robert Macgregor, "The economics of erosion control in a subtropical watershed: A Dominican case", *Land Economics*, Vol. 61 (1985), pp. 145–55.

4. For example, erodability is often defined as "the ease with which soil particles are being detached and carried away by the impact of falling rain" (see World Bank, *Indonesia – Java Watersheds*, op. cit.). The major soils of Java are commonly divided into four classes of susceptibility– recent volcanic (low erodability), pliocene volcanic (low – medium), pliocene sedimentary (high), and miocene sedimentary (very high). See Karl Kucera, *et al.*, *Micro Model Farm Assessment of Land Resources*, Directorate

General of Reforestation and Land Rehabilitation, Department of Forestry (GOI and USAID: Citanduy, Ciamis, Indonesia, May 1986).

5. World Bank, *Indonesia – Java Watersheds*, op. cit. Off-site sedimentation may also yield some benefits, notably the provision of very fertile silt for agricultural activity downstream. Although there is anecdotal evidence of these benefits for the lower watersheds of Java, this effect has not been formally studied and valued. It may be extremely important in some areas. As a result, any evaluation of the off-site costs of upper watershed degradation should also look at this and any other potential benefit from downstream sedimentation.

6. William B. Magrath and Peter Arens, "The costs of soil erosion on Java – A natural resource accounting approach" (World Resources Institute: Washington, DC, November 1987).

7. A formal analysis of the incentives for upland farmers to invest in soil conservation packages is provided in Barbier, "The economics of farm level adoption", op. cit.

8. Bungaran Saragih, Paul C. Huszar and Harold C. Cochrane, "Model farm program benefits: The Citanduy watershed" (USAID: Jakarta, Indonesia, July 1986).

9. Kucera *et al.*, op. cit.

10. Achmad M. Fagi and Cynthia Mackie, "Watershed management in upland Java: Past experience and future directions", paper presented at "Soil and Water Conservation on Steep Lands" (Soil Conservation Society of America: San Juan, Puerto Rico, 22–27 March, 1987).

11. R. Bernstein and R. Sinaga, "Economics" Technical Appendix 6, Government of Indonesia/USAID, *Composite Report of the Watershed Assessment Team* (Jakarta, Indonesia).

12. Kurianto Dwiwarsito and Jan de Graff, *Economic Impact of Watershed Development Activities at the Village Level* (Kali Konto Project: Malang, Indonesia, August 1987), p. 40.

13. Bernstein and Sinaga, op. cit.

14. Dwiwarsito and de Graff, op. cit., Chapter 4.

15. Bernstein and Sinaga, op. cit.

16. Ibid.

17. Brian Carson and KEPAS East Java, *A Comparison of Soil Conservation Strategies in Four Agroecological Zones in the Upland of East Java* (KEPAS: Malang, Indonesia, July 1987).

18. S.M.H. Tampubolon and Bungaran Saragih, "Model farm upland farming technology in the Citanduy River Basin; A state of the art" (USESE: Ciamis, Indonesia, 1986).

19. Saragih, Huszar and Cochrane, op. cit.

20. Bernstein and Sinaga, op. cit.

21. Achmad Sumitro, "Tree crop management" Technical Appendix 5, Government of Indonesia/USAID, *Composite Report of the Watershed Assessment Team*, Vol. 3 (Jakarta, Indonesia, 1983).

22. For further discussion of these points, see Edward B. Barbier, "Cash crops, food crops and agricultural sustainability: The case of Indonesia", forthcoming in *World Development*, Vol. 17 (1989).

23. Bruce Glassburner, "Macroeconomics and the agricultural sector", *Bulletin of Indonesian Economic Studies*, Vol. 21 (1985).

24. Although only 10 % of cassava is exported, 97 % of exports are to the EEC. See Faisal Kasryno, "Analysius of trends and prospects for cassava in Indonesia", (Center for Agroeconomic Research, Agency for Agricultural Research and Development; Bogor, Indonesia, April 1987).

25. World Bank, "Indonesian agricultural policy: Issues and options", Vol 1: The Main Report (World Bank: Washington, DC, July 17 1987), p. 38.

26. World Bank, "Indonesia – agricultural policy: Issues and options", op. cit, p. 48.

27. World Bank, "Indonesia – agricultural policy", op. cit., Technical Annex E, Table 1.
28. Bambang Irawan, "Executive summary: Marketing analysis for dryland farming development in Citanduy River Basin" (USESE: Ciamis, Indonesia, 1986).
29. World Bank, "Indonesia – agricultural policy", op. cit.
30. Frederick C. Roche, "Sustainable farm development in Java's critical lands: Is a 'Green Revolution' really necessary?" (Division of Nutritional Sciences, Cornell University: Ithaca, New York, May 1987).
31. See World Bank, "Indonesia – Java watersheds", op. cit.
32. Barbier, "Natural resources and economic policy framework", op. cit., p. 16.
32. See World Bank, "Indonesia – Java watersheds", op. cit.; and Carson *et al.*, op. cit.
34. Peter E. Kenmore, "Status report on integrated pest control in rice in Indonesia with special reference to conservation of natural enemies and the rice brown planthopper (*Nilaparvata lugens*)" (FAO Indonesia: 13 October 1986).
35. World Bank, "Indonesia – agricultural policy", op. cit.
36. World Bank, "Indonesia – Java watersheds", op. cit.
37. This amounts to US$ 150 million from a reduction in the fertilizer subsidy, US$ 25 million and US $ 40 million from the abolishment of the pesticide and sugar credit subsidies respectively, and US$ 30 million each for the reallocation of research and extension funding.
38. See, in particular, William L. Collier, Soentoro, Gunawan Wiradi, Effendi Pasandaran, Kabul Santoso and Joseph F. Stepanek, "Acceleration of rural development on Java", *Bulletin of Indonesian Economic Studies*, Vol. 18 (1982), pp. 84–101; and Douglas D. Hedley, "Diversification: concepts and directions in Indonesian agricultural policy" (Workshop on Soybean Research and Development in Indonesia, The CGPRI Centre: Bogor, Indonesia, 24–26 February 1987).

# 8
# *Conclusion*: An Economics of Sustainable Development

The implications of Natural-Resource Scarcity for welfare have always been considered an economic problem. As, at different times, economists have seen scarcity in different functions of the environment, economic perspectives or views of it necessarily change.

This book has primarily been concerned with these changing economic perspectives. The main theme has been that the emergence of a new class of scarcity problems – products of cumulative and often irreversible environmental degradation – demands an alternative view of natural-resource scarcity. Therefore, most of the book has been taken up with exploring the main differences, as well as the similarities, between more conventional approaches to environmental and resource problems, and an alternative approach. The previous two chapters have tried to provide specific illustrations of the type of scarcity effects, their impacts on welfare, and the policy implications (to which the alternative view is particularly applicable). The last chapter, discussing the problem of upper watershed degradation on Java, focusses mainly on appropriate policy responses. The ultimate aim of such a response must clearly be to counteract environmental degradation and foster more sustainable economic development.

But what exactly constitutes "sustainable" development and what modifications and restraints does it require of economic–environmental interactions? What new developments in economic analysis are in turn required to help policymakers ensure that a development path is inherently "sustainable"? How far are we along the road towards an economics of sustainable development and how much further do we have to go?

## SOME DEFINITIONS AND CONDITIONS

The broad objective of sustainable economic development is to find the optimal level of interaction between three systems – the biological and resource system, the economic system, and the social system – through a dynamic and adaptive process of trade-offs.[1] This optimal level would therefore be the most sustainable development that these three crucial systems can support. To be truly useful and operational however, sustainability must be applicable to all forms of economic and social activity, ranging from agriculture and forestry to industry and human settlements. At the moment, this goal needs to be made more concise, systematic and rigorous before it can usefully be applied in policymaking and planning.

Nevertheless, a broad consensus does exist about the conditions required for sustainable economic development.[2] Two interpretations are now emerging: a wider concept concerned with sustainable economic, ecological *and* social development; and a more narrowly defined concept largely concerned with environmentally sustainable development (i.e., with optimal resource and environmental management over time).

The wider, highly normative view of sustainable development (endorsed by the World Commission on Environment and Development) defines the concept as "development that meets the needs of the present without compromising the ability of future generations to meet their own needs".[3] More specifically, a sustainable development approach – particularly as applied to the Third World – requires that

> the strategies which are being formulated and implemented are environmentally sustainable over the long-term, are consistent with social values and institutions, and encourage "grassroots" participation in the development process.... In general terms, the primary objective is reducing the absolute poverty of the world's poor through providing lasting and secure livelihoods that minimize resource depletion, environmental degradation, cultural disruption, and social instability.[4]

In contrast, concern with optimal resource and environmental management over time – the more narrowly defined concept of environmentally sustainable development – requires maximizing the net benefits of economic development, subject to maintaining the services and quality of natural resources.[5]

The term "natural resources" should be interpreted in the broad sense used by the alternative view of natural-resource scarcity (see Chapter 5). It includes *renewable* resources such as water, terrestrial and aquatic biomass; *nonrenewable* resources such as land, minerals, metals and fossil fuels; and *semi-renewable* resources such as soil quality, the assimilative capacity of the environment, and ecological life-support systems.[6]

Note that maintaining the services of a natural capital stock does not necessarily imply maintaining the physical stock intact which, in any case, may be neither desirable nor feasible. By definition, any positive-use rate for exhaustible resources will physically deteriorate this total capital stock.

However, it is possible to maintain the value of the services at some approximately constant level while allowing the stock of exhaustible resources to decline. This calls for increased technological change to enhance environmental quality and the level of environmental services, and the removal of incentives to deplete resources in an unsustainable fashion.

Sustainable development also implies caution in assuming that an irreversible loss of the natural capital stock is justified if it results in the formation of more reproducible (manufactured) capital. As stressed throughout this book, some of the functions of the environment are not replicable, such as complex life-support systems, biological diversity, aesthetic functions, micro-climatic conditions and so forth. Others might be substituted but not without unacceptable cost. In addition, degradation of one or more parts of a resource system beyond some threshold may lead to a breakdown in the integrity of the whole system, dramatically affecting recovery rates and the resilience of the system. The total costs of such a breakdown may often exceed the value of the activity causing it.

Harvesting tropical forests is a valuable activity. Continual depletion and degradation of a forest system, however, might impair nutrient and water cycling, soil composition and run-off and energy flows. The cumulative result may be a breakdown in the ability of the forest system to recover and regenerate sufficiently to avoid damage to micro-climatic conditions, soil and water conservation, and to the general ecological stability and resilience of the forest system and neighbouring agricultural systems. Clearly, developing economic indicators of sustainability – or alternatively, improving economic analysis of this type of scarcity effects – is essential to the goal of sustainable development.

To ensure environmentally sustainable development, economic decision-makers must design policies, investment strategies and incentive structures that can deal effectively with the type of scarcity effects emphasized by the alternative view. In general, there is a need to recognize the importance of the irreversible effects of development and of the valuation of any benefits lost through the reduction of the natural capital stock in such a way that its flow of services is affected. Thus, the first step in devising economic indicators of sustainability is the proper valuation of the economic consequences of natural-resource degradation over time (see below).

Ultimately, the full integration of environmental considerations into development objectives must imply a convergence between the two interpretations of sustainable development. Then one can clearly consider as sustainable develoment any economic activity that raises social welfare with the minimum amount of environmental degradation allowable within given economic, social and technical constraints. This is not to argue that the wider interpretation is superior to the narrower or *vice versa*. However, it is clearly apparent that tackling the problem of environmentally sustainable development is a necessary precondition to understanding the conditions required to achieve overall sustainable development. This is particularly true for economies and economic systems in developing countries which are dependent on the exploitation of natural resources. In these countries, the *efficient* use of natural capital stock is essential for maximizing current efforts towards development. At the same time, *sustainable* use must be the foundation upon which emerging structural developments in industry and services can safely and continuously be built.

Similarly, in the case of agriculture – or more accurately agro-ecosystems – the application of the concept is self-evident as these systems are directly dependent on environmental resources and essential ecological functions for sustainability. This becomes apparent if we take Conway's more specific definition of agricultural sustainability as discussed in Chapter 2: "the ability of a system to maintain its productivity when subject to stress or shock".[7] The unchecked abuse of resources within an agro-ecosystem (whether as a result of the inappropriate use of agro-chemicals and fertilizers, the overcropping of erodable soils, poor drainage, etc.) can affect the overall sustainability of the agro-ecosystem by increasing the susceptibility to stress, shock, or both. The key lies in reducing the degradation of resources and, therefore, the stresses and shocks associated with it, to a level where the natural processes and functions of the agro-ecosystem – appropriately subsidized by human-made inputs and innovations – can counteract these disturbances and so preserve overall sustainability.[8]

Of course, the crucial element in all this is that the productivity of the agro-ecosystem is essential to human livelihoods. In developing countries in particular, we are really talking about sustainable livelihoods. Chambers points out that this requires "a level of wealth and of stocks and flows of food and cash which provide for physical and social wellbeing and security against becoming poorer."[9] This quickly gets us back to the wider concept of sustainable development, in which the appropriate balance is struck between the need for the poor to gain better livelihoods against the needs of future generations. Consequently, especially in rural settings in developing countries where livelihoods are dependent on the productivity of agro-ecosystems and its equitable distribution, we come back to Conway's view of agricultural sustainability. We must therefore consider the appropriate trade-offs among, on the one hand, ensuring the long-term sustainability of such agro-ecosystems and, on the other, the potential sacrifices (if any) in short-term productivity, stability and equity.[10]

We are also back to Page's conservation criterion for ensuring intergenerational equity: if the opportunity of equal access to natural resources is a condition for each generation's survival, or at least a condition for achieving "sustainable livelihoods", this suggests a permanent livability criterion ensuring that the resource base is kept intact. That is, unless all generations can be made better off by degradation of the resource base, then it should be managed as though it were jointly owned over time.[11]

This implies that the resource base itself must be equal across generations. In physical terms, such a rule is clearly self-defeating as any current extractions of non-renewable resources will reduce the stock available to future generations. On the other hand, as argued by Pearce, if the resource base is viewed as a composite of renewables and non-renewables, if users are indifferent about which is used, and if the renewable-resource use rate never exceeds the regeneration rate, then exhaustables can safely be diminished by current generations.[12] Limiting use of renewable resources within regeneration rates should allow the steady substitution of renewables for non-renewables over time, as stocks of the latter decline and increase in relative scarcity. As a result, the composite stock of resources can be maintained across generations.

Maximizing the net benefits of economic development, subject to maintaining the services and the quality of the stock of natural resources over time, is an essential criterion for sustainable development. As Pearce and others have consistently argued, this criterion means observing certain biophysical constraints.[13] That is, if the resource base is a composite of exhaustables and renewables (including semi-renewables and waste-assimilative capacity), sustainability requires:

i) utilizing renewable resources at rates less than or equal to the natural or managed rates of regeneration;

ii) generating wastes at rates less than or equal to the rates at which they can be absorbed by the assimilative capacity of the environment; *and*

iii) optimizing the efficiency with which exhaustable resources are used, as determined by the rate at which renewable resources can be substituted for exhaustables and by technological progress.

Failure to obey these constraints will lead to a process of environmental degradation as the resource base is depleted, wastes accumulate and natural ecological processes are impaired. In turn, this will lead to the kinds of natural-resource scarcity effects suggested by the alternative view. This of course assumes that:

i) the services, or functions, of the environment are essential to the economic system;

ii) there are insufficient substitution possibilities between reproducible capital and these environmental functions; *and*

iii) these environmental functions are not augmented by a constant positive rate of technical progress.[14]

The conditions governing the optimal trade-off between environmental quality and consumption over time have been analysed in various models of economic-environmental interaction.[15] Although these models assume some form of environmental degradation, and thus implicitly assume the transgression of biophysical constraints by the economic system, no attempt is made to examine explicitly how an economy might respond to the limits imposed by these constraints and hence the optimal conditions for sustainable economic growth.

In contrast, a simple model developed in the appendix to this chapter characterizes the conditions necessary to maintain the environmental sustainability of an economic system over time. The results of the model indicate that the initial level of environmental quality as well as the rate of social time preference are significant factors in determining the optimal choice between sustainable and unsustainable growth. For example, with an initial low level of environmental quality and a high rate of social discount, environmentally unsustainable economic growh may be an optimal strategy, as the benefits of increased consumption occur in the present whereas environmental degradation and collapse is a future problem. Moreover, the initial level of environmental quality influences the minimum bound on discount rates, so a historically lower initial level of environmental quality leads to a high rate of discount and *vice versa*.

## SUSTAINABLE DEVELOPMENT AND ADVANCED ECONOMIES

The concept of sustainable economic development is certainly relevant to advanced industrialized countries. That is, the continuing emphasis on resource-intensive, growth-oriented development in these countries has culminated in the following pattern of resource allocation:

- a decrease in the labour/output ratio (less labour per unit of output);
- an increase in the capital-intensity of production (requiring more investment per unit of output);
- an increase in the long-term use of energy and raw materials per unit of output; *and*
- an increase in environmental degradation and ecological stress.[16]

In short, the continued substitution of capital and natural resources for labour in the production process is a pattern of economic development that may be unsustainable, in the long run. If advanced economies seek to increase economic growth in this manner without adequately analysing the trade-offs in terms of long-term sustainability then problems of high unemployment, resource scarcity, environmental degradation and misallocation of capital resources may get worse.

In fact (as Chapter 6 illustrates in the case of the greenhouse gas problem), even if the advanced industrialized economies manage to slow down or steady their current rate of use of global resources, this may not be sufficient to avert the damage already inflicted on the biosphere. Already, with global problems such as the greenhouse effect, acid rain, tropical deforestation and so forth, we face crucial choices of trade-offs between resource-intensive growth and more sustainable resource use. With the current global economic development path modelled on the resource-intensive, growth-oriented development of the handful of 'successfully' industrialized advanced economies, the world is hardly ensuring the criterion of intergenerational equity.

Moreover, this resource-intensive growth path is hardly equitable for present generations either. As Table 8.1 shows, the advanced economies – with only 26 % of the world's population – consume a disproportionate share of global resources. To bring developing countries' energy consumption up to industrialized country levels by 2025 would require increasing global energy use by a factor of five. In terms of industrialization, a five to tenfold increase in manufacturing output – and therefore an inevitable rise in resource demand – will be needed just to raise consumption of manufacturing goods by Third World countries to industrialized-world levels.[17] The crucial question is whether the global resource base – including its assimilative capacity – can sustain these increased demands as long as the advanced economies continue to hang on to their disproportionate share.

Certainly, it is desirable that the industrialized nations continue the recent shifts in the content of their growth towards less material and energy-intensive activities and to use their technological capacity to improve the efficiency of energy and material use. Nevertheless, it is clear that profound transformations, i.e. committed policies to and incentives for resource-saving development, are required beyond what has already

**Table 8.1: Distribution of World Consumption, Averages for 1980–82**

| Commodity | Units of Per Capital Consumption | Developed Countries (26 per cent of population) | | Developing Countries (74 per cent of population) | | Relative Consumption |
|---|---|---|---|---|---|---|
| | | Share in World Consumption | Per Capita (1) | Share in World Consumption | Per Capita (2) | (1) ÷ (2) |
| Food: | | | | | | |
| Calories | Kcal/day | 34 | 3,395 | 66 | 2,389 | 1.42 |
| Protein | gms/day | 38 | 99 | 62 | 58 | 1.71 |
| Fat | gms/day | 53 | 127 | 47 | 40 | 3.17 |
| Paper | kg/year | 85 | 123 | 15 | 8 | 15.38 |
| Steel | kg/year | 79 | 455 | 21 | 43 | 10.58 |
| Other Metals | kg/year | 86 | 26 | 14 | 2 | 13.00 |
| Commercial Energy | mtce/year | 80 | 5.8 | 20 | 0.5 | 11.60 |

*Source:* World Commission on Environment and Development, *Our Common Future* (Oxford University Press: Oxford, 1987), Table 1.2.

been achieved. For example, between 1973 and 1983 – during the era of high natural gas and oil prices – energy consumption per unit of GDP in OECD countries dropped by 1.7 % annually, and the general productivity and efficiency of resource use has improved over the last two decades.[18] At the same time, however, *total* energy consumption in OECD countries still grew by one per cent between 1973 and 1983,[19] which means that these countries' per capita energy consumption has hardly been dramatically reduced (see Table 8.1). With energy prices now falling in real terms, an even greater policy commitment is required if energy saving is to be accelerated.

The key issue is that there appears to be no automatic economic mechanism on the horizon for ensuring a more sustainable pattern of energy use in advanced economies. There have been no technological advances to produce energy (e.g., backstop technologies or the discoveries of new resources), nor do the present market mechanisms for fossil fuels work properly to curb consumption. Hence, there is an economic rationale, from a sustainability point of view, for a greater policy commitment to energy saving.

Such a commitment – if it is seriously to be about shifting advanced economies to a resource-saving development path – will inevitably require the reallocation of economic and environmental resources to different patterns of use. This will cost more than simply stimulating the same pattern of resource use (i.e., the current structure of growth-oriented development) simply to produce more. There is no magic solution. The reallocation of resources called for involves real opportunity costs that cannot be avoided.

The costs of reducing resource use and pollution in advanced economies – marginal though these reductions may seem – has been high. In the US, pollution abatement expenditures for manufacturing amounted to 3.3 % of total new expenditures ($ 4.53 billion) in 1984; for chemicals it was 3.8 % ($ 580 million). For steel in Japan, such expenditures accounted for 21.3 % of total investment in 1986 and for around 5 % currently.[20] Clearly, much more new investment in improving resource efficiency, pollution abatement, materials recycling, waste treatment and environmental improvement services is required in advanced economies, even though it may come at the expense of structurally neutral investment to stimulate economic growth. For example, technologies to remove sulphur and nitrogen emissions from coal combustion may increase investment costs by 15–25 %,[21] which is bound to affect the end-use price of energy and thus the costs of economic production in general.

The crucial question really becomes whether advanced industrialized societies are willing to pay these costs for a transition to a more resource-saving development path. On the one hand, public concern for the problems of environmental degradation and – perhaps more importantly – the increasing acceptance by more and more individuals of the need to pay for measures to overcome these problems, suggest that advanced economies may be willing to make a more rapid transition to a development path that conserves resources.

On the other hand, as has been stressed throughout this book, the scarcity effects generated through environmental degradation tend to manifest themselves outside market forces as ecological stresses and shocks. They are not easily amenable to "the measuring rod of money". Moreover, these effects are often cumulative and interactive. As a consequence, we still know very little about their impacts on ecological functions and resource systems and therefore about their implications for economic activities and human welfare. Given such uncertainties, it is difficult to sort out the economic costs and benefits of alternative choices for investment. For example, whether the sulphur emissions of coal-burning plants should be reduced by 30 % or more, whether research into renewable energy supplies should be subsidized, whether recycling would be encouraged by a selective tax on raw materials, and so on.

These and other key economic questions need to be addressed if advanced industrialized countries are to commit themselves decisively to whole-scale structural changes for a more resource-saving economy. Up to now, such political will has been lacking. This is not surprising because, until very recently, for the populations living *within* the advanced industrializsed countries, the permanent livability criterion for inter-generational equity has more or less been met. That is, each subsequent generation living within these countries has been assured access to a relatively intact resource base. However, it has been kept intact not through conserving resources but through *extending* consumption to include more and more of the *global* resource base. In the absence of conservation, the disproportionate consumption of world resources is the only means of guaranteeing an effectively intact resource base. Upon this foundation is built the alluring dream of material wealth that advanced countries have always offered their citizens.

In the last decades of the twentieth century, we now know that further extensions of the resource base may no longer be possible. The first – albeit only brief – indications of this were probably the energy crises of the 1970s. Perhaps the real lasting indications are the scarcity effects of cumulative environmental degradation highlighted in this book. To this must now be added the increasing – and necessary – resource demands of developing countries. Putting all these concerns together may yet induce sufficient political will in the advanced economies to make the transition to a more resource-saving development path. Let us hope that this is the case.

## SUSTAINABLE DEVELOPMENT AND DEVELOPING ECONOMIES

The growing recognition that environmental considerations must be incorporated into development strategies is starting to have some influence on policymaking and planning in developing countries. This may appear to be a curious (and dubious) trend, given that the resource demands of these countries are increasing and that purely economic development goals – such as generating foreign exchange earnings, increasing agricultural production, servicing debts, etc. – would suggest a short-term policy horizon.

On the other hand, direct dependence on natural-resource exploitation to sustain economic livelihoods is most evident in the Third World, where in some regions the combination of poverty, unequal distribution of land and other resource assets, and demographic pressure have led to over-exploitation. Moreover (assuming no change in the distribution of land and other resource assets) the number of subsistence farmers, pastoralists and landless – groups that represent three-quarters of the agricultural households in developing economies – will increase by 50 million to nearly 220 million by the year 2000. Without opportunities for adequate livelihoods, these resource-poor households will be caught in a poverty trap that induces them to over-exploit existing resources simply to survive.[22]

The problem faced by these resource-poor millions is neatly summarized by the model presented in the appendix to this chapter: a low initial level of environmental quality forces resource users to discount the future heavily. That is, poor people faced with marginal environmental conditions often have no choice but to opt for immediate economic benefits at the expense of the long-term sustainability of their livelihoods. This particularly holds for the marginal lands of the Third World, which are areas characterized not only by lower quality and productivity but also by greater instability, especially in terms of micro-climatic, agro-ecological and soil conditions.[23] If economic development is to offer the resource-poor the opportunity of sustainable and secure livelihoods, then sustainable-resource management must become a primary development goal.

At the national level, a large number of low and lower-middle income economies are directly dependent on natural resources for the over-whelming majority of their exports (see Tables 8.2 and 8.3). In many instances, export earnings are dominated by one or two primary commodities. These economies are therefore heavily dependent on their resource stocks for current and future development efforts. Efficient use of their natural capital stock is essential for maximizing current develop-ment efforts, and sustainable use is necessary as the foundation upon which emerging structural developments in industry and services can be safely and continuously built. The danger of an unsustainable path is the risk that the successful transformation from a resource-dependent to a fully developed economy may not be complete before the resource base and its essential environmental functions are irreversibly degraded and depleted.

For low and lower-middle income resource-based economies, the

**Table 8.2: Low Income Economies with High Export Concentration in Primary Commodities**[a]

| | Contribution of 33 main commodities to total exports | Main Export Commodities 1 | 2 |
|---|---|---|---|
| | *over 90 %* | | |
| Zaire ($170) | 100.0 | Copper (58.5) | Petroleum (19.0) |
| Angola ($270) [b] | 100.0 | Petroleum (93.1) | Coffee (6.1) |
| Burundi ($230) | 98.5 | Coffee (91.2) | Cotton (2.8) |
| Uganda ($230) [b] | 98.0 | Coffee (94.0) | Cotton (1.8) |
| Zambia ($390) | 96.8 | Copper (92.4) | Zinc (2.7) |
| Equatorial Guinea | 95.4 | Cocoa (71.5) | Timber (18.5) |
| Rwanda ($280) | 94.7 | Coffee (66.6) | Tin (17.0) |
| Malawi ($170) | 91.9 | Tobacco (49.8) | Sugar (19.8) |
| Cuba | 90.2 | Sugar (88.5) | Tobacco (0.8) |
| | *over 80%* | | |
| Burma ($190) | 81.2 | Rice (43.2) | Timber (29.0) |
| | *over 70%* | | |
| Togo ($230) | 74.9 | Phosphate (46.5) | Cocoa (11.0) |
| Ethiopia ($110) | 71.7 | Coffee (61.5) | Hides and skins (6.8) |
| | *over 60 %* | | |
| Chad | 65.1 | Cotton (60.7) | Hides and skins (4.5) |
| Solomon Islands | 63.7 | Timber (34.6) | Copra (13.6) |
| Nepal ($160) | 63.5 | Rice (26.0) | Hides and skins (16.9) |
| Central Afr. Rep. ($260) | 63.2 | Coffee (28.7) | Timber (25.4) |
| Tanzania ($290) | 60.0 | Coffee (29.8) | Cotton (13.3) |
| | *over 50%* | | |
| Guinea ($320) | 55.6 | Bauxite (52.2) | Coffee (2.2) |
| Benin ($260) | 50.8 | Cotton (20.7) | Cocoa (14.2) |
| Burkina Faso ($150) | 50.6 | Cotton (45.0) | Hides and skins (4.0) |
| Vanuatu | 50.6 | Copra (38.4) | Cocoa (4.4) |

*Notes:* [a]Calculated in terms of percentage contributions to the value of total merchandise exports in 1981–83. U.S. dollar figure after each country listed indicates GNP per capita in 1985. Low-income economies are those with GNP per person of $400 or less in 1985.
[b]GNP per capita in 1984.

*Sources:* World Bank, *Commodity Trade and Price Trends*, 1986 edn, Washington, DC, 1986; and World Bank, *World Development Report* (1986 and 1987 edns), (World Bank: Washington, DC, 1986 and 1987).

**Table 8.3:  Lower Middle Income Economies with High Export Concentration in Primary Commodities[a]**

| | Contribution of 33 main commodities to total exports | Main Export Commodities 1 | 2 |
|---|---|---|---|
| | *over 90%* | | |
| Congo, P.R. ($1,110) | 97.3 | Petroleum (93.1) | Timber (3.1) |
| Liberia ($470) | 95.2 | Iron ore (63.5) | Rubber (15.0) |
| Nigeria ($800) | 92.6 | Petroleum (90.5) | Cocoa (1.7) |
| | *over 70%* | | |
| Guyana ($580)[b] | 76.6 | Sugar (34.4) | Bauxite (29.4) |
| Papua New Guinea ($680) | 76.4 | Copper (36.5) | Coffee (13.9) |
| Nicaragua ($770) | 74.0 | Coffee (28.5) | Cotton (23.9) |
| Honduras ($720) | 71.8 | Bananas (28.2) | Coffee (22.7) |
| Egypt ($610) | 70.9 | Petroleum (55.8) | Cotton (13.7) |
| | *over 60%* | | |
| Syria ($1,560) | 69.4 | Petroleum (59.8) | Cotton (7.2) |
| Ecuador ($1,160) | 69.2 | Petroleum (51.8) | Bananas (8.1) |
| El Salvador ($820) | 67.3 | Coffee (56.5) | Cotton (7.0) |
| Ivory Coast ($660) | 67.1 | Cocoa (24.2) | Coffee (19.4) |
| Mauritius ($1,090) | 61.8 | Sugar (59.9) | Tea (1.9) |
| Paraguay ($860) | 60.9 | Cotton (37.0) | Timber (17.7) |
| Costa Rica ($1,300) | 60.6 | Bananas (25.2) | Coffee (25.0) |
| Chile ($1,430) | 60.0 | Copper (46.1) | Fish meal (6.6) |
| | *over 50%* | | |
| Colombia ($1,320) | 59.9 | Coffee (49.2) | Bananas (4.6) |
| Indonesia ($530) | 58.9 | Petroleum (47.9) | Rubber (3.3) |
| Dominican Republic ($790) | 58.3 | Sugar (38.0) | Coffee (9.1) |
| Mauritania ($420) | 57.2 | Iron ore (54.7) | Fish meal (2.5) |
| Guatemala ($1,250) | 50.5 | Coffee (28.9) | Cotton (6.6) |

*Notes:*  [a]Calculated in terms of percentage contributions to the value of total merchandise exports in 1981–83. US dollar figure after each country listed indicates GNP per capita in 1985. Lower middle income economies are those with GNP per person of $1,600 or less in 1985.
[b]GNP per capita in 1984.

*Sources:*  See Table 8.1.

failure to manage resources sustainably undoubtedly means increased vulnerability to the economic stresses imposed by external debt. Since 1970, external debt as a percentage of GNP for these economies has increased dramatically (See Tables 8.4 and 8.5). Debt servicing, as both a percentage of GNP and of exports, has also risen substantially in virtually all of these economies. In some cases, debt servicing in 1985 consumed more than 10 % of export earnings. For these economies, the ability to meet debt repayments for some time to come and *simultaneously* induce further economic development will depend upon continued successful exploitation of their resource base. Unless this is managed efficiently and sustainably, the debt burden may become a severe constraint on development efforts.

In general, the design of effective natural-resource management policies for sustainable development will require more substantive and extensive analyses. These analyses must examine the natural-resource implications of macro-economic, trade and sectoral policies; better nationally aggregated and co-ordinated information on the micro-economic decisions affecting natural resource use (particularly at the village, farm and agro-ecosystem level); and greater investment in environmental-institution building, especially the development of inter-sectoral co-ordination. The failure to carry out these analyses may perpetuate erroneous assumptions about the relationship between economic policy objectives and the environment, such as the belief that export-oriented agricultural development is inherently less sustainable than production aimed at achieving food self-sufficiency.[24] More importantly, however, it will lead to the design of economic policies that, in the long run, promote the inefficient use of both economic and environmental resources.

At present, four important initiatives are being explored that could make a potentially substantial contribution to integrating sound natural-resource management principles into all levels of economic policymaking in developing countries. These initiatives will be referred to as environmental cost-benefit analysis, resource accounting, macro-economic policy-making and applied sustainability research.

As pointed out by the authors of the classic *UNIDO Guidelines*, the main rationale for conducting social cost-benefit analyses is "to subject project choice to a consistent set of general objectives of national policy".[25] As perceptions of national policy objectives in Third World countries have changed, for example emphasizing the need for scarce foreign exchange and equitable income distribution, project appraisal and planning have expanded to reflect the new objectives.[26] Consequently, the recent emphasis on the role of environmental quality and the long-term productivity of natural-resource systems in sustaining economic development has led to further extensions of social cost-benefit analyses to include environmental impacts.[27] That is, in contrast with traditional

**Table 8.4: Debt and Debt Service Ratios in Resource-Dependent Low Income Economies[a]**

| | *External public debt[b] as % of GNP* | | *Debt Service as percentage of* | | | |
| | | | *GNP* | | *Exports* | |
| | *1970* | *1985* | *1970* | *1985* | *1970* | *1985* |
|---|---|---|---|---|---|---|
| *over 90%* | | | | | | |
| Zaire (100.0) | 9.1 | 111.8 | 1.1 | 7.9 | 4.4 | 8.6 |
| Angola (100.0) | x | x | x | x | x | x |
| Burundi (98.5) | 3.1 | 39.7 | 0.3 | 2.0 | 2.3 | 16.6 |
| Uganda (98.0) | 7.5 | x | 0.4 | x | 2.9 | x |
| Zambia (96.8) | 36.0 | 150.8 | 3.6 | 4.0 | 6.3 | 10.2 |
| Eq. Guinea (95.4) | x | x | x | x | x | x |
| Rwanda (94.7) | 0.9 | 19.1 | 0.1 | 0.9 | 1.2 | 4.3 |
| Malawi (91.9) | 44.2 | 75.7 | 2.2 | 7.4 | 7.7 | x |
| Cuba (90.2) | x | x | x | x | x | x |
| *over 80%* | | | | | | |
| Burma (81.2) | 5.0 | 42.1 | 1.0 | 2.8 | 17.2 | 51.4 |
| *over 70%* | | | | | | |
| Togo (74.9) | 16.2 | 121.0 | 0.9 | 13.7 | 3.0 | 27.5 |
| Ethiopia (71.7) | 9.5 | 37.1 | 1.2 | 2.2 | 11.4 | 10.9 |
| *over 60%* | | | | | | |
| Chad (65.1) | 9.9 | x | 0.9 | x | 4.2 | x |
| Solomon Islands (63.7) | x | x | x | x | x | x |
| Nepal (63.5) | 0.3 | 22.5 | 0.3 | 0.5 | x | 4.0 |
| Cen. Afr. Rep. (63.2) | 13.5 | 44.9 | 1.7 | 2.0 | 5.1 | 11.8 |
| Tanzania (60.0) | 20.1 | 48.5 | 1.3 | 1.0 | 5.2 | 16.7 |
| *over 50%* | | | | | | |
| Guinea (55.6) | 47.2 | 70.2 | 2.2 | 3.6 | x | x |
| Benin (50.8) | 15.2 | 66.9 | 0.6 | 2.2 | 2.3 | x |
| Burkina Faso (50.6) | 6.6 | 46.4 | 0.7 | 2.5 | 6.8 | x |
| Vanuatu (50.6) | x | x | x | x | x | x |

*Notes:* [a]Percentage figure after each country listed indicates contribution of 33 main primary commodities to total exports as indicated in Table 8.1. Low-income economies are those with GNP per person of $400 or less in 1985.
[b]External public debt outstanding and disbursed.
x = figures not available.

*Sources:* World Bank, *Commodity Trade and Price Trends* (1986 edn), (Washington DC, 1986); and World Bank, *World Development Report* (1987 edn), (World Bank: Washington, DC, 1987).

**Table 8.5:  Debt and Debt-Service Ratios in Resource Dependent Lower-Middle Income Economies**[a]

| | External public debt[b] as % of GNP | | Debt Service as percentage of | | | |
| | | | GNP | | Exports | |
| | *1970* | *1985* | *1970* | *1985* | *1970* | *1985* |
|---|---|---|---|---|---|---|
| *over 90%* | | | | | | |
| Congo, P.R. (97.3) | 52.4 | 86.5 | 3.4 | 15.9 | x | 19.6 |
| Liberia (95.2) | 39.4 | 85.3 | 4.4 | 1.7 | x | 3.8 |
| Nigeria (92.6) | 4.6 | 17.2 | 0.6 | 5.3 | 4.2 | 30.8 |
| *over 70%* | | | | | | |
| Guyana (76.6) | x | x | x | x | x | x |
| Papua New Guinea (76.4) | 6.2 | 49.0 | 0.2 | 6.0 | x | 10.4 |
| Nicaragua (74.0) | 19.5 | 185.2 | 3.0 | 1.6 | 10.5 | x |
| Honduras (71.8) | 13.6 | 68.8 | 0.9 | 5.4 | 3.1 | 17.6 |
| Egypt (70.9) | 23.1 | 61.9 | 4.6 | 7.8 | 36.8 | 30.9 |
| *over 60%* | | | | | | |
| Syria (69.4) | 10.8 | 16.9 | 1.7 | 2.2 | 11.2 | 14.8 |
| Ecuador (69.2) | 11.8 | 60.9 | 1.4 | 8.0 | 8.6 | 28.8 |
| El Salvador (67.3) | 8.6 | 39.6 | 0.9 | 5.3 | 3.6 | 16.3 |
| Ivory Coast (67.1) | 18.8 | 88.5 | 2.9 | 9.0 | 7.0 | 17.4 |
| Mauritius (61.8) | 14.7 | 39.8 | 1.4 | 6.6 | 3.2 | 11.5 |
| Paraguay (60.9) | 19.2 | 55.8 | 1.8 | 5.6 | 11.8 | 12.9 |
| Costa Rica (60.6) | 13.8 | 105.1 | 2.9 | 13.3 | 10.0 | 36.6 |
| Chile (60.0) | 25.9 | 90.3 | 3.0 | 8.7 | 19.1 | 26.2 |
| *over 50%* | | | | | | |
| Colombia (59.9) | 18.5 | 28.5 | 1.7 | 4.3 | 12.0 | 29.2 |
| Indonesia (58.9) | 25.2 | 32.0 | 0.9 | 4.8 | x | 19.9 |
| Dominican Rep. (58.3) | 14.5 | 58.6 | 0.8 | 5.1 | 4.4 | 16.1 |
| Mauritania (57.2) | 13.9 | 208.2 | 1.8 | 12.0 | 3.3 | 19.0 |
| Guatemala (50.5) | 5.7 | 19.8 | 1.4 | 2.3 | 7.4 | 21.3 |

*Notes:* [a]Percentage figure after each country listed indicates contribution of 33 main primary commodities to total exports as indicated in Table 8.2. Low-middle income economies are those with GNP per person of $1,600 or less in 1985.
[b]External public debt outstanding and disbursed.
x = figures not available.

*Sources:*  World Bank, *Commodity Trade and Price Trends* (1986 edn), (Washington, DC, 1986); and World Bank, *World Development Report* (1987 edn), (World Bank: Washington, DC, 1987).

project evaluation, which considers only the direct project benefits and costs, "the expanded approach includes the external and environmental improvement benefits (plus the benefits from environmental protection), as well as the costs of external and/or environmental damages and of environmental control measures".[28] The basic methodology is first to identify and measure the environmental effects, and then to translate them into monetary terms for inclusion in the formal project analysis.

Extending cost-benefit analysis to incorporate the environmental impacts of projects involves a number of problems. First, physical estimation of environmental effects is often difficult. Secondly, as most environmental resources are non-marketed common-property goods, economic valuation of their services is not straightforward. Thirdly, little consensus exists regarding methods for monetary valuation of intangible environmental goods, such as the need to preserve unknown species for their intrinsic value.[29]

As this expanded approach inevitably raises issues of inter-temporal choice, the interest rate chosen to discount the future may determine whether environmental degradation is optimal – as demonstrated formally in the model in the appendix of this chapter. It is often stressed that the appropriate discount rate should emerge from the project appraisal process.[30] In practice, imperfect capital markets, inconsistent data on the productivity of capital and large variances in domestic borrowing for investment make it difficult to establish an economic accounting rate of interest for developing countries.[31]

Introducing environmental considerations further complicates the picture. As Markandya and Pearce observe, natural resources are more likely to be over-exploited at high discount rates than at low ones, whereas low discount rates discriminate against projects with an environmental dimension that have a long gestation period.[32] Given the additional problems posed by environmental risk and irreversible impacts, these authors conclude that it is generally preferable to adjust the project costs and benefit values and adopt additional sustainability criteria, than to adjust the discount rate.

As discussed above and demonstrated in the appendix to this chapter, in many examples of poverty-induced environmental degradation, the sacrifice of long-term sustainability for immediate economic returns implies a high discount rate. For example, one of the consequences of deforestation and the depletion of fuelwood supplies is that it forces poor households to use dung for fuel rather than for fertilizer. The present value of the dung as fuel is higher than its value as a soil nutrient, but "the context is one where there is no choice anyway since there are neither fuel nor fertilizer substitutes to which households can gain access." Therefore, this behaviour is itself "the result of the resource degradation process which compels actions to be taken which imply high discount rates".[33] In other words, the apparently high discount rates are a reflection of the constraints imposed by environmental degradation rather than the desired social choice.

The second initiative, usually referred to as resource accounting, involves adjusting national income accounts to register both the direct costs inflicted by environmental degradation and the depreciation of natural capital to allow for losses in future production.[34] Although the national accounts record the income earned from harvesting resource stocks (e.g., fish catch, timber, meat, etc.), the loss of future income through declining resource stocks and deteriorating environmental quality is excluded. By allowing for such depreciations in the natural capital stock, the net contributions of resource degradation to national income are much lower and more accurately reflect the impact on economic welfare. For example, preliminary estimates of the depreciation of the forest stock in Indonesia due to deforestation, forest degradation and timber extraction suggest a cost of around US $ 3.1 billion in 1982, or approximately 4 % of GDP.[35]

Because resource accounting uses the existing system of national accounts, it appeals to economic policymakers. Nonetheless, there are a number of limitations on its application. Measuring the stock of economic capital and its rate of depreciation in developing countries is in itself a complicated task. Given the difficulties in quantifying environmental "goods", extending depreciation accounting to the stock of "natural" capital would prove even more difficult. Some natural resources, such as forest timber, oil and fish stocks, are more readily counted as discrete units. Others, such as soils and watersheds, are not easily measurable as stocks.

There is also disagreement among some economists over the method of valuing the depreciation of natural capital stocks. In the standard economic accounting approach, if an environmental asset is to be treated like any other capital asset, its economic depreciation should be composed of two components: the value of its physical depreciation and any change in the current price valuation of stocks (i.e., capital gains or losses). Thus an asset (such as the stock of standing Indonesian hardwoods) can suffer some degree of physical deterioration and still increase in present value, implying negative depreciation or a net capital gain.[36] Other economists argue, however, that international commodity prices for natural resources fluctuate dramatically with little impact on projected extraction and production schedules. "Including unrealized capital gains from natural-resource price changes in current income could therefore lead to significant swings in income between successive periods".[37] These economists advocate that depreciation accounting should include only the value of physical changes in the resource stock.

Perhaps a more serious limitation is that a resource accounting approach that limits itself to just one function of an environmental asset – its production of valuable and marketed raw material – can only cover part of the economic costs of environmental degradation. Such an approach does not include all the externality, or off-site, environmental quality effects (i.e., the value of environmental assets in assimilating waste and in providing ecological support for economic systems and human welfare).

In Indonesia, for example, the true value of the forest stock must include not only its productive value as a commodity but also its value in supporting other economic activities dependent upon its existence (e.g., husbandry of non-timber forest products, traditional shifting cultivation, etc.). It must also include other economic values (e.g., the option and existence values of preserving biological diversity, micro-climatic functions, etc.). Favourable external impacts on, say, neighbouring agricultural activity (the maintenance of fertility and cohesion, hydrological cycles, etc.) must also be included.[38] Together, these values represent the full opportunity cost of forest depletion. Therefore, the figure of $ 3.1 billion for the direct depreciations of the forest stock of Indonesia must be well below the full cost.

Yet despite such difficulties, resource accounting is a major advance over the present procedure by which natural capital is valued at zero. Moreover, by starting to measure environmental values, resource accounting approaches ensure that better techniques for measuring such values will be developed.

Resource accounting could be considered as part of a large initiative to design macro-economic policies which can correct problems of environmental degradation in developing countries. This is proposed in two ways:

i) through the design of investment programmes supporting environmental and natural-resource objectives; *and*
ii) through promotion of economic, social and institutional policies and incentives that influence the environmentally related behaviour of government agencies, major-resource users, and countless small-scale resource-using activities which occur throughout a nation's economy.[39]

The appeal of such an approach is that it would rely on traditional economic tools and concepts, such as marginal opportunity cost, to measure the total environmental costs borne by society of resource degradation and depletion.[40] Moreover, some existing economic policies in developing countries (e.g. agricultural input subsidies, fiscal and financial inducements for livestock rearing, and agricultural export taxation) may be encouraging both environmental degradation and economic inefficiency.[41] Correcting these policies may therefore offer the opportunity to pursue both environmental and development goals.

In designing appropriate incentives for sustainable development, a distinction should be made between *user enabling incentives* focused on the resource user (e.g., changes in land and resource rights, increased participation in decision making and appropriate projects); *policy enabling incentives* focused on the policymaker and implementing agencies (e.g., institutional strengthening and flexibility, political conditions); and *variable incentives* focused on price changes facing producers and consumers (e.g., altering input and output pricing, exchange-rate modification, tax and subsidy reform, adjusting middlemen margins, etc.).[42] User-enabling incentives are the main micro-level concerns for sustainable development, whereas appropriate policy-enabling and variable incentives are the macro-level issues. Working with only one set of these incentives is likely to be ineffective. We need at least one policy instrument for each objective. As the case studies of Amazonian deforestation and upper watershed degradation on Java illustrate, the challenge for economic policy is to design the right combination of incentives for a given target group and a given environmental degradation problem.

The design of appropriate incentives is fraught with difficulties. For example, it is often assumed that getting producer prices in agriculture closer to world prices will increase the incomes of farmers, which will in turn encourage resource conservation investments. The counter-argument, however, is that price increases encourage switches between crops but may have no effect on aggregate output. Farmers may not have an extra surplus to invest in resource conservation. In addition, in the case of the upper watershed degradation on Java, the relationship between increased profitability of farm-level production and additional investments in land-management and farming systems improvement is not a straightforward one. In general, "the current state of research is simply not adequate to pronounce on the nature of the linkage from producer price to agricultural supply response to natural resource effects" to engender confidence over the design of appropriate incentives and investment strategies.[43]

Nevertheless, macro-economic policies and incentives for natural-resource management are, in the long run, essential for sustainable development. Donor agencies, led by the World Bank, are making a major effort in co-operation with the governments of some developing countries to conduct studies of how best to design an appropriate natural-resource and economic-policy framework for sustainable development.[44] As these studies are indicating, before any practical policy gudelines can be successfully formulated, there is a need for substantive and extensive analysis of the natural-resource implications of various macro-economic, trade and sectoral policies in developing countries. At the more micro level, there is a need for a greater analysis of the economic costs of environmental degradation and of the natural-resource allocation decisions by villages and farmers. This should be co-ordinated and reviewed consistently at the national level so as to be useful for policy and investment decisions.[45]

If sustainable development is to succeed in dealing with these micro-level issues, the three initiatives discussed so far need to be complemented by a fourth – the applied analysis of the sustainability of farming and other production systems at the village, community and household level. For example, in agriculture, the "farmers' needs pull" form of farming systems research and extension takes the analysis of existing farming systems as its starting point. It then goes on to determine the needs, problems and constraints to which subsequent technological innovation is directed. The use of agro-ecosystem analysis and rapid rural appraisal techniques are crucial to this approach.[46]

An even broader, and more difficult, task is the analysis of the problems of attaining sustainable and secure livelihoods. For example, rural livelihoods do not rely exclusively on farming but also on skills employed on the farm, in the manufacture of handicrafts and in other cottage industries, on natural resources (such as timber, fuelwood, fodder, wild plants, fish and other wild animals) that may be harvested, on opportunities for off-farm employment, or most commonly on some combination of these. Thus a livelihood typically relies on ownership of, or access to, resources, and access to product- or income-generating activities. Therefore, it is measurable in terms of both the stocks (i.e., a household's reserves and assets) and the flows of food and cash. In practice, rural families decide on livelihood goals and then determine the optimal mix of activities depending on their environmental and social circumstances, and the skills and resources at their disposal. Sustainable-livelihood analysis must take into account this decision-making process at the household level, as well as the set of institutions, customs and systems of rights and obligations at the community level that determine much of what individuals and households can and cannot do.[47]

These four initiatives indicate the need for a multi-level, as well as a multi-disciplinary, approach to integrating sound natural-resource management at all levels of economic policy making and planning. Sustainable development cannot be based solely, or even largely, on resource accounting, cost-benefit analysis, macro-economic policy, or farming systems research and sustainable-livelihood analysis. Each of these four initiatives needs to be developed in its own right and in relation to the other approaches, and this totality of analysis used as the basis for sustainable development.

Perhaps one constraint common to all these approaches is the lack of a database and the methodology needed to evaluate the impacts of environmental degradation on the resource base. Current databases in developing countries, where they are reliable, are disaggregated by administrative and political boundaries (i.e., region, province, district, sub-district, etc.). It is often extremely difficult to obtain the same economic and environmental data by major agro-ecological and resource system zones (e.g., watersheds, semi-arid lands, uplands, forests and coastal resource systems). It may be equally difficult to obtain reliable data on certain key socio-economic groups, such as agro-pastoralists, nomads, upland farmers, shifting cultivators, indigenous tribes, etc. In addition, although valuation techniques for measuring the environmental impacts of economic policies and projects have been developed in recent years, they have yet to be disseminated and applied extensively in developing countries. Thus developing the data and methodology requirements for all levels of analysis in developing countries should be a major priority.[48]

## SUMMARY AND CONCLUSION

If there is one basic principle underlying the diverse body of knowledge we call economics, it is that there is no such thing as a free lunch. In other words, there is always a cost for whatever we do. Somehow, conventional economic theory has tended to forget this when considering the functions that the environment provides for economic activity and human welfare. The message of this book is therefore just a simple reminder to economics of one of its basic principles: if the environment is being increasingly exploited for one set of uses (say, to provide new sources of raw material and energy inputs and to assimilate additional waste), the quality of the environment may deteriorate. The consequence is an increasing relative scarcity of essential environmental services and ecological functions. Moreover, in circumstances where ecological stress is extreme, which is more likely in resource-poor environments where ecological processes are fragile and highly variable, environmental degradation over time may pose an absolute constraint on economic-environmental systems.

This proposition may seem simple. However, like other simple observations, further exploration reveals more complex yet highly instructive insights. In developing this theory – or alternative view – of natural-resource scarcity, this book has explored its relationship with early economic theories of natural-resource scarcity, non-economic influences, and more conventional views of resource and environmental problems. The conclusion is that this alternative view is applicable to a new class of problems arising from environmental degradation that have not been adequately dealt with by conventional economic approaches. In addition, this alternative view provides insight into the type of economic strategies required to tackle the new class of problems of environmental degradation. Thus, the second part of this book examines three examples of environmental degradation – the global greenhouse effect, Amazonian deforestation and upper watershed degradation on Java – in order to illustrate the type of scarcity effects that can be explained by the alternative view and to indicate the type of policy responses that such problems require. Although the policy tools and instruments – variable or price incentives, user-enabling incentives, policy-enabling incentives and direct investment programmes – are the standard means for dealing with any economic problem, only the right combination of these is appropriate for a given problem of environmental degradation. The alternative view of natural-resource scarcity, as developed in this book, not only provides insight into the economic consequences of environmental degradation but also provides the rationale and the guidelines for an appropriate economic policy in response to these consequences.

The basis of this rationale is the need for environmentally sustainable development. As this chapter makes clear, the concept of sustainable economic development has to be carefully examined, and has different implications for the advanced industrialized economies compared with the developing economies. On the other hand, an economics of sustainable development must naturally emerge from further explorations of the type of scarcity effects that concern the alternative view and from the analysis required for designing appropriate economic strategies to overcome the problems of environmental degradation that undermine economic sustainability.

The overall message of this book is that if the sustainability of the ecological processes underlying economic activity is recognized to have value, then sustainability must be explicitly included as one of the objectives to be pursued by economic policymakers and planners. Undoubtedly, the pursuit of sustainable economic development will require reconciling crucial trade-offs – not the least being the trade-off between resource-using economic growth and appropriate resource-management objectives. As "no one model provides the means for understanding how the ends of both economic growth and ecological sustainability might be achieved",[49] perhaps an important contribution of this book is to try to explore and model this trade-off a bit more rigorously. Maybe future explorations will develop this theory and empirical analysis further into a true economics of sustainable development.

## *APPENDIX*: A MODEL OF OPTIMAL SUSTAINABLE ECONOMIC GROWTH[50]

The purpose of the following model is to analyse optimal-growth paths for an economy faced with the choice of operating under the three long-term biophysical constraints: harvesting of renewable resources within their natural and managed rates of regeneration; extracting exhaustible resources at the rate at which renewables can be substituted for them (which, in the long run, implies a zero rate of exhaustion of the composite resource); and emitting wastes within the assimilative capacity of the environment. The analysis will be based on a modified and extended version of the model developed by Forster, which examined optimal economic growth under one of these constraints, namely that waste levels should not exceed the assimilative capacity of the environment.[51]

The key to this model is the assumption that at any time t, the rate of environmental degradation $\dot{S}$, is equal to any flow of waste emitted from the economic process W, in excess of the amount of waste assimilated by the environment A; plus the flow of renewable resources harvested from the environment R, in excess of the (managed or natural) biological productivity of these resources G; plus the flow of exhaustible resources extracted from the environment E:

$$S = (W - A) + (R - G) + E, \tag{1}$$

where $(W - A) = 0$ if $W = A$

and $(R + E) - G = 0$ if $(R + E) = G$.[52]

Since resources are extracted and harvested and wastes are emitted by the economic process to provide consumption C, it is assumed that:

$$W = W(C), W'(C) > 0, W''(C) > 0 \tag{2}$$

$$R = R(C), R'(C) > 0, R''(C) > 0$$

$$E = E(C), E'(C) > 0, E''(C) > 0.$$

Similarly, if X is some measure of environmental quality,[53] then it is assumed that the amount of waste assimilated and the biological productivity of the environment are both increasing functions of X:

$$A = A(X), A'(X) > 0, A''(X) < 0 \tag{3}$$

$$G = G(X), G'(X) > 0, G''(X) < 0.[54]$$

Substituting (2) and (3) into (1) yields:

$$S = [W(C) + R(C) + E(C)] - [A(X) + G(X)] \tag{4}$$

$$= N(C) - Q(X),$$

where $N(C)$ indicates the increasing environmental degradation resulting from the various resource demands of the economic process and $Q(X)$ can be thought of as the environmental resilience in the face of these resource demands.

Given (2) it is assumed that:

$$N(C) > 0, N'(C) > 0, N''(C) > 0, C > \underline{C} \tag{5}$$

$$N(\underline{C}) = 0, C = \underline{C},$$

where $\underline{C}$ is the level of consumption where the economy is consuming accumulated resource stocks, with pollution abatement ensuring that $W = 0$. Hence, an economy at consumption level $\underline{C}$ is making no additional resource demands on the environment.

Similarly, from (3) it is assumed that:

$$Q(X) > 0, Q'(X) > 0, Q''(X) < 0, X > \underline{X} \tag{6}$$

$$Q(\underline{X}) = 0, X \leq \underline{X},$$

where $\underline{X}$ is the minimum sustainable level of environmental quality. That is, if environmental quality falls below $\underline{X}$, ecosystems are no longer capable of assimilating waste and generating biological productivity.

Finally, it is assumed that there is an inverse relationship between $\dot{S}$ and $\dot{X}$; i.e., if environmental degradation is increasing over time, then environmental quality must be falling:

$$\dot{X} = -aS \qquad (7)$$

$$= a[Q(X) - N(C)].$$

It is now assumed that social welfare at any point in time is measured by a strictly concave utility function U of current C and the current stock of X:

$$U = U(C,X), \qquad (8)$$

with $U_c > 0$, $U_{cc} < 0$, $U_x > 0$, $U_{xx} < 0$, $U_{cx} = 0$, $\lim\limits_{C \to 0} U_c = \infty$,

and $\lim\limits_{X \to 0} U_x = \infty$.

Equations (1) and (7) were deliberately constructed to reflect the criteria for sustainability, that of observing the biophysical constraints. That is, a minimum condition for an economic growth path to be sustainable over the long run is $W = A$ and $(R + E) = G$, which ensures that no environmental degradation will occur (that is, $\dot{S} = 0$). Thus, one possible choice open to society is to plan for a growth path that, in the long run, produces zero environmental degradation.

Conditions (1) and (7) also indicate, however, that as long as some environmental degradation is continuing to occur, environmental quality will decline. Equation (6) suggests that there is a lower limit to environmental quality. If X is driven below $\underline{X}$, environmental degradation will have destroyed the natural clean-up and regenerative processes in the environment. This is tantamount to an environmental collapse, and economic growth leading to such a collapse can be said to be environmentally unsustainable. Nevertheless, there may be conditions under which society may have no choice but opt for an unsustainable growth path.

The purpose of this model, therefore, is to examine the optimal conditions leading to sustainable versus unsustainable economic growth. Given a positive rate of time preference r, the planning problem is to find solutions which will

$$\max \quad \int_0^\infty e^{-rt} U(C,X) \, dt \qquad (9)$$

subject to $\dot{X} = a[Q(X) - N(C)]$,

$X(0) = X_o$, $X(\infty)$ free.

Given the continuous function P(t), the Hamiltonian of the problem is:

$$H = e^{-rt} \left([U(C,X) + Pa[Q(X) - N(C)]\right) . \qquad (10)$$

The first-order conditions are:

$$\frac{dH}{dC} = U_c - PaN' = 0, \tag{11}$$

or $P = U_c/aN' > 0$.

$$\dot{P} - rP = -\frac{dH}{dX} = -U_x - PaQ', \tag{12}$$

or $\dot{P} = [r - aQ']P - U_x$, and

$$\dot{X} = a[Q(X) - N(C)]. \tag{13}$$

$P(t)$ is the costate variable, which can be interpreted as the social value, or shadow price, of environmental quality. Condition (11) gives C as an explicit function of P with:

$$\frac{dC}{dP} = \frac{aN'}{U_{cc} - aPN''} < 0. \tag{14}$$

From (12) and (13), the behaviour of the system from any initial point, $(X_0, P_0)$, is governed by:

$$\dot{P} \; \underset{<}{\overset{>}{=}} \; 0 \quad \text{if } [r - aQ']P \; \underset{<}{\overset{>}{=}} \; U_x, \tag{15}$$

$$\dot{X} \; \underset{<}{\overset{>}{=}} \; 0 \quad \text{if } Q(X) \; \underset{<}{\overset{>}{=}} \; N(C). \tag{16}$$

One possible configuration of the phase diagrams of these equations is given in Figure 8.1. Note that:

$$\lim_{\substack{X \to 0}} P \Big|_{X=0} = \lim_{\substack{X \to 0 \\ C \to \underline{C}}} \frac{U_c(C,X)}{aN'(C)} = \frac{U_c(\underline{C},0)}{aN'(\underline{C})}. \tag{17}$$

Also, the $\dot{X} = 0$ curve and the trajectories in Figure 8.1 are kinked at $X = \underline{X}$, since Q' is not continuous at this point. The slopes of the stationary loci are given by:

$$\frac{dP}{dX}\Big|_{\dot{P}=0} = \frac{aPQ'' + U_{xx}}{(r - aQ')} < 0, \tag{18}$$

$$\frac{dP}{dX}\Big|_{\dot{X}=0} = \frac{aQ'}{aN' \, dC/dP} < 0. \tag{19}$$

In Figure 8.1, $(X_1{}^\star, P_1{}^\star)$ and $(X_3{}^\star, P_3{}^\star)$ are stable equilibria, whereas

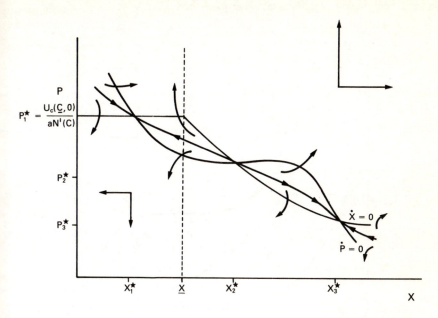

**Figure 8.1: Multiple Equilibria Solution to Phase Diagram**

$(X_2^\star, P_2^\star)$ is totally unstable. If $X_0 > X_2^\star$, then the optimal policy is to select $P_0$ so as to place the economy on a growth path that ends at the stable equilibrium $(X_3^\star, P_3^\star)$. This represents environmentally sustainable growth, given the assumption that if $\dot{X} = 0$ and $X > \underline{X}$, then biophysical constraints are being observed. If $X_0 = X_2^\star$, then it is optimal to remain at $X_2^\star$ for ever. If $X_0 < X_2^\star$, assuming sufficiency conditions are satisfied for the non-concave region, then the growth path of the economy heads to $(X_1^\star, P_1^\star)$. However, this growth path is unsustainable, for on the one hand, the assimilative and regenerative capacity of the environment has been destroyed, and on the other, the economy is forced to consume existing internal resource stocks. Eventually, the latter will be consumed and the economy will collapse.

Thus, with a low initial level of environmental quality, environmentally unsustainable economic growth may be an optimal strategy. Since the benefits of increased consumption occur in the present whereas environmental degradation and collapse is a future problem, this strategy is made optimal by a high rate of discount on future utility. Consequently, both the initial level of environmental quality as well as the rate at which future utilities are discounted are significant factors in determining the optimal choice between sustainable and unsustainable growth as one would expect.

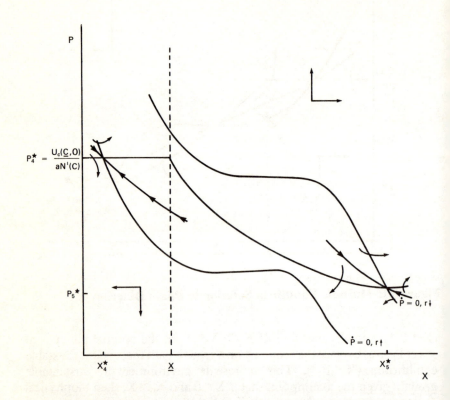

**Figure 8.2: The Effects of Changes in r**

It is apparent from (15) that an increase in the discount rate would have the effect of shifting down the $\dot{P}=0$ curve. As shown in Figure 8.2, the end result may be a unique equilibrium, but one that only allows unsustainable growth (i.e., $X_4^\star < \underline{X}$). In contrast, lower discount rates would shift the $\dot{P}=0$ curve up, leading to a unique equilibrium of sustainable growth (i.e., $X_5^\star > \underline{X}$). These results appear to confirm the conclusions of Forster of the role of discount rates in determining the sustainability of the economic process.[55]

The minimum bound on the social rate of time preference, r, is not independent of the historically given level of environmental quality, $X_0$. Note that in (15), for $\dot{P}=0$ it is a requirement that $r > aQ'$. Given the properties of $Q(X)$ outlined in (6), a lower initial X will have a higher $Q'$, thus requiring a high rate of discount to keep $\dot{P}=0$. Conversely, a higher $X_0$ will have a lower rate of discount. As shown in Figure 8.3, therefore, the initial level of environmental quality influences choice of r and imposes a lower limit on any changes in r.

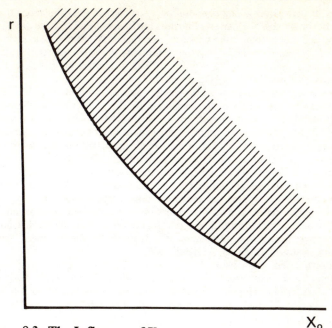

**Figure 8.3: The Influence of $X_0$ on r**

# NOTES

1. Edward B. Barbier, "The concept of sustainable economic development", *Environmental Conservation*, Vol. 14 (1987), pp. 101–10. For further elaboration on the views of sustainability expressed throughout this chapter see also Edward B. Barbier, *New Approaches in Environmental and Resource Economics: Towards an Economics of Sustainable Development* (IIED and the New Economics Foundation: London, 1987); David W. Pearce, "Sustainable development: Ecology and economic progress", draft paper (IIED/UCL London Environmental Economics Centre, 1988); and David W. Pearce, "The meaning and implications of sustainable development", Report of a Workshop on Sustainable Development (Economics and the Environment Secretariat, OECD: Paris, France, 12–13 November 1987). The members of the Workshop were David W. Pearce, R. Kerry Turner, Edward B. Barbier, Peter Nijkamp and the Secretariat. See also David Pearce, Edward B. Barbier and Anil Markandya, *Sustainable Development: Environment and Economics in the Third World* (Edward Elgar: London, forthcoming in 1989).
2. See the references listed in note one.
3. World Commission on Environment and Development (WCED), *Our Common Future* (Oxford University Press: 1987).
4. Barbier, "The concept", op. cit.
5. This definition and the following elaboration is based on Pearce *et al.*, "The meaning", op. cit.
6. "Economic development" implies structural change in the economy and society, and can be conventionally defined as the "process whereby the real per capital income of

a country increases over a long period of time – subject to the stipulations that the number below an 'absolute' poverty line does not increase, and that the distribution of income does not become more unequal". See Gerald M. Meier, *Leading Issues in Economic Development* (3rd edn), (Oxford University Press: New York, 1976).

7. See Chapter 2 and Gordon R. Conway, "The properties of agroecosystems", *Agricultural Systems*, Vol. 24 (1987), pp. 95–117.

8. For example, the resource degradation may be reduced to a level where the natural processes can be subsidized in the long term by the appropriate applications of external inputs (e.g., agro-chemicals, fertilizers, tools, machinery, etc.). Counteracting resource degradation often requires innovations in techniques, organization or land management. Examples of the former include integrated pest management and the optimal mix of organic and inorganic fertilizers. Examples of appropriate innovations were discussed in Chapter 8 (i.e., the adoption of land-management and farming-system techniques to improve soil and water conservation). More often than not, a combination of approaches rather than one single response is required for counteracting the stresses and shocks imposed by environmental degradation.

9. Robert Chambers, "Sustainable livelihoods: An opportunity for the World Commission on Environment and Development" (Institute of Development Studies: University of Sussex, Brighton, England, 1986).

10. See Conway, op. cit., and Chapter 2.

11. See Chapter 5 and talbot Page, *Conservation and Economic Efficiency: An Approach to Materials Policy* (Johns Hopkins University Press: Baltimore, Maryland, 1977); and David W. Pearce, "Foundations of an ecological economics", *Ecological Modelling*, Vol. 38 (1987), pp. 9–18.

12. See Pearce, "Foundations", op. cit.

13. See, in particular, Pearce, "Foundations", op. cit.; David W. Pearce, "The limits of cost benefit analysis as a guide to environmental policy", *Kyklos*, Vol. 29 (1976), pp. 97–111; David W. Pearce, "Optimal prices for sustainable development" in D. Collard, D.W. Pearce and D. Ulph ed, *Economic Growth and Sustainable Environments* (Macmillan: London, 1988); Page, *Conservation*, op. cit.; and Edward B. Barbier, "Alternative approaches to economic-environmental interactions", Paper presented at the 13th Annual Eastern Economic Association Conference (Washington, DC, 5–7 March, 1987), forthcoming in *Ecological Economics*. See also the discussion and references cited in Pearce, "Sustainable development", op. cit., and in Herman E. Daly, "The economic growth debate: What some economists have learned but many have not", *Journal of Environmental Economics and Management*, Vol. 14 (1987), pp. 323–336.

14. These conditions ensure that the environmental degradation resulting from the failure to observe the biophysical constraints poses a threat to the long-term sustainability of the economic process; alternatively, the violation of any one of these conditions would alleviate this threat. This follows from an extension of the analysis presented in Partha Dasgupta and Geoffrey Heal, *Economic Theory and Exhaustible Resources* (Cambridge University Press: 1979), Chapter 7. For example, if the three important economic functions of the environment are broadly considered to be the production of useful material and energy inputs $E_1$, the assimilation of waste $E_2$, and the provision of human, ecological and life-supporting services $E_3$, then each of these $E_i$ functions is essential if, in its absence, feasible consumption must necessarily decline to zero in the long run. On the other hand, if reproducible capital, or a laobour–capital composite, can be sufficiently substituted for each $E_i$, then it is no longer essential. Equally, even in the absence of such substitution possibilities, if each $E_i$ could be augmented by a constant positive rate of technical progress, the loss of that function could be managed to ensure that its technically enhanced services are bounded away from zero.

15. See Chapter 5 and Barbier, "Alternative approaches", op. cit.; Robert A. Becker,

"Integenerational equity: The capital–environment trade-off", *Journal of Environmental Economics and Management*, Vol. 9 (1982), pp. 165–85; Karl-Göran Mäler, *Environmental Economics: A Theoretical Inquiry* (Johns Hopkins University Press: Baltimore, Maryland, 1974); and Neil Vousden, "Basic theoretical issues of resource depletion", *Journal of Economic Theory*, Vol. 6 (1973), pp. 126–43.

16. Edward B. Barbier, "The potential for reviving economic growth: The political economy of resource misallocation", Paper presented at The Other Economic Summit (London, 6–9 June 1984).

17. World Commission on Environment and Development, op. cit. See also Edward B. Barbier, "Is sustainable economic growth our common future?", *New Economics*, Issue 3 (1987), pp. 7–9.

18. World Commission on Environment and Development, op. cit., p. 216.

19. Organization for Economic Co-operation and Development, *The State of the Environment 1985* (OECD: Paris, 1985), p. 212.

20. WCED, op. cit., p. 212.

21. Ibid., p. 172.

22. Ibid., pp. 13 and 142.

23. See, for example, Edward B. Barbier, "Sustainable agricultural development and the resource poor: Policy issues and options", LEEC Paper 88-02, IIED/UCL Environmental Economics Centre, 1988; Robert Chambers, "Sustainable livelihoods, environment and development: putting poor people first", Discussion Paper 240 (Institute of Development Studies, University of Sussex: Brighton, England, December 1987); Gordon R. Conway and Edward B. Barbier, *After the Green Revolution: Sustainable Agriculture for Development* (Earthscan Publications: London, 1989); and Gordon R. Conway, Ibrahim Manwan and David S. McCauley, "The development of marginal lands in the tropics" *Nature*, Vol. 304 (1983), p. 912.

24. See Edward B. Barbier, "Cash crops, food crops and agricultural sustainability: The case of Indonesia" (IIED: London, 1987), forthcoming in *World Development*.

25. United Nations Industrial Development Organization, *Guidelines for Project Evaluation* (United Nations: New York, 1972).

26. See I.M.D. Little and J.A. Mirrless, *Project Appraisal and Planning for Developing Countries* (Heinemann: London, 1974); and Lyn Squire and Herman G. van der Tak, *Economic Analysis of Projects* (Johns Hopkins University Press: Baltimore, Maryland, 1975).

27. See, for example, John A. Dixon, Richard A. Carpenter, Louise A. Fallon, Paul B. Sherman and Supachit Manopimoke, *Economic Analysis of the Environmental Impacts of Development Projects* (Earthscan Publications: London, 1988); John A. Dixon and Maynard Hufschmidt (eds), *Economic Valuation Techniques for the Environment* (Johns Hopkins University Press: Baltimore, Maryland 1986); and Maynard M. Hufschmidt, David E. James, Anton D. Meister, Blair T. Bower and John A. Dixon, *Environment, Natural Systems and Development: An Economic Valuation Guide* (Johns Hopkins University Press: Baltimore, Maryland, 1983).

28. Dixon and Hufschmidt, op. cit., p. 7.

29. Robert J. Goodland and George Ledec, "Neoclassical economics and principles of sustainable development" (World Bank: Washington, DC, July 1986).

30. See UNIDO, op. cit.

31. David A. Phillips, "Pitfalls in estimating social discount rates: A case study", *Project Appraisal*, Vol. 1 (1986), pp. 15–20.

32. Anil Markandya and David W. Pearce, *Environmental Considerations and the Choice of the Discount Rate*, Environment Department Working Paper No. 3 (World Bank: Washington, DC, May 1988).

33. David W. Pearce, "The economics of natural resource degradation in developing countries" in R. Kerry Turner (ed.), *Sustainable Environmental Management: Principles and Practices* (Westview Press: Boulder, Colorado, 1988).

34. See Yusuf J. Ahmad, Salah El Serafy and Ernst Lutz (eds), *Environmental and Resource Accounting and Their Relevance to the Measurement of Sustainable Development*, Selected Papers for Joint UNEP/World Bank Workshops (World Bank: Washington, DC, May 20 1988); William B. Magrath and Peter Arens, "The costs of soil erosion on Java – A natural resource accounting approach" (World Resources Institute: Washington, DC, November 1987); and Robert Repetto, Michael Wells, Christine Beer and Fabrizio Rossini, "Natural resource accounting for Indonesia" (World Resources Institute: Washington DC, May 1987).

35. Repetto, Wells, Beer and Rossini, op. cit.

36. See Henry M. Peskin, "Environmental and nonmarket accounting with references to Indonesia", Chapter 10 in Ahmad, El Serafy and Lutz (eds), op. cit.

37. Repetto, Wells, Beer and Rossini, op. cit., p. 36. For example, this study's calculation of the 1982 depreciation of the Indonesian forests ($ 3.1 billion) represents only the value of net changes in this stock. The capital gains arising from changes in the price valuation of forests assets over 1982 are not included as part of depreciation but noted in a separate "revaluation reserve" account.

38. Edward B. Barbier, "Natural resources policy and economic framework", Annex 1 in James Tarrant *et al.*, *Natural Resources and Environmental Management in Indonesia* (USAID: Jakarta, October 1987). Peskin, op. cit., provides a methodological framework for including all the nonmarket functions of environmental assets in a resource accounting framework. Magrath and Arens, op. cit., attempt to estimate both the on-site and off-site impacts of soil erosion in the uplands of Java as part of their "resource accounting" approach.

39. Jeremy J. Warford, "Natural resources management and economic development" (World Bank: Washington, DC, 1986).

40. David Pearce and Anil Markandya, "Marginal opportunity cost as a planning concept in natural resource management", Paper prepared for the Western Science Association, Special Session on Environmental Issues and Economic Development (Kona, Hawaii, 18–21 February 1986); Warford, "Natural resources", op. cit.; and Jeremy J. Warford, *Environment, Growth and Development*, Development Committee Paper No. 14 (World Bank: Washington, DC, 1987).

41. For a general exposition on this point see Robert Repetto, "Economic policy reforms for natural resource conservation" (World Resources Institute: Washington, DC, 1986). See Chapters 7 and 8 for the specific examples of the contribution of inappropriate economic policies to Amazonian deforestation and upper watershed degradation on Java.

42. David Pearce, Edward Barbier and Anil Markandya, "Environmental economics and decision-making in sub-Saharan Africa", LEEC Paper 88–01, Paper for the Conference on Swedish Development Co-operation with Sub-Saharan Africa in the 1990s, 6–8 September 1988.

43. Ibid.

44. For examples of these studies see David W. Pearce, *Natural Resource Management in West Sudan* (World Bank: Washington, DC, July 1987); World Bank, *Indonesia – Forests, Land and Water: Issues in Sustainable Development*, draft report (World Bank: Washington, DC, March 1988); World Bank, *Renewable Resource Management in Agriculture* (Operations Evaluation Department, World Bank: Washington, DC, 24 June 1988); and Environmental Resources Limited (ERL) and MacDonald Agricultural Services, *Natural Resource Management for Sustainable Development: A Study of Feasible Policies, Institutions and Investment Activities in Nepal with Special Emphasis on the Hills*, Interim Report, 2 Vols (ERL: London, July 1988). The author participated in the Indonesia and Nepal studies.

45. See the discussion in Barbier, "Natural resources policy", op. cit.

46. See Conway and Barbier, op. cit., Chapters 8 and 9.

47. For discussions of the concept of livelihood in development and "sustainable

livelihood" analysis see Chambers, op. cit.; Conway and Barbier, op. cit., Chapter 8; and World Commission on Environment and Development, *Food 2000: Global Policies for Sustainable Agriculture* (Zed Books: London, 1987).

48. See Edward B. Barbier, "Economic valuation of environmental impacts", *Project Appraisal*, Vol. 3, No. 3 (September 1988); and Pearce, Barbier and Markandya, op. cit.

49. Richard Norgaard, "Environmental economics: An evolutionary critique and a plea for pluralism", *Journal of Environmental Economics and Management*, Vol. 12 (1985), pp. 382–94.

50. An earlier version of this model appeared in Edward B. Barbier, "Sustainable natural resource management as a factor in international economic security", Paper presented at the Centre for Economic Policy Research Workshop on Economic Aspects of International Security (London, 18 March 1988). The author is indebted to other members of the workshop for their comments on this model, in particular Shanti Chakravarty, and to Anil Markandya, Karl-Göran Mäler and David Pearce.

51. See Bruce A. Forster, "Optimal consumption planning in a polluted environment", *Economic Record*, Vol. 49 (1973), pp. 534–45; Bruce A. Forster, "Optimal control with a nonconstant exponential rate of decay", *Journal of Environment Economics and Management*, Vol. 2 (1975), pp. 1–6; and Bruce A. Forster, "Consumption-pollution trade-offs" in J.D. Pritchard and S.J. Turnovsky (eds), *Applications of Control Theory to Economic Analysis* (North-Holland: Amsterdam, 1977).

52. As W is total waste from the economic process and thus comprises waste from exhaustible resource extraction, from renewable resource harvesting and production and consumption, it may appear that equation (1) is double counting. But equation (1) is not accounting for the flow of material through the economic system but for the total impact on the environment (i.e, the "composite" resource base) of the waste generation and resource depletion created by the economic system. For example, a forest might be depleted faster than its rate of regeneration, whereas the total waste generated by the harvesting plus production and consumption of the wood products might not exceed the assimilative capacity of the environment. Looking at the total impact on the environment of this economic activity would therefore require accounting for both the impact of the total waste generation (which is negligible in this case) and the impact of the harvesting – which is significant.

Note that, as stated, equation (1) is symmetrical; that is, if the biophysical constraints are observed (i.e., $W \leq A$ and $(R + E) \leq G$ in the long run) then the rate of environmental degradation will be zero or there may even be an improvement in environmental quality. These effects will be made more explicit later in the model. However, it is worth nothing that observed environmental impacts are more likely to be asymmetrical; i.e., in some economic-environmental systems, it may take a long time before observation of the biophysical constraints leads to any improvement in environmental quality, whereas failure to observe these constraints may cause rapid environmental degradation.

53. "Environmental quality" is defined as in Chapter 5. That is, following Becker, op. cit., and Mäler, op. cit., it is assumed that environmental quality is measured by a stock of environmental goods that yield a flow of services proportional to that stock in each time period. However, Becker defines this stock variable as "the differences between the level of pollution for which life ceases and the current level of pollution". Similarly, Mäler's intertemporal models consider only the quality and flow of waste residuals and recycling to have an impact on environmental quality. Here it is assumed that environmental quality may be affected not only by (net) waste generation but also by resource depletion, as both of these may contribute to environmental degradation if biophysical limits are exceeded (See equation (1)). This implies a fairly broad, but perhaps more realistic, concept of the stock of environmental goods. For a given type of ecosystem with its associated energy flow,

a measure of environmental quality may include (in addition to Becker's definition) the ecosystem's biomass (i.e., the volume or weight of total living material found above or below ground) plus some measure of the distribution of nutrients and other materials between the biotic (living) and abiotic (non-living) components of the ecosystem.

54. As the previous note indicates, the concept of environmental quality adopted by this model is fairly broad and essentially synonymous with the entire stock of environmental goods. The three basic functions, or services, of this stock are the assimilation of waste, the production of material and energy inputs for the economic system and the provision of amenity, life support and general ecological services. This allows the model to assume that, for all intent and purposes, A and G are increasing functions of X.

55. Forster, "Optimal control", op.cit.

# Index

absolute ecological constraint, xv–xvi, 36, 97, 98, 99, 100, 103, 104, 109, 111, 112, 115, 126, 204
absolute scarcity, xii, 1–2, 3, 10, 23, 92–3, 97, 98, 103, 113
   see also scarcity
adaptive measures, 150
advanced economies
   effect on biosphere, 99, 117n
   energy consumption, 190–91
   and greenhouse effect, 139–42
   resource allocation pattern, 189
   and sustainable development, 189–92
agricultural rent, see rent
agriculture
   Amazonian, 124–5, 126, 127, 129–32, 133
   and greenhouse effect, 135–42
   performance indicators, 49
   policy in Indonesia, 167–81
   productivity, see productivity, agricultural
   uneven impacts from global warming, 139–42
   see also crops
agro-ecosystems, 47–8, 50–51, 55–6
   sustainability, 50, 51, 56, 115n, 121–2, 187
agroforestry in Java, 164–5, 166–7, 171, 175
alternative economic approaches, xi, xv–xvii
   features of, xv–xvi
Amazonian tropical forests, see forests, Amazonian
amenity services, see environmental services
American Conservation Movement, 34
applied sustainability research, 202–203
arbitrage model, 66
atmospheric general circulation, 128

Babunovic, M., 66
Barber, William J., 16
Barnett, Harold J., 1, 4, 6, 24, 34, 35, 66
Barrow, M., 66

Baumol, William J., 75, 80
beaches, effects of sea-level rise, 145
Becker, Robert A., 118n
Beckerman, Wilfred, 32n
biophysical constraints, 188–9, 205, 207, 212n, 215n
biosphere, exploitation of, 97–9, 117n
biotic potential, 39
boreal forests, 144
Brazilian Amazon, economic policies, 129–32
Broecker, Wallace S., 146
Brown, Gardner, Jr, 84
brown planthopper, 174, 176, 178
Bryson, Reid A., 157n
BULOG, 169

capital accumulation, 112, 113–14
capital-labour substitution, 8–9, 27–9, 189
capitalism, 20, 21
carbon dioxide, 133, 134, 136, 138, 156n, 157n
cassava, 170, 171, 172, 173, 175, 177, 178–9, 180, 182n
cattle ranching in Amazonia, 124, 125, 126, 129, 130–31, 154–5n
cereals, 139, 140, 141, 142, 143
Chambers, Robert, 187
chlorofluorocarbons, 134, 151, 157n
Ciriacy-Wantrup, S.V., 83
Citanduy II project, 163–4, 166
climatic change
   in Amazonia, 126, 128–9
   from greenhouse effect, 134–6, 146–51, 152
cloves, 172, 175
coal
   mining, 12, 14, 17–18
   pollution, 76–80
Coal Question, The, 14
Coase, R.H., 79

Coasian bargaining, 79, 88n
coffee, 170, 172, 175
colonist settlement in Amazonia, 124–5,
    130, 131, 133, 156n
commodities
    commodity fetishism, 20
    export concentrations in, 193–4
    world distribution of, 190
common property, 67–9, 73n, 94, 98, 116n
community ecology, 39–40
composition of output, changes in, 105
conservationism, 34–8, 58n, 106
    resource-saving criteria, 36
consumption, world distribution of, 190
Conway, Gordon R., 47, 187
corn, 7, 9, 15, 169, 170, 172, 175, 178–9
cost-benefit analysis, environmental, 196,
    199–200
costs
    monetized and unmonetized, 149–50
    opportunity, 82, 101
    production, 2, 9
    residual, 149–50
    social, 75–8, 81, 85
    soil conservation, 165–6
    *see also* prices
credit, farmer, 130, 174–5, 176
*Critique of the Gotha Programme*, 20
crop yields, 138, 158n, 162, 177, 178–9
cropping patterns, improved, 163–4
cropping systems, 106, 126, 177
crops
    area planted in Java, 177
    exported, 170, 172, 175
    production in Java, 177–8, 180
    share of major producers, 140, 141
    *see also* agriculture

Daly, Herman E., 31n, 97
Dasgupta, Partha, 64, 65, 66, 212n
databases, 203
debt and debt servicing, 196–8
decay of ecological processes, 86
deforestation
    Amazonian, 99, 120–33, 144, 152–6
        effects of, 126–9
        pattern of, 124–6
        rates of, 124
    Indonesian, 200
depletion of resources, *see* resource
    depletion
depreciation of natural capital, 200–201,
    214n
Desai, Meghnad, 20

descriptive ecology, 39
desertification, 99, 138–9, 150
design, changes in, 105
developing countries
    data and methodology requirements,
        203–204
    energy consumption, 190
    financial assistance to, 142, 150, 151
    food imports and aid, 142, 143, 158n
    and greenhouse effect, 139–42, 150, 151
    manufacturing transferred to, 117n
    and sustainable development, 192–204
diminishing returns
    in agriculture, 2, 4, 7, 9, 12, 13, 14, 16,
        17, 26–9, 30n, 32n
    in exhaustible resources, 17
discount rates, 147–8, 159n, 199, 209–10
discounting the future, 193, 199
diseases, 126, 154n
donor agencies, 202
dung as fuel, 199

ecological decay/collapse, 86, 98–9, 109,
    132, 207, 209
ecological succession, 40
ecology, 38–51, 55–7
economic development, 211–12n
economic growth
    constraint on, 4, 5, 6, 7, 8, 14, 16
    effect on scarcity, 4
    optimal sustainable (model of), 189,
        205–10, 215n
    and resource savings, 105, 107
    and technological change, 12, 116n
    and thermodynamics, 52–5
economic incentive for deforestation,
    Amazonian, 131–2
economic policies
    Brazilian Amazon, 129–32
    Java, 167–81
    for sustainable development, *see*
        sustainable development
economic-environmental interaction
    flow diagram, 101–103
    models of, 100–104, 110–15, 189
economically valuable resources, 24, 25, 35,
    95, 97
economics, neo-classical definition of, xii
ecosystems
    Amazonian, 121–4, 126, 128
    biomass, 118n
    classified by energy source and level, 44,
        121
    description of, 38–9

modification by man, 40–43, 46
  resilience of, 43, 45, 46, 47, 55, 59–60n,
    97, 116n
  shocks to, 44–5, 192
  stability of, 42, 43–5, 46, 47, 55, 59–60n,
    97, 103, 116n, 128
  total energy flow, 43, 44
efficient resource conversion and use, 105
emission permits, 81
energy consumption, 190–91
entropy, 52–55, 56, 100, 117n
environment
  economic dependence on, 8
  economic functions of, *see* environmental
    services
  productive function of, 86–7
  quality of, xvi, 96, 103, 106, 108, 110–14,
    118n, 126, 188–9, 204, 206–10,
    215–16nn
  value to humanity, 35, 82–3, 85
environmental cost-benefit analysis, 196,
  199–200
environmental costs of economic activity,
  75–87, 101
environmental degradation, xvii, 8, 75, 94,
  96–8, 99–100, 103, 105, 107–14 *passim*,
  115n, 118n, 119n
  in Amazonia, 126
  and biophysical constraints, 188, 207
  as entropy, 54–5, 56
  and macro-economic policies, 201–202
  reducing, 101, 105, 187, 212n
  and sustainable growth, 205, 206, 207,
    209
  and underdevelopment, 21
  *see also* pollution; upper watershed
    degradation in Java
environmental economics, non-economic
  influences on, xi, 34–61
environmental management, 106, 110–14,
  118n
environmental services, 13–14, 18, 23, 71,
  82–3, 85, 94–6, 101, 103, 110, 119n, 212n
environmental standards, 79–80, 81
equilibrium state, 107, 210
equitability, 50, 51
erodability of land, 161, 167, 181n
*Essay on Population, An*, 6
evolutionary ecology, 39
exchange value, 7, 16, 20, 21, 22
  *see also* value
exclusive ownership, 66, 79
exhaustible resources, xiv–xv, 17–18, 23,
  63–6, 185–6, 188, 205, 206

existence value, 89n
exploitation
  Amazonian trees, 122, 125, 153n
  difficulties of, xix
  of lower-grade resources, 26
  of renewable resources, 66–70
exports
  concentrations in commodities, 193–4
  crops, 170, 172, 175
  of low and lower-middle income
    economies, 193–4
externality
  definition of, 87–8n
  pollution as an, 75–8, 95
extraction costs, 24, 63, 66

factor substitution, 105
FAO, 163, 174
farmer terms of trade, 171, 172
farming, *see* agriculture
feedback mechanisms, 40, 41
fertility of land, 2, 9
fertilizers, xviii, 47, 163, 172, 173–4, 176,
  179, 183n, 199
FINAM, 130
fishing, 67–9, 99, 115n, 126
flood plains, Amazonian, 121, 122, 124, 126
flooding, 126, 136–7, 145, 155n, 161–2
food production, 140, 142, 143
food security, 140, 142, 150, 158n
forests
  Amazonian, 46, 99, 120–33, 144, 152–6
  functions and uses, 122, 123
  and greenhouse effect, 142, 144
  Indonesian, 200, 201
Forster, Bruce A., 205, 210
fossil fuels, 133, 150–51
Frank, J., 66
free good, definition of, xix
fruits, 166, 169, 170, 171, 173, 175
functional ecology, 39
Fundo de Investimento da Amazonia, 130
future options, 83

genetic materials, 122, 126
Georgescu-Roegen, Nicholas, 53
global warming, *see* greenhouse effect
Goldstein, Jon H., 84
Gowdy, John M., 20
Grande Carajas Program, 129–30
Green Revolution, 169, 172
greenhouse effect, 99, 129, 133–52, 156–9
  and advanced economies, 139–42
  climatic change from, 134–6, 146–51, 152

costs of responses to, 147, 149–50
and developing countries, 139–42, 150, 151
impacts and policy responses, 148
long-term changes, 144–6
need for research, 151
policy responses to, 146–51, 152
share of major producers in crops and livestock, 140, 141
short-term changes, 135–44
sources of, 133–4, 156n
groundnuts, *see* peanuts
growth, *see* economic growth; population, growth
*Guidelines for Project Evaluation*, 196

harvesting, *see* exploitation
hazardous wastes, xviii
Heal, Geoffrey M., 64, 65, 66, 212n
higher yielding varieties (HYVs), 169, 173, 179, 180
Holling, C.S., 47
Hotelling, Harold, 23, 63, 66

igapos, 121
import controls, 169, 170, 175
incentives
investment, Brazilian Amazon, 130–32
soil conservation, Java, 163–7, 171, 179, 181–2n
for sustainable development, 201–202
income tax, Amazonian, 131, 132
industrialized countries, *see* advanced economies
innovations, 105–106, 107, 108
*see also* technological change
integrated pest management, 174, 176
intercropping, 165
intergenerational equity, 106, 187–8, 192
intertemporal theories, 69–70, 118n, 199
investment incentives, Brazilian Amazon, 130–32
investment strategies, Java, 167–9, 171, 172, 175, 176, 179–81
iron law (Malthus), 6, 9
irreversible development, 82–3, 85, 186, 199
irrigation, 169, 172, 173, 174, 175
Ise, John, 57n
islands, effects of sea-level rise, 145

Java, upper watershed degradation, 160–83
Jevons, William Stanley, 11–12, 14–16, 23

Kali Konto Project, 164

Kamien, Morton I., 65
Kemp, M.C., 66
Kitching, Gavin, 22
Krautkraemer, Jeffrey A., 87
Krutilla, John V., 24, 94

labour
as constraint on growth, 7
dependency, 11, 23
substitution by capital, 8–9, 27–9, 189
terracing projects, 165–6
theory of value, 10, 19–20, 22
land-management improvements, 167–8, 171
land scarcity, *see* scarcity
land titling in Amazonia, 131, 132
land values, 131
limit to resource availability, 4
limited territory concept, 6, 7, 10
livelihoods, sustainable, 187, 203, 214–15n
livestock
share of major producers, 141
upper watershed projects, 164, 165, 166
Long, N.V., 66
long-term scarcity, 97, 103, 104
low-income food-deficit countries, 142, 143

macro-economic policies, 201–202
macro-micro analogy, 94, 109, 115n
Maddox, John, 157n
mahogany, 125
maize, 173, 177, 180
Maler, Karl-Goran, 118n
Malthus, Thomas R., xiv, 1, 2, 4, 6–8, 9, 22–3, 26–9
Malthusian scarcity, *see* absolute scarcity
management techniques, 106, 110–14, 118n
marginal social damage of pollution, 80
Markandya, Anil, 199
markets
imperfection, 66
prices, 5, 9, 18, 76, 81
and resource allocation, 97
Marsh, George Perkins, 35, 36, 55
Marshall, Alfred, 11, 12, 16–19, 23, 77
Marx, Karl, 19–22
material-energy balance, 52, 100–101
material-energy inputs, 87, 95, 97
Mill, John Stuart, 1, 11, 12–14, 23, 31–2n, 82
mineral exploitation, Amazonia, 133
mining, scarcity, 12–13, 14–16, 17–18
monetized and unmonetized costs, 149–50
monopoly, 66, 79

moral issues, 36–7, 55
Morse, Chandler, 1, 4, 6, 24, 34, 35, 66
multicropping, 106, 171

national income accounts, 200
natural environments
  and pollution, 75–91
  preservation over time, 81–4
natural growth rate, 67, 68, 69
natural law theories, 4–5
natural resources
  definition, 94
  scarcity of, *see* scarcity
nature
  "bounty of", 5, 6
  heterogeneity of, 35, 36
  limited productivity of, 10
  Marx and, 19–20
  nature-man continuum, 35, 36, 55
  and scarcity, 13–14, 18
navigation, obstruction of, 162
neo-classical economics, xiv, 11–12, 20, 23
new materials, 26
Newell, R.E., 128
non-economic influences, xi, 34–61
nonrenewable resources, 185, 188
Norgaard, Richard, 101
Northern countries, *see* advanced economies
nurseries, 165
nutrient cycles, 126, 128, 144

Oates, Wallace E., 75, 80
Odum, Eugene P., 40, 43
O'Hare, G., 42
open access, 67–8, 69, 73n
opportunity costs, 82, 101
optimal rates of depletion, 62–74, 87, 101
optimal sustainable economic growth,
  model of, 189, 205–10, 215n
option values, 83
Oram, P.A., 138, 139
organization, 16–17, 32n, 105
over-exploitation, 67–8, 99, 193, 199
overgrazing, xvii, 131

paddy, 171, 173, 177, 178–9, 180
  *see also* rice
Page, Talbot, 36, 101, 105, 187
Paglin, Morton, 11
Pakistan villages, impacts on system
  properties of, 51
Paris Biosphere Conference, 37
pasture formation, effects of, 125, 126, 127,
  129, 130

peanuts, 170, 172, 177, 178–9, 180
Pearce, David W., 86, 188, 199
pesticides, xviii, 47, 163, 172, 173, 174, 179,
  183n
pests, 122, 126, 174, 176, 178
petroleum vs coal, 15
physical limits of resources, 34
Physiocrats, 5, 6
Pigou, A.C., 77
Pigouvian taxes, 75, 76–81, 88n, 89n
planning problem, 73n, 112, 207
plants, Amazonian, 122, 126
polar ice-caps, 134, 135, 146, 157n
policy enabling incentives, 201, 202
pollution
  abatement costs, 77–8, 80, 81, 191
  as an externality, 75–8, 95
  and market failure, xv, 81
  and natural environments, 75–91
  optimal control of, 78–81
  taxes on, 75, 76–81, 88n, 89n
  *see also* environmental degradation; waste
    generation/assimilation
population
  decline, 126, 154n
  ecology, 39
  effects of sea-level rise, 146
  growth, 6, 7, 8, 9, 11, 12, 23, 140, 146,
    150
potatoes, 174, 177, 178–9, 180
poverty trap, 193
preferences for environmental functions,
  108
preventive measures, 150–51
prices
  in agriculture, 202
  pricing policies, Indonesia, 169–71
  resource allocation by price, xiii
  resource-price movements, 66
  and scarcity, xiii, 2–4, 5, 7, 9, 17–18,
    24–5, 106
  shadow price, 85, 108, 208
  true value vs market price, 5
  *see also* costs
*Principles of Political Economy* (Malthus), 6,
  29
*Principles of Political Economy* (Mill), 12
*Principles of Political Economy* (Ricardo), 10
product quality, changes in, 105
production costs, 2, 9
productivity
  agricultural, xiii, 5, 10, 47, 50, 51, 125,
    138, 140, 142, 143, 158n, 161, 162,
    163–4, 166, 167, 168, 169, 187

extractive process, 26
food, 140, 142, 143
profitability and soil erosion, Java, 167, 168, 171
profits, decline in, 7, 9, 11, 23, 27, 29
protection rates, 169–70, 175
public bads, 77

quality of environment, *see* environment, quality of
quality of resources, decline in, xiii, xix, 2

rainfall patterns, 129, 133, 134, 135–6, 138, 144
Ramsey, Frank, 23, 63, 72n
reciprocal pollution externality, 80
Redclift, Michael, 21
relative scarcity, xii–xiii, 2, 3, 4, 11, 13, 18, 23, 96, 100, 103, 109, 112, 113, 116n
*see also* scarcity
renewable resources, 36, 66–70, 95, 185, 188, 205
rent, 6–7, 9, 30n, 32n
replanting, 151
research, agricultural, 176
residential land, 13
residual costs, 149–50
residuals, 53–4, 61n, 75, 118n
resilience of ecosystems, 43, 45, 46, 47, 55, 59–60n, 97, 116n
resource accounting, 200–201
resource depletion, xiv–xv, 2, 23, 24, 86, 98, 99, 118n, 215n
optimal rates, 62–74, 87, 101
resource-price movements, 66
resource-saving, *see* innovations; technological change
re-use of waste, 26, 36, 61n 98, 101, 103, 105, 110, 111, 112, 113, 118n
Ricardian scarcity, *see* relative scarcity
Ricardo, David, xiv, 1, 2, 4, 9–11, 22–3, 26–9
rice, 168–9, 172, 173, 174, 175, 176, 177, 178
ricefield as agro-ecosystem, 48
*see also* paddy
rivers, flow and storage of, 136–8, 161–2
road building in Amazonia, 124
Rondonia, 124, 125, 154n, 155–6n
royalties in mining, 17–18
rural credits, 130, 174–5, 176

scarcity
alternative view, 92–119
classical approaches to, 4–11
historical approaches to, 1–33
mining, 12–13, 14–16, 17–18
modern conventional view, 22–6, 62–3
*see also* absolute scarcity; relative scarcity
Schwartz, Nancy, L., 65
sea-level rise, 135, 144–6, 151, 152, 157n, 159n
sedimentation, 161, 162, 181n
semi-renewables, 95, 185, 188
shadow price, 85, 108, 208
shifting cultivation, 121–2, 126
shocks to ecosystems, 44–5, 192
short-run scarcity, 96
smallholder production in Java, 166, 167, 169, 172
Smith, Adam, 5–6, 7, 22
Smith, V. Kerry, 24, 66, 94
Smith, V.L., 67
social costs, 75–8, 81, 85
social value, 47, 50, 63, 64, 67, 95, 96, 103, 110–14
soil composition changes, 126, 127
soil conservation
costs, 165–6
incentives for, 163–7, 171, 179, 181–2n
soil erosion, 20–21, 22, 99, 108, 126
Java, 160–64, 166–9, 171, 174
on and off-site effects, 161–2
and profitability, 167, 168
strategy for reducing, 162–3
soil run-off, 126
solar energy, 101, 105
Solo Watershed project, 163
Solow, Robert M., 65
South America, affected by Amazonian deforestation, 128
soya beans, 170, 172, 173, 175, 177, 180
squatting, 131–2, 155n
stability
agro-ecosystem, 50, 51, 56
ecosystem, 42, 43–5, 46, 47, 55, 59–60n, 97, 103, 116n, 128
stagnation, 8, 23
stationary state, 12, 14, 31n, 69
Stiglitz, Joseph E., 65, 66
stock depletion, *see* resource depletion
stock of environmental goods, 118n
subsidies, 165, 169, 170, 172–4, 175–6, 183n
subsistence, 6, 7, 15
substitutability, 24, 25
substitution, xii, xiv, xviii, 2, 4, 15–16, 25–6, 64–6
substitution of capital for labour, 8–9, 27–9

sugar, 169, 170, 171, 173, 175, 183n
Superintendency for the Development of the Amazon (SUDAM), 130, 131, 155n
surveying methods, 85–6
sustainability
   agro-ecosystem, 50, 51, 56, 115n, 121–2, 187
   ecological, xvi, 47, 50, 51, 55, 59–60n
sustainable development, 37, 38, 103
   and advanced economies, 189–92
   definitions and conditions, 184–9
   and developing countries, 192–204
   incentives for, 201–202
sweet potatoes, 170, 177, 178–9, 180

tax incentives, 130, 131, 132
taxes on pollution, 75, 76–81, 88n, 89n
technological change, xiv, 4, 11, 12, 14, 15, 26, 28, 29, 64, 65, 69, 83, 98, 116n, 186
   *see also* innovations
temperature change, 134, 135, 136, 137, 138, 139, 144
*terra firme*, Amazonian, 121
terracing, 163–4, 165–6, 167, 175
thermodynamics, 51–5, 56, 100, 107
throughput concept, xv, xix
timber exploitation in Amazonia, 122, 125, 130, 154n
Tivy, J., 42
trace gases, 133, 134, 150, 151, 156–7n
trade-offs, xvi, xviii, 38, 87, 92, 93, 108, 109, 113, 147, 185, 187, 188–9, 190, 205
trash dumping, 77, 88n
trees
   Amazonia, 122, 125, 153n
   growing in Java, 164–5, 166–7
tropical forests, 121, 152–3nn
   *see also* forests, Amazonian

uncertainty, 70, 71n, 80, 81–2

underdevelopment and environmental degradation, 21
unidirectional pollution externality, 80
UNIDO, 196
United Nations Conference on the Human Environment, 37
unsustainable development, xviii
upper watershed degradation in Java, 160–83
   *see also* environmental degradation
use values, 20, 21, 22
   *see also* value
user enabling incentives, 201, 202

valuation of natural capital depreciation, 200–201
value, 5, 7, 9, 10–11
   *see also* exchange value; land values; use values
value theory, 10, 19–20, 22
variable incentives, 201, 202
*varzeas*, 121, 122, 124, 126

Washington, DC, Conference, 37
waste generation/assimilation, xv, 24, 47, 57, 86, 95–96, 97, 98, 99, 118n, 188, 205, 206, 215n
   *see also* pollution
water pollution, 162
water recycling, 128
water run-off, 126, 128, 171
welfare, 47, 50, 63, 64, 67, 95, 96, 103, 110–14
West, Edward, 9
whaling, 70
wildlife reserves, 84, 90n
World Bank, 160, 174, 202
World Commission on Environment and Development, xviii, 185
*World Conservation Strategy*, 38